AF699605

The Art and Science of

MAKING MONEY

EARNING, INVESTING, AND SPENDING YOUR WAY TO GREATER PERSONAL WEALTH

The Art and Science of

MAKING MONEY

EARNING, INVESTING, AND SPENDING YOUR WAY TO GREATER PERSONAL WEALTH

by
Shane Roberts

McMahon Publishing

Copyright © 1993 by Shane Roberts

All rights reserved. No part of this book may be reproduced or transmitted in any form or by any means, electronic or mechanical, including photocopying, recording, or by any information storage and retrieval system, without permission in writing from the publisher.

Published by McMahon Publishing, P.O. Box 96, Nevada City, CA 95959

Printed in the United States of America

Library of Congress Catalog Card Number 92-61032
Roberts, Shane
The art and science of making money: earning, investing, and spending your way to greater personal wealth
Shane Roberts — 1st ed.
1. Investments. 2. Small Business — Management. 3. Finance, Personal. 4. Wealth. 5. Career

ISBN 0-9633122-9-4

First Edition

ACKNOWLEDGMENTS

This book would not have been possible without the love, support, and patience of my wife Maggie and my two daughters Amble and Journey. The help of my editor, Gretchen Kelly, was invaluable. Also thanks to: Fred Marks, whose wisdom, enthusiasm, and encouragement energized the project; Peter DeMille, who helped clarify the information in the stock market and real estate chapters; my neighbor, Rich Briggs, a businessman who shared important insights; and John Klus, who carefully read the real estate chapter and shared his expertise. Belden Johnson, a fellow writer, was very generous to me, as was my old friend, Zen Player, who helped design the book. So many encouraged me and gave me confidence, including: Marge Brodhead, Michael and Tommie Conlen, Jan Fishler and Yuri Federoff, Mark Greishaber, Kate and Ken Hite, William and Janet Kopiecki, Ray and Kathleen Lynch, Ann Martin, Edith McKenna, Bill McMahon and Sandy Suter McMahon, Ruth and Russ McMahon, Nancy and Rojelio Novey, Alan Berkowitz and Kathy Poore, George Roberts, Rip Roberts, Marta Roberts, and Liz and Olie Stephenson.

This book was written to provide information regarding the subject matter contained herein. However, the author and publisher are not engaged in rendering accounting, legal, investment, or tax advice or services through this publication. No statement in this publication is to be construed as a recommendation to buy or sell securities. Before acting on any suggestion contained in this book, legal or other professional assistance should be sought.

This publication is designed to give correct and helpful information, but there may be errors and mistakes in content. Care should be taken to use this book as a general guide to financial information and not as the ultimate source of this type of information.

The purpose of the opinions and information contained in this book is to educate and entertain the reader. The publisher and author of this book shall not have liability nor responsibility to any person or other legal entity in regard to any loss or damage caused or alleged to be caused either directly or indirectly by the information or the use of the information contained in this book.

CONTENTS

CHAPTER ONE

Making Money

When I was a little boy I dreamed of growing up and becoming rich. But as I grew, I watched my parents struggling for money, continually falling back into debt, poverty, and despair of wealth. Nobody ever taught me how to handle money. When I had it, I spent it.

By the time I was a hippie in the late sixties, I decided that the struggle for money was an establishment plot to yoke the spirit of the people. My dream of making a lot of money changed to a dream of living in a beautiful forest. I would live off the land and commune with nature, living a self-sufficient life away from the rat race.

Neither of my dreams came true for many years. I could never find the resources within myself to make my dreams a reality. That was 20 years ago, and I wish I'd had this book then.

If I could speak to my younger self now, I would want to say all the things I have said in this book on making money and becoming wealthy. Then I would have had everything I needed to fulfill either of my dreams—to make a lot of money and become rich, or to charge off into the wilderness and stake my claim on the wealth of the natural world. If I had known then what I know now, I would have realized that my two dreams were really very similar. They were both about becoming wealthy and finding fulfillment.

There is of course no way to reverse time and avoid the 20 years of struggle and exploration it took to learn and understand the principles of wealth-building. But I am thankful that as I approach mid-life, I have achieved the knowledge and success to make the rest of my life comfortable and satisfying.

Along the road I traveled, I was never alone. I made friends with a few wealthy individuals and shared some of the comforts of the "good life," but mostly my travel companions were people of average means who never had a lot of money, and did not know how to get a lot of money. They struggled to survive from month to month. Some of my friends were really poor and had difficulty holding down jobs. Others had good jobs but could never stretch their money beyond the end of the month. I knew a few people who had worked for many years, bought a home, and lived in relative comfort, but paid such a high price for so little, they perhaps wondered what the use of it all was.

In other words, most of the people I have known could not figure out how to become wealthy. And for a long time this was my problem, too.

In this book I will show you how to avoid my early fate, and the fate of most of the people I have known. By the time you finish this book, you will understand why my two dreams—making a lot of money and living off the wealth of nature—were really very similar. The secret of wealth would have given me the power to make either of these dreams come true.

This is not your typical money book; we all need money, but money is not what we are really after. What we want is what money can buy, or the freedom, security, or status that money makes possible. Real wealth is about well-being, but don't worry, this is not a new age book about finding your true happiness within. That is where you will find true happiness, but it is not what I am attempting to teach you.

What I am going to give you in this book is a complete understanding of how money works, what wealth is, and how to acquire wealth in all its forms. Not just cash and cars, but the whole condition of wealth, a prosperous life according to *your* definition, not mine.

Making money is not that hard once you know how to go about it. Becoming wealthy is a little more difficult, because it requires you to understand who you are and what you want out of life. Not everyone wants to become a stressed-out Wall Street financier, or a go-go business-person, constantly struggling to surpass the competition in order to acquire wealth. And although much of what we read and learn about making money brings these images to mind, they are false conceptions of what making money requires. You don't have to become a Ross Perot, Leona Helmsley, Michael Milken, or any of the other famous or infamous rich people, to achieve wealth. The best way to become wealthy is to do it on your own terms. Follow a plan customized to who you are and what you want out of life.

Learn the techniques explained in this book that turn making money into an exciting and fulfilling adventure, instead of a sentence to drudgery, frustration, and anxiety. This book will lead you on an exploration of all the different paths to wealth. It will give you the financial tools that are the source of all the money of the rich. And it will give you the knowledge to understand *true* wealth. You will learn why you have to know what wealth is, before you can earn money. Then making money is pretty easy. But the trick to becoming wealthy is not just getting a lot of money. It involves creating quality of life for yourself.

Wealth is quality of life, not just money.

As an American schoolchild, all kinds of ideas about wealth and money floated around in my head, telling me how difficult it is to make money and become wealthy. It clouded my future and caused me to despair of wealth, just like my parents. There were stretches during my career when I almost gave up, just coasting along on what I knew and surviving. I was no longer striving to better my life. I just accepted how it all seemed to be, putting up with the hassles of working, paying the bills, and never having enough money.

But my spark of ambition never completely died. I *had* to learn how this whole money and wealth thing worked. I finally became so obsessed that I burned with the desire to become wealthy. When I began my struggle for financial independence I looked for the right tools. I read books. I talked to people. I went to seminars. I sniffed rich people up and down to discover their secrets. And what I discovered was that few systematic approaches to creating wealth existed. That surprised me. Making money is such an important subject, I expected an avalanche of information, but all I found was a trickle. Our grade school and university educational systems don't adequately teach financial principles, or how to achieve financial independence. The secrets of making money and accumulating wealth are well-known on the one hand, and mysteriously hidden on the other.

I could have gone to business school and learned many of the business and financial principles presented in this book. But I had a family to support by the time I was serious about building my own wealth. And fortunately it was not necessary. Much of what you learn in business school is not really about making money and becoming wealthy anyway. It is about solving business problems. That is why the title of one popular book is *What They Don't Teach You at Harvard Business School.*

When I discovered how little information was available for general readers like myself, I hit the books. I studied the stock market, real estate investing, commodities, collectibles, textbooks on accounting, finance, starting your own business. My friends couldn't believe it. They thought I was obsessed, and they were right. I was obsessed. I had to figure this thing out. How do you achieve financial security? How do you make a lot of money? Where does money come from, what is it, how does it work?

I made some interesting discoveries. Here are some of the basics.

Number 1.

A lot of experts have a lot to say about nothing. Do you get my point here? You have been patiently reading along as I tell you my story, but how much have you learned so far about making money? That's my point! All of the "experts" love to go on and on, but where's the beef?

When you read the experts and you cannot understand what they are saying, nine times out of ten it is because they aren't saying anything.

It's not because you are dumb. It's because they aren't saying anything.

I was intimidated by a lot of the reading I did to learn about wealth because so much of it did not make sense to me. Now looking back, with greater knowledge and wisdom to apply to what I read, I realize many experts make much ado about nothing. They don't really get to the point, which is, what is making money and becoming wealthy really all about? This book is my solution to the problem of too much information that says too little. I have made every effort to simplify the subject and get to the point, including only the ideas and information that you will need to maintain an efficient and effective wealth-building program for yourself.

Number 2.

There are only a few basic principles of creating wealth. Creating wealth, making money, is no big secret. You could have fooled me. I was born poor, raised poor, and stayed poor. As far as I could see, whatever the secret of making money was, nobody was letting me in on it.

What I didn't know was that Benjamin Franklin said everything there is to say about making money 200 years ago. Benjamin Franklin loved money. The two most important things in the world to him were being an upstanding citizen and making money. Ben formed a club of young businessmen when he was only 20. He kept this club going for years, with the sole purpose of networking and finding more ways to make money. Eventually Ben revealed his secrets for making money in his famous essay "The Way to Wealth."

Ben had making money down pat. He knew so much about making money he is still doing it. He established several trusts for the benefit of Philadelphia, his adopted home, and to this day those trusts are earning a lot of money.

So the second interesting discovery I made is that creating wealth is no big secret.

Number 3.

The secret of making money is finding or creating value, and earning a good return on your time, effort, and money, year after year.

I just gave you the complete and only secret to creating wealth.

It may not look like much, but everything else I have to say in this book builds on the foundation of this secret. You will soon realize that this is the one and only secret of wealth that has been used since civilization began.

Before I can give you the details of how to use this secret in your life, I need to talk about some other ideas first. You must appreciate not only how powerful this secret is, but also that you, whoever you are, can use this secret. Anyone in good health and of average ability can build whatever amount of wealth he or she chooses, using the principles contained in this secret.

Here are some of the basic ideas:

—Finding or creating value is about exchanging one form of wealth for another. When you work at your job, or run your own business, you are selling something of value—the value of your labor and ideas—in return for money.

—When you buy something at a low price and sell it at a high price, you are finding value. When you come up with a good idea for making money, you are creating value.

—Earning a good return on your time, effort, and money, year after year, is about how fast you improve your life. The faster you make money or wealth, the easier it is to accumulate more than you spend. It is also about knowing how to spend your time, and how to invest your effort and money to get the most in return.

These are the basics and you may be getting a little suspicious at this point. Somewhere inside your mind a little voice is saying that this is all very familiar. These ideas are common sense. You already know that this is how the world works.

And you are right! You do.

You will discover as you read this book that I am going to show you things you already know about yourself and how life works. But I also have many new ideas to share. These ideas will combine with what you already know to give you the power to make money and to become wealthy. I have developed a system for doing this. I call it the **wealth-building equation**. This is a set of tools for empowering you to succeed in your wealth-building plan. Here it is:

Attitude + Knowledge + Skills + Effort + Resources

= Power to Build Wealth

By using the wealth-building equation, you will be able to apply the secret of making money to your life. I have devoted a chapter to the explanation of how the wealth-building equation works and how to use it—how to overcome all the obstacles to building wealth, so that your success will be guaranteed.

Of course the wealth-building equation is not magic. It is not a gimmick that will cure all of life's problems for you. But if you are of sound body and mind, you have everything you need to become wealthy. **Not just a little wealthy, but very wealthy.**

The wealth-building equation and the secret of making money can overcome any obstacles to your wealth-building program. Not even deep indebtedness can prevent you from becoming wealthy. Because so many people are in debt, and have difficulty staying out of debt, I have written a chapter to explain how to cope with debt and begin your wealth-building program at the same time. Debt is a troubling and painful experience that produces a lot of stress and anxiety. Debt is also the most common cause of despair of wealth. Once people fall into debt, they feel as if they can never become financially successful.

This is a wrong assumption that you must correct in your thinking!

Many wealthy individuals have gotten out of debt and become very rich. Sometimes more than once.

A friend of mine who has been in debt for many years, and struggled to earn more than a subsistence wage in her job as a corporate marketing professional, recently told me my book could not help her. "How can I even think about making money, when I don't even know how to get out of debt?"

I was flabbergasted at first, since it is exactly for such a person that this book has been written. Then I began to talk with her about despair of wealth. This incapacitating condition afflicts so many of us. It discourages our efforts to understand and practice wealth-building principles.

After we discussed my ideas and the "secret" power of my book, she realized that she had been stymied by her own ignorance of the principles of making money. She felt her ability to build wealth was already doomed by the burden of debt she lives under. She did not realize that her debts are but one of many symptoms of her financial and wealth-building ignorance.

My friend, and the majority of Americans who live aimlessly uneducated about the basic principles of making money and accumulating wealth, suffer poverty for much of their lives. They are in despair of wealth.

In the chapter "Surviving Debt" you will discover that debt can be overcome. I know that is hard to believe when you have been struggling with it for years on end. Easy for me to say, you might think. But I have lived in debt and suffered its burden. I know exactly how it feels. I now have no debts, and I know that making money is not that difficult, and neither is getting out of debt. Not once you understand how it all works.

Other stumbling blocks to wealth are the ideas we get from listening to the news every day. Bad news is the news that sells best and the bad news we hear about the economy can be very discouraging. It makes us feel that we are losing ground. The good old days are gone. Maybe we have a right to despair of wealth.

Unemployment is always a problem that makes the news, because full employment is a difficult goal to achieve. The truth is, only socialist economies have "full employment." An economy that has full employment can accomplish this only with "make work" jobs for those who are currently unemployed. As the old Russian joke goes, "We pretend to work, and the government pretends to pay us."

One way to think of unemployment is the philosophical attitude about viewing a glass as half empty or half full. It is a matter of your point of view. The worst unemployment we have seen in this country was in 1933 at the height of the Great Depression. You could say it was terrible that one in four workers did not have a job, or you could say that even then, three out of four workers had jobs. Those were awful and frightening times, but the country held together and some of our most inspiring American success stories are born of that time.

In the middle of 1992, just coming out of a recession, unemployment was higher than it had been since 1985, at just over 7% of the work force. But that still means that more than nine out of ten workers had a job.

Much of the news about unemployment applies to people who have lost jobs that are disappearing overseas. This is because much of our manufacturing work is now being done by cheap labor somewhere else, or because there are now machines to do it.

When I was a child, my father took me into the print shop of the newspaper where he was a photographer, and showed me the typesetters positioning their lead type in rows, one letter at a time, to set up the printing plates for the next edition of the paper. Today, none of those jobs exist. They are all computerized.

Automobile manufacturing, office filing, bookkeeping, package delivery, grocery checkout counters, banking, warehousing, and blue-collar and white-collar occupations are being increasingly automated. This reduces the need for a human labor force.

The idea of losing jobs to "foreigners" or machines is upsetting to most people. They feel their way of life is being attacked. Human beings don't like change and uncertainty; it makes us anxious and uncomfortable.

I don't want to minimize or gloss over the problems of unemployment or low wages. But the blaring headlines of the newspapers and the evening news can distort the picture and create unnecessary anxiety and discouragement. Some people, for a variety of reasons, have a hard time finding or holding a job. But the vast majority of people who want to work are able to find and keep a job. Of the less than one out of ten people who are currently unemployed, many of those are simply in between jobs and will find new work.

The good news is that America is not losing jobs overall. We have created more new jobs than any other country in the world over the last twenty years. The problem our workers are experiencing is that many of the old kinds of jobs are disappearing and being replaced by new types of work. Our economy is becoming a service and information economy. The main problem of unemployment in America today is sustaining a level of education and skill in our work force that will qualify people for good jobs at good wages. And that is what this book addresses.

The Art and Science of Making Money is a valuable source of hope to people who are concerned about their jobs and careers. I will show you how to move firmly into the category of those who stay employed at good wages. I will give you the knowledge and tools to manage your career and your money, to guard against the uncertainties of our rapidly changing modern economy.

The nickname for the science of economics is "the dismal science." Many of the original theories upon which the modern science of economics is based were developed by people with bad attitudes. The same gloomy world of work and foul existence that Charles Dickens wrote about is the world that the original economists grew up in. Their point of view was one of scarcity and poverty.

The world has changed a great deal since then, and many of the old theories of economics (which still play a part in the thinking of today's economists) have been discredited.

Our economy is still the largest and strongest economy in the world. Despite the marvelous growth that has taken place in the economies of Japan, Germany, Korea, France, and many other countries of the world, the American economy is still in the lead. We have better universities, technology, natural resources, roads, transportation, and all the other things necessary to a healthy economy than anyone else.

The *Harvard Business Review* has stated that all the dire predictions of America's decline are basically false. Just because other economies of the world have taken giant steps forward does not mean that our economy is falling behind. There is no reason for our economy to stagnate and degenerate, unless the American people lose their spirit of enterprise and fall into despair. Despite the bickering and complaining that goes on in this country, we still have a free enterprise system that provides opportunity for every hard-working individual. Not all of us may be ambitious enough to overcome obstacles in our way, and take advantage of our system of free enterprise. But there is nowhere else in the world where better opportunities exist.

Our economy has been growing and prospering for over 200 years—more than any other nation in the world. There is no reason to believe our economy will not continue to thrive in the future.

Economies always go through cycles. Our economy is just coming out of a downward cycle during which we experienced a recession. But guess what? Japan, Germany, and many other countries also experienced economic difficulties during this time. That is normal.

But the news always sounds like Chicken Little running around shouting that the sky is falling, when a leaf has landed on his head. Every time America enters one of its many downward economic cycles, politicians and the news media start running around shouting and pointing fingers, trying to lay blame and find fault. It is like trying to find out who is to blame for bad weather.

When people are pessimistic and discouraged about their earning power and what the future holds, bad economic news just fuels their cynicism, futility, and hopelessness. When life colors your attitude in these ways, **your attitude becomes an obstacle to financial success.**

When your outlook on the world is gray and dismal, you lose all motivation. You just cannot muster the energy to succeed. It doesn't seem worth it, so you end up procrastinating, despairing of wealth.

I have lived through all kinds of different economic conditions, some of which produced widespread panic about what would happen to the future of America. In 1980 when inflation was 13.5%, nobody knew what to expect. I read gloom and doom books and newsletters that made it sound like the end of the world. This was very discouraging to me. I thought the "good old days" of economic prosperity in the 1960s were gone for good. I had been born at the wrong time. I missed the boat.

Instead, none of the dire predictions I read came true. Quite the contrary, the 1980s were boom times for our national economy.

So I have learned to take both good news and bad news with a grain of salt. I exercise my skepticism and stick to my own knitting. Let all the pundits and experts argue over the future, which no one can predict anyway. I will keep working my own wealth-building plan for continued success.

When you hear of all these terrible things in the news about the economy, unemployment, foreign competition, and American decline, don't get too upset about it. The sky is not falling. My attitude is that it doesn't pay to worry about the big picture too much. You cannot do anything about it anyway, except get anxious and depressed and fall into despair of wealth. The big picture may help you think about how to manage your business and investments, if you are at that stage in your wealth-building cycle of life. But it will not help you become more optimistic, unless you can look beyond the news of the day, and look at the *BIG,* big picture—the long-term miracle of the American economic experience.

The twentieth century is the dividing line between humankind as primitive nontechnological creatures, and modern existence where people make extensive use of knowledge and technology to enhance their lives. Dramatic changes have taken place in our use of technology. Our standard of living began to rise a couple of hundred years ago with new approaches to scientific thinking, but these changes happened much more rapidly in the twentieth century. With advances in transportation and communication, new scientific discoveries could be shared more easily. One new idea quickly added to another, and all sorts of new inventions and technologies were created.

Radio, television, magazines, newspapers, telephones, and now computers and worldwide satellite communication systems allow us to share our ideas with almost everyone in the world in an instant. These technological breakthroughs dramatically enhance our ability to create wealth. Nowadays it is much easier to get information and generate new ideas. It is also easier to communicate new ideas to other people, and use them to make money or build wealth.

The development and communication of new ideas and information over the last 200 years has greatly increased the wealth of a large portion of the world population. It is not merely the elite of society who have benefited; the condition of the common person in western civilization has also been vastly improved.

The average income of colonial Americans was $1,000 a year in today's dollars. Because there were so few goods and services available, they were not so much deprived of money as they were deprived of food, shelter, clothing, transportation, communication, entertainment, health care, indoor plumbing, books and literature, and almost all of the other modern "necessities" we take for granted. Our grandparents or great-grandparents may have been wealthy for their day, but compared to what we can buy and do with our money today, they were our poor relations.

The average income of American families today, at around $28,000 per year, is 28 times that of our colonial forebears. As Americans we enjoy one of the highest standards of living in the world, and we have access to the largest supply of consumer goods and services. But even though we may have more now than our ancestors had, we also expect more. The cost of our modern "necessities" stretches a $28,000 budget very thin. To pay for a minimum lifestyle leaves little room for what we consider to be luxuries.

The negative side of our thought revolution, our advanced technology and new wealth, is the unequal distribution of its benefits. We are each liable to benefit from, or be deprived of, all that is new and wonderful in our world. And largely the determining factor is how much money we have. We feel frustrated when we see people who are living so much better than ourselves, even though we have it much better than our grandparents or great-grandparents.

In today's economy we face the same challenge to survive—to feed, clothe, shelter, and provide for ourselves and our families—as our ancestors did. In some ways this is easier to do today because there are more resources to draw upon, more goods and services available to meet our needs. In other ways, this challenge is even more difficult than it was for our parents. Many in their generation attended school, graduated, took employment in a stable or growing company, put in a lifetime of work, and retired with a home and a comfortable pension.

Our new world is much more dynamic and complicated than this. Changes are happening too quickly and dramatically for any company today to realistically offer a lifetime of employment and benefits. Employees in today's world are naive if they entrust their future to a company that is powerless to guarantee it for them. There is no company in today's economy that can be assured of its long-term survival and success.

There are all kinds of changes that are taking place in our economy. These changes affect the kinds of jobs that are available and what education and skills people must have to earn a good living. In the past if you had good manufacturing skills, and a willingness to do hard work, you might have a job for life. This is no longer true. Today you cannot blindly accept the same kind of work your mother or father did. You have to be aware of how you fit in, and what you are going to have to do to survive and prosper.

We are all faced by these challenges, the changes from an industrial worker economy to a knowledge worker economy. For some people these changes may pass with hardly a ripple. There are businesses that go on for years and will continue to do so, without being affected. But for others the changes will be wrenching, as they transition from a lifetime of guaranteed employment to unemployment and few employable skills.

There is no end to the products and services our imagination can create to enhance our enjoyment and well-being. There is no end to the need for knowledge workers who can invent and implement technologies and ideas to produce these goods and services. For this segment of our society there is unlimited future employment.

You have the opportunity to use the knowledge and ideas in this book to guarantee your individual success, no matter what happens in the overall economy. That is the point of this book. It will show you how to take control of making money and building wealth, so you are not dependent on what happens to businesses and the economy in general. This book will teach you how to plan ahead and to react appropriately under changing conditions. You can take responsibility for your own economic fate. The fundamental principles of making money and building wealth are ancient, and therefore timeless. They are applicable under any circumstances.

America is the richest country in the world. The American phenomenon of economic prosperity is unprecedented in the history of the world. It is a miracle. I am now one of the richest people in the world, and I am even one of the richest people in America. Now let's not get this out of context. I am certainly not about to be elected to the *Forbes Four Hundred* list of the richest Americans. But my income and my assets put me in the top ten percent in our country, and in the top one percent of the world population. That is exciting to me. It is a dream come true. Twenty years ago, when I was homeless and living in a pickup truck, trying to finish high school, I never would have believed it. The future looked dismal. I thought I was a failure—that I couldn't learn to be successful, that the economy was going wrong, that the government was going wrong, that my *life* was going wrong. I ended up way off track. I finally came to my senses when I studied the history of American prosperity and realized that I was a part of something really big. There was an awakening that took place in me, a realization that I was already part of something great. All I had to do was get on board.

Remember though, wealth is not just about money. Wealth is about value—the values you hold dear in your life. I now own a nice home in the country in a quaint little Victorian gold mining town where I want to raise my kids. Clean air, no crime, wild flowers and wild animals all over our property. That was important to me. Those are the values I hold dear, and that was my dream come true.

But to get there I had to adjust my attitudes. I had to set my sights on what I wanted and pursue my dreams until they came true. I have written this book to show you how you can achieve wealth and well-being *on your own terms.* I don't offer any get-rich-quick schemes. But I won't discourage you from getting rich quickly, slowly, or at whatever pace suits you. You can use the knowledge contained in this book to master all the financial principles of wealth creation. These include maximum career earnings, the highest investment returns, success in business (still the surest way to riches), and the quality of life and work you truly desire.

The true secret of making money is to increase your earning power. But even more important than making money is the power to build wealth. This involves more than an understanding of making money; you must also understand what wealth is and where it comes from. These are the secrets contained in this book. And as I have said, they are mysterious secrets because, although some of them are well known, they are not well understood. If you tell people you have found a book that contains the secret to building wealth they may not believe you, because we live in a cynical age in which everything is already known, and there are no miracles. But finding the truth about making money can seem like a miracle, once you discover the power in it.

This is not a "get-rich-quick" book, this is a "get rich if you work for it" book. If you are willing to learn and apply the principles taught here, you will become rich in time. I promise you. It is an easy promise to make, because the principles work. But it is no guarantee that you will become rich. Unless you study the principles and apply them, they will not work.

You will have to change your thinking as you read this book. I am going to take many of your ideas and challenge them. I am planning to turn your parents, teachers, friends, even the government and its economists, on their heads, and spin them like a top. I am going to turn their ideas around to a better point of view, so you will see your future in a brighter light.

So this is your chance. If you already know how to become rich, to accumulate wealth, you don't need this book. If you have read other books and become discouraged, take heart. This book gives the true story. You have been fooled for the last time.

The news today is full of stories about the lost American Dream, our falling standard of living, and massive company layoffs. Making money and building wealth have nothing to do with waiting for economic prosperity to descend on the nation. If that is what you are hoping for, you already missed the boat. America is still the richest nation in the world, and getting richer. If you are not on board, *now* is the time to sign up.

CHAPTER TWO

What Wealth Is

You want wealth. That is why you are reading this book—to find ways to acquire wealth. We all want money to satisfy our desire for wealth.

When I set out to become rich, I tried to figure out the best way to make money. Could I win a jackpot, gambling? Maybe I could find the right formula for winning at blackjack or poker. What could I invent that would be so new and ingenious I could sell it to a lot of people? I racked my brain to come up with ideas for businesses that I could start, to make a lot of money. Perhaps I had a long-lost relative who was rich and might help me. No luck there. All of my relatives were poor.

I tried to imagine which jobs paid the most, to decide what occupation I might go into. We always hear that doctors and lawyers make the most money. What about that? I used to study contest rules on packages at the supermarket, wondering if there was some way to trick the game and win the grand prize. I would sometimes daydream about money that bank robbers may have buried after a big theft. Or maybe there was some tricky way to figure out where gold is buried, like the treasure-hunting team in Florida that uncovered tens of millions of dollars of Spanish gold from a sunken galleon a few years ago.

Eventually, I felt stymied by my daydreams of wealth. I knew that it was possible to get a lot of money in any of these ways. But I wasn't interested in these pursuits, except for the money. I was fixated on money. I thought that to be wealthy I had to "get money." For some years I remained stuck with that idea. How could I get a lot of money?

By fixating on money, I kept missing the opportunity to create or acquire wealth. I was thinking like P. T. Barnum, the famous circus owner who said: "There's a sucker born every minute, and two to take him." I was trying to invent ways to separate people from their dollars. I wasn't trying to be dishonest. I never hurt anyone or took money illegally.

I just knew that I wanted a lot of money, and to have it I would have to think of ways to get other people to give up their money to me.

When I wrote the title of this book, I played a trick on you. I called it *The Art and Science of Making Money.* What I really should have called it was *How to Build Wealth.* But I figured you might be a lot like I was—more interested in how to make money than in building wealth. If you made the same mistake I did, you think money is wealth.

I completely misunderstood what wealth is, and how to acquire it. **Wealth is not money.** But if wealth is not money, what is it?

Wealth is whatever helps to satisfy human wants.

To understand the mystery of what wealth is, and where it comes from, you have to appreciate how ideas and technology are used to satisfy human wants. For example, imagine the earth before there was any life on the planet: a big ball of dirt and rocks, floating in space, with some water on it, and some air, all burning under the relentless heat of the sun. There was not much there to satisfy human desires. The planet Mars is pretty much like that, and I cannot think of too many people anxious to live there.

Now think of the earth today, with all the things it contains to satisfy human wants. Where did all of that wealth come from? It came from ideas and technology.

The first wealth to arrive on the planet was life. Most of the value added to the planet before humankind arrived was in the form of some living thing. The genes that are the blueprint for life are the same as ideas. They are like having an idea and writing it down, or using it to draw a design or plan.

Living cells use their genes as the ideas that control the technology of life. A 300-foot-tall redwood tree is built from the ideas and technology contained in a little seed.

It is the same process as baking a cake. You start out with the idea of what you want, and you turn something basic—the raw ingredients—into something more interesting and useful to human beings. You have added value. You have created more wealth.

That is why it costs more to buy a cake than it costs to buy the flour, eggs, salt, sugar, and other ingredients used to bake it. You are paying for the extra value in the cake. You are buying the ideas and technology that went into converting the ingredients into a delicious treat to satisfy human desire.

The Earth was transformed from a ball of dirt into a fertile planet, rich with life, through the use of ideas and technology. This may sound strange to you if you think ideas and technology belong only to human beings. Genes store ideas, and biology is technology. Wealth was added to the earth by the ideas and technology inherent in the evolution of life forms.

And life is one of the most valuable forms of wealth we have.

These ideas may seem very abstract, as if they have little to do with your life and how to make money. Quite the contrary, if you want to be wealthy, *really* wealthy, these are exactly the ideas you need.

I made the mistake of thinking that I could get money without finding or creating wealth. I did not even know what wealth is. But money was not invented to make people rich, **money was invented only as a way to exchange wealth.** Money is a convenience for people who already *have* wealth, a token to use as a measure of wealth that is to be exchanged.

To illustrate the power of creating wealth from ideas and technology, rather than simply acquiring money, and to broaden my definition of what wealth is, I have composed a little story. It goes like this:

There was a man named Jim who had a horse to trade. He was approached by a pig farmer named Honest John, who offered him ten pigs for his horse. Jim thought this was a pretty good trade until Honest John suggested that he accept 10 red pieces of paper to seal the bargain. Jim thought this was a strange idea and started to laugh. Then Farmer John showed him what was written on each red piece of paper; "Good for one fat healthy pig at any time. You have my word on it. Signed Honest Farmer John." This caused Jim to stop and think. Perhaps this was a great deal after all. He gets rid of his horse, which he has to feed and take care of, and gets ten pig promises in return. He trusts Honest John, who is known for his sincerity and good will, and is sure to be good for the pigs. The red pieces of paper could be very valuable. Jim doesn't have to feed and shelter them; he can hide them under his mattress. Whenever he runs out of bacon, he can head on over to Honest John's and pick out a pig, leaving one of his pig promises in exchange.

Now think about that. Where is Jim's wealth? Under his mattress? No, his wealth is over at Honest John's farm. The red paper under his mattress is a promise to pay wealth to him at any time. The actual wealth is his horse and those pigs over at the farm. He doesn't care about the red paper. He values what it represents in terms of pigs and horses. And the pigs and horses were produced by ideas and technology.

This is how money works. We trust that people will let us use it to buy items of value, to exchange it for wealth.

Honest Farmer John had the idea of clearing some land, cutting up trees for building fences, and getting himself a sow and a boar to breed little piggies. He understood the technology of producing pork and used his ideas to take care of pigs and raise them for sale. He used his ideas to create wealth.

Honest John came up with another idea for producing wealth. He had offered Jim ten pigs for a horse. When Jim agreed, he suggested that since pigs are a lot of trouble to take care of, he would be willing to do it for him. How about if Jim took ten pig promises and just came around for his pigs when he needed them? Jim decides it's a great idea because he only wanted to eat the pigs in the first place. He doesn't want to have to take care of them. But Honest John knows that, too. Jim is not going to come around next week and ask for ten pigs. He is only going to ask for one. It will take Jim three years to eat ten pigs! So Honest John is not going to keep Jim's pigs around and take care of them. He is just going to make sure he has new pigs when Jim needs them. He has only *one* of Jim's pigs ready for him. Jim has ten pig promises, but there is only one pig to back them up. But Jim doesn't know that, and he never will, because Honest John knows how fast Jim eats pigs. Neat idea, huh?

That is how business credit works, which is another form of money. Jim loaned Honest John some of his wealth, so he could create more wealth and pay Jim back in the future.

Honest John now has Jim's horse to help him build more pig fences, and plow more acreage to grow pig food. And it cost him only one pig, due maybe next week, and nine other pig promises, due over the next three years. Pretty slick.

Now where is the wealth? It just vanished into thin air.

All of Jim's pig promises are worth only the value of Honest Farmer John's ideas and technology, as well as his health and good intentions. If Jim's horse steps on Honest John and kills him, or John takes to the booze and turns mean, sacrificing the value of his good reputation, Jim might as well eat his pig promises. He won't be seeing anymore bacon on the table from that farm.

So the value of credit depends on the future prospects of the borrower. If you are lending your wealth, you have to trust whom you lend it to. Or if you are borrowing wealth, the lender has to trust that you will pay it back.

Since Honest John traded his promises to Jim for his horse, he figures he has a good thing going. He is mortgaging the future output of his ideas and technology, everything he can produce from his pig farm, against the value of wealth he can receive from others, today. He trades pig promises for all sorts of goods and services. He buys a plow from the blacksmith. He hires help to work the farm. He buys seed corn to grow food for his pigs. Even the dry goods store in town agrees to accept his pig promises for clothing and other household necessities.

Honest John has figured out how to use the value of his future wealth (in the form of the pigs he is going to raise) to acquire wealth in the present from people willing to trust him. They base their trust on his integrity, his good intentions, the value of his word, and the evidence of his future prosperity—represented by his highly successful pig farming operations. All of these are part of his total wealth.

His creditworthiness is a form of wealth he can use to create more wealth. He builds his creditworthiness by working hard and demonstrating his reliability in paying back his pig promises.

All of a sudden the whole town owns Farmer John's pig promises, his little red pieces of paper. Now they start trading pigs with one another. The blacksmith already went out to the farm and picked up a pig. He doesn't need anymore pork for now. But he still has some pig promises left. He heads over to the local saloon and talks the bartender into taking a pig promise in exchange for 100 hundred shots of whiskey. They sit down together over a drink and make up a sheet of paper with 100 little glasses on it. Every time the blacksmith wants a drink, the bartender takes out their accounting sheet of the drinks, and the smithy crosses off a glass and signs his name next to it.

Now where are the money and the wealth?

The saloon has a pig promise from the blacksmith. That is money, a medium of exchange. It is worth one pig, or 100 shots of whiskey.

The saloon did not get the pig promise for free, though. It had to establish a drink account for the blacksmith. That is money too—a store of value, a promise to pay drinks. The blacksmith spends his drink account money every time he goes to the saloon and checks off glasses from his accounting sheet.

So the money is the little red pig promises, and the drink account paper. The wealth is pigs and whiskey. They satisfy the human needs or desires for food and drink. Money is the paper they use to represent the value of pigs and whiskey. But nobody is passing money around for nothing. They expect it to be backed up by real wealth, things people would be interested in buying with the money. Even if the wealth does not exist now, like the pigs that Honest John has not yet raised, it is expected to be there when people get around to spending their money.

One day the bartender went out to Honest John's farm to pick up a pig. He needed more pork for the saloon restaurant. He was talking to John about the pig promises, and how he had set up a drink account for the blacksmith. Then he and John got to musing about money and wealth, and John mentioned his idea of having to raise pigs only as fast as people turned in their pig promises. This got the bartender thinking. How fast could the blacksmith drink whiskey?

He seems to show up at the saloon every day at about seven o'clock, spends an hour having a drink or two, signs his drink account and goes home. At that rate, it should take him at least a couple of months to drink all of that whiskey. The 100 drinks the blacksmith started with in his account will require about five bottles of whiskey to satisfy. That is a lot of whiskey to keep on the shelf of the saloon just waiting for the blacksmith to use it up.

A sly grin crosses the face of the bartender. He realizes that if he accepts pig promises in return for setting up drink accounts for his customers, he can have all of the pork he needs for the saloon restaurant. They will never run out of ham and bacon. And he does not even have to keep all the whiskey around to pay off the drink accounts. He just needs enough whiskey to pay on people's drink accounts as fast as they use them up.

Now the bartender can push pork in the restaurant and bring in lots of customers for the saloon. He does not even have the whiskey to pay for the pork. He is buying it on the promise of future drinks. He is using his ideas and the technology of the saloon business to build his wealth. He has some money he can spend, in the form of pig promises. But those are just promises to pay. They are only part of his wealth. Most of his wealth is in his saloon business, and what it owns—the building, the whiskey, and the pigs that belong to him out at Farmer John's place. His wealth is also in his ideas and his reputation in the community for honoring his drink accounts.

His ideas are a form of wealth because, without them, he would never have set up so many drink accounts and received a lot of pork for the restaurant. His reputation is a form of wealth because it provides customers with the confidence to give him pig promises in exchange for drinks they will not get until the future.

This is how many forms of contracts, bank loans, insurance, bonds, and other credit instruments work. Because businesses or individuals trust each other, they are willing to lend or give money today, in return for the promise to receive wealth in the future. Usually this is because we expect to get more wealth in the future by letting someone use our wealth to create more wealth for us. That is what investing is. By getting the use of Jim's horse, in exchange for pig promises, Honest John was able to create more pigs.

About this time a little trouble settles over our happy community. It seems Farmer John is a happy and hardworking pig producer, and he has been doing his best to raise enough pigs to keep up with the pig promises turned in to him. But he has been so busy, he just hasn't managed to keep up on the construction of pigpens. He has also had some trouble getting the local farmers to supply him with enough hay.

One night the temperature began to plummet. Farmer John was surprised at this freak weather so early in the season, and his pulse began to race with concern.

He quickly rounded up his helpers and began herding pigs into their pens. But Farmer John did not have enough pens for all the pigs and many were left unprotected.

Catastrophe had struck Honest John's business enterprise and attacked the very heart of the community's wealth. All of those pig promises depended on there being pigs to back them up. How much would those little red pieces of paper be worth after one half of Farmer John's pigs died in the cold?

It did not take long for word to get around that a bunch of John's pigs were lost. The whole town showed up at Farmer John's waving their red slips of paper and shouting at each other and at Farmer John. The bartender was there too, and he looked almost as upset as John. He kept seeing visions of the crowd in front of his saloon screaming, "We want our whiskey."

What is happening here is a "credit crisis." When things go wrong with business or the government, people get worried about all the promises that were made to back up the forms of their money. Will your insurance company pay your claims? Should the bank trust you to pay your credit card? Can the bank collect enough money to pay interest on your savings account? Are junk bonds any good?

The money and credit in our economy is not just backed up by wealth that exists today, it is also based on our faith that future wealth will be produced.

When you want money to buy things, you have to earn it in exchange for wealth you produce now, or you have to convince people to trust you with their money now, in return for money or wealth you will produce in the future.

The mayor took charge of the situation and quieted down the crowd. "Look, folks," he said. "We have all known Honest John here a long time. He has always worked hard, taken good care of his pigs, and kept his word with us. Farmer John has run into some bad luck here. We can all see that. But I think you all know that Honest John is going to work hard and get his pig production back up to where it was before. He just needs you to maintain your faith and give him another chance. Don't worry about your pig promises. I have spoken to Honest John and you will get your pigs. Just be patient. Those of you who have an immediate need for pork, please stand by and we will hold an auction. The rest of you good folks go on home."

The mayor's speech saved the day. Jim felt reassured by what he had to say. It was just plain common sense. Jim thought for a minute about demanding his horse back, but he no more wanted his horse now than he did when he sold it to Farmer John for pig promises. And the more he thought about it, the more he realized that the *horse* was his wealth, and his pig promises were still backed up by the horse, even if there were not enough pigs to go around. Without his horse, Farmer John would just have more trouble making bacon for him.

The rest of the community felt about the same as Jim did, so most of them went on home. But the ones who remained wanted their pigs, including the bartender, who was worried about supplying his saloon restaurant.

The town banker now presided over an auction for the 50 pigs Honest John said he could afford to sell that day. The reason for the auction was that even after most of the folks had gone, there was still more demand for pigs than there was a supply of pigs to sell.

The banker auctioned off the pigs to whoever bid the most pig promises. Because they wanted pigs, and there were not enough to go around, some people were willing to pay more than one pig promise per pig. The bartender managed to buy five pigs for his restaurant by winning a bidding round with an offer of nine pig promises. This is a basic question of economics—how to match supply and demand, and at what price? How is wealth valued relative to money?

Suddenly the value of pigs had become inflated from one pig promise to almost two pig promises. This inflation reduced the value of a pig promise. The same amount of money no longer represented the same amount of wealth in pigs.

Nervous people with pig promises in their pockets were willing to pay a higher price for those pigs. This happens all the time in our economy. When there is more money than there are goods and services, prices go up. That is inflation.

When there are more goods and services than there is money, prices go down. That is deflation.

When people demand a lot of something in short supply, it goes to the highest bidders, just like the auction at Farmer John's place.

Cash is money and so is credit. When it is easy for businesses and individuals to borrow money, there can be too much credit around. Too large a supply of money drives up prices. When people have money to spend, their desire for wealth increases. They want to buy things.

Sometimes the government clamps down on the supply of credit, because too much money causes inflation. When there is inflation, money is not worth as much.

Money is the same as Honest Farmer John's pig promises. It is valuable only as long as Honest John is busy taking good care of his business and backing up his promises with pigs.

Wealth is produced from ideas and technology, which creates value for other human beings. Honest John created wealth from raw materials. He planted corn and raised pigs to sell. The bartender provided services as a form of wealth. He sold whiskey and pork. He also found wealth for his business by establishing a system of credit. His customers gave him pig promises so he could get the pork for his restaurant right away. In return he promised to pay them back in future whiskey.

That is how credit works. It is the promise to pay future wealth, in return for the use of present wealth. The only reason people would give up present wealth and wait for future wealth, is to be rewarded for waiting with an increase to their wealth.

That is how interest on a loan works. Whoever lends money gets paid interest over and above the original amount of money—the principal—that he loaned. When you put money in a bank savings account, the bank pays you interest for the use of your money. When you buy the bond of a business, it pays you interest for the use of your money, money that is used to create new wealth—whatever products and services that business produces.

(Actually you are getting a raw deal when you deposit money in a bank savings account. A bank will pay you 5% interest for using your money. Then it will turn around and loan that money out at 8% interest and pocket the difference.)

When you understand that wealth is everything of value to human beings, and that money is only one form of wealth—a token of stored wealth or a promise to pay wealth—you can understand the secret of making money better.

The secret of making money is finding or creating value, and earning a good return on your time, effort, and money, year after year.

Honest Farmer John was creating value when he raised pigs. He was also creating value when he invented pig promises. It was valuable to people not to have to take care of pigs in order to have their bacon. Jim got value from Honest John when he got rid of his big hungry horse and received convenient little pig promises in exchange.

The bartender found value in the pig promises as a way to exchange liquor for pork, and as a convenient way to store pigs until he needed them.

He also found value in "networking" with Farmer John. He learned about supplying only enough pigs to pay off the pig promises as they came in. This knowledge saved him a lot of money because he realized he needed to keep on hand only as much whiskey as people would drink right away. This is how he learned that **knowledge is wealth.**

Information is just as important a form of wealth as tangible objects.

Knowledge is power. Knowledge is what makes all of our modern technologies possible. All of our advances in medicine, transportation, manufacturing, education, and all other endeavors, result from the power of knowledge.

Honest John's pig promises are a great idea that anyone can use to create value. You can create pig promises yourself in the form of contracts. If you find a way to provide goods or services to someone else in exchange for money or some other form of value they offer in return, a contract can be written to specify how the arrangement will work. **Contracts are another form of money.** They are a promise to pay wealth in the future.

Most people think of contracts as a formal document written by a lawyer. But anyone can write a contract. I have written many business contracts without a lawyer. There are even books you can buy with standard contracts in them.

Part of the secret of making money is "earning a good return on your time, effort, and money, year after year." That is what Honest Farmer John did. He worked hard to produce the most pigs in the shortest amount of time. When he bought Jim's horse, he got a better return on his effort when plowing his fields. He got more field plowed for the amount of time and effort he put into the job, because the horse provided more plowing power and speed.

Honest John also got a good return on his money. Remember, money is a token of wealth, a medium of exchange, and a promise to pay future goods and services. When Honest John went around town handing out pig promises to buy supplies and equipment, he was using his future as collateral. He was trading on the value of his future. He then used what he bought to produce more wealth. He continued to do this for a good return on his money, year after year.

Honest John created his own money in the form of pig promises. You might think you cannot just go out and print money, since only the government is allowed to print money. This is because people have to be able to trust money. It must be backed by real wealth, real goods and services. People don't ask questions if you hand them a dollar to buy something, because your money is backed by the full faith and credit of the United States Government. The government is responsible for controlling the money supply and making sure there is not too much. Otherwise it becomes worth less, because of inflation.

But you can create your own money, just as Honest Farmer John did. Credit is money too. If you look at a dollar bill, you will notice that it says: "This note is legal tender for all debts, public and private." Anyone can create a "note." Most stationery stores provide standard forms for a "promissory note." If you can convince people to loan you money, because they trust you in the same way people trusted Honest John and his pig promises, you can secure the loan with a promissory note.

But if you are going to borrow money, you had better use it to create more wealth, as Honest John did with his pig farm. Otherwise, you will not have any wealth with which to repay the loan, and you will lose the value of your reputation for honesty and ability to produce wealth.

Remember, your creditworthiness is a form of wealth.

When I was a little boy and dreamed of becoming rich, all I knew about wealth was that you could buy things with money. I did not understand how to *create* wealth.

As a teenage hippie, I thought money should just be given out "for free." Why can't we all just share the wealth, giving and getting out of love and kindness? I did not want to labor at a job and have some employer "exploit" my body, mind, and spirit. I did not understand that **wealth is the product of a dedicated body, mind, and spirit.** If I wanted wealth, I needed to dedicate myself to achieving it. I could not expect the government to give it to me. That has been the failure of socialism—the expectation of an economic free ride.

I thought I was rejecting money and wealth by choosing to live in the woods and commune with nature, away from money and greed, exploitation and oppression. I did not realize then that **wealth is quality of life.**

By choosing to live in the woods, I was only exchanging one form of wealth for another, one quality of life for another.

I once read a book about a successful and affluent couple who decided to escape the rat race. They homesteaded some land in a remote wilderness of Canada, hacking out a primitive existence. They built a log cabin near a river, shot bear and other wild animals for food, planted a garden in summer, learned to identify edible plants, and wrote "back to nature" books to supplement their income.

I say their writing "supplemented" their income because their main income was not money; it was the product of their survival craft, their harvest of whatever the wilderness could offer. They chose a lifestyle imbedded in the economy of nature. They drew their wealth from the natural beauty and elemental sensations of their wilderness existence. Apparently they preferred living this way, without the comforts of the big city they came from. This is obviously not a popular lifestyle, but it is one that you cannot buy with dollars. They had to earn the quality of their existence by choosing and living it.

Chuck Berry, the rock-and-roll star, dreamed of having a million dollars. Not just a million dollars in assets, but a million dollars cash in the bank. A million dollars in cash was a symbol of status, achievement, and security for him. But working to bank a million dollars is too simple a way of thinking about money and wealth. There is more to financial success and wealth than that.

Because wealth is quality of life, you must consider who you are. What fulfills you? What do you need from life? How much money you have to spend is only part of the equation. There are other forms of wealth to consider as well such as love and friendship, knowledge and skill, travel and entertainment, self-esteem and pride of accomplishment, pleasure and comfort, freedom and security. And you cannot acquire all of these forms of wealth just by spending money.

Money is a means to life enrichment, not an end in itself. The value of money is in the goods and services we exchange it for.

You earn money by creating or acquiring goods and services of value to others and selling them. And to do so you have to invest your time, thoughts, emotions, effort, and life experience into that process.

How you benefit from that process depends on how clearly you comprehend yourself and the process as a whole, and succeed in achieving the maximum value from it. Whether you enjoy your work, where you live, how much money you have to spend, what you own, whom you know, and how you spend your spare time, all depend on the choices you make for how to live your life. Your choices determine your life enrichment.

Wealth does not always depend on how much money you earn. Wealth is also measured by the cost of personal sacrifices you make to achieve it.

What good is a lot of money, if you hate what you do to earn it?

If work life is Monday morning blues and "Thank God it's Friday," then no amount of money can compensate for that dissatisfaction. Understanding money and wealth means understanding your own ability to create the values in your life that money is only a symbol for.

The most sophisticated and meaningful approach to money is to see it as a system of values that you can trade on to enhance the quality of your life. And the ultimate equation is that you are drawing on universal energy and packaging it to produce a more worthwhile existence for yourself and other human beings. You can transform raw ideas and materials into objects and services of value to yourself or others.

I am a licensed building contractor, so I like to work on my house myself. When we bought our home in the country, I spent a couple of months working on it. It is a big house with a lot of land, so there are plenty of jobs I could have hired out to others. But I like doing them. I save money and have fun at the same time. Losing myself in these simple tasks, my mind wanders away from the stresses of business and investments, and I experience the pleasures of physical exercise, easy accomplishments, and the great outdoors. For me that is heaven, the sort of personal fulfillment I had always hoped to achieve.

For some people, having a big house also means having people to take care of it. Their idea of wealth may be completely different from mine. They would choose a different quality of life, going by different guidelines for what they want from living.

To become wealthy is to know what you want from life, and get it.

Imagine that our metaphorical friend Honest Farmer John is now content with his life. He knows there are many compromises to be made in life, to achieve what he wants, but on balance it has all worked out. Farmer John enjoys his work. He likes animals and finds pig breeding interesting and full of new challenges. He also feels great satisfaction with his stature in the community. He is respected for his honesty and hard work.

Honest John is secure in the knowledge that as long as he stays healthy and no unexpected misfortunes befall his family, he should be able to sustain the quality of his existence for the rest of his life, because of the wealth he has accumulated.

But how did Honest John achieve his present status in life?

As a boy, Honest John was very poor. His parents were uneducated and discouraged by life, living in hopelessness and despair of wealth. Honest John went to school but was never well educated. He had a talent for something though. He loved animals and treated them well.

As a teenager things grew so difficult at home that Honest John set out on his own. Life became even more difficult. With no place to live, little education, few skills, and no money, Honest John had to struggle even to survive. He slept in barns and begged for his food.

As you might imagine, poor Honest John was in deep despair of wealth. He had no wealth and perhaps never would. Or so he thought.

It never occurred to John that, in exchange for food and shelter, he might offer to work. He felt so worthless and helpless, full of self-pity, and preoccupied with his own troubles, that he did not think of what others might need or want from him or of what he had to give.

One day John's hunger drove him to the front door of an old, wise, and kindly woman. She offered Honest John some food, then sat in her rocker on the front porch and began to chat. John found himself pouring out his troubles. She assessed John's situation in her mind and, sizing up his character, decided he might be of use to her. She also felt moved by his story and wanted to help him.

Honest John did not understand it at the time, but he had just stumbled onto a treasure trove of wealth. **A powerful ally or mentor is a source of wealth.**

The old woman offered to take Honest John in. She explained that there was a lot of work to do around her little farm, and being so old, she could no longer keep up with it. John was thrilled at this suggestion. Full of excitement at his good fortune, visions of a secure home and regular meals danced in his mind.

Soon John had fallen into a regular routine around the farm, taking care of the animals, tending the vegetable garden, mending fences, and working at countless other chores. And it so happened that the old lady kept quite a few pigs around the place.

Fate had now taken control of his destiny and set him on the road to becoming "Honest Farmer John." Like so many people, Honest John had stumbled into his career without realizing it. He had lived in such despair of wealth, it never occurred to him to take charge of his own destiny and pursue a course of wealth-building. He did not think of the long life in front of him and how he might spend it for both enjoyment and the accumulation of prosperity and happiness. He did not weigh his options and decide he could find the most happiness and make the most money as a pig farmer. His despair of wealth simply led him down the path of least resistance.

For many months Honest John worked around the farm. At first he was grateful for the old lady's kindness and thankful for his good fortune. But gradually he grew restless and discouraged. Falling into despair of wealth again, he grew lazy and began to slack off his work. His original visions of food and shelter now paled in his mind. He took the comforts of home for granted and wondered what more to life there might be than just the drudgery of farm work.

The old woman noticed John's fallen spirit and neglectful attitude toward his chores and she sat him down for a talk. Honest John felt ashamed and weak when she mentioned his poor attitude and demoralized behavior. But then she expressed her sympathy and explained his mistakes were part of human nature. He should not feel bad, but take heart instead. In fact, she said, this might be a moment of great opportunity for him. Then she told him the story of her life and how she had acquired her wealth and wisdom.

The old woman's husband Tom had been a very wealthy man, and understood the secrets of making money. When Tom was young he had been handsome and kind, full of high ideals. Later he became preoccupied with money. He forgot that true wealth is quality of life. Tom's obsession with his business led him away from his affections for their family. His heart grew cold and his mind preoccupied.

For her part the woman enjoyed the luxuries that wealth had brought to them. But she also fell into despair of wealth as she saw Tom's greed and insecurity grow, and the quality of their family life deteriorate.

As the years passed, Tom's business ventures became riskier and riskier. His obsession grew and he became overconfident in his abilities. He lost sight of the original principles of wealth on which he had built his fortune, and finally, after borrowing too much money against his faltering enterprises, Tom was ruined when an economic recession struck.

They lost their riches, and were left with one last possession, this little farm. Tom now fell into despair of wealth. He was full of grief and remorse over his foolish obsession, his wasted life, and ultimate failure. Gradually Tom's health failed, and he grew ill and died.

With all the troubles she had suffered, the woman could not help but wonder at how her beautiful life had withered. She pondered the meaning of it all and realized the power of her late husband's business philosophy. His principles of financial success had catapulted him into riches. But in pursuing money with a narrow focus of intent, he had missed the other half of the equation that gives value to life. **Wealth is quality of life, not just money and property.**

Everything people desire can be bartered for wealth and money. You must have something people want, and offer it in exchange, if you expect them to give up something of value to you.

This is the secret of the con man. He knows how to create a desire so strong that you will give him your money in exchange for false promises. But the con man is always living on thin ice, because he refuses to offer real value. He is living in despair of wealth just like most people. He does not know how to create wealth. He knows only how to create the *illusion* of wealth and barter it.

The worst con men end up in jail. But the world of business contains many con men who continually advertise their products and services with false promises to their customers. They believe that their customers will continue to be fooled and fail to recognize the poor quality and lack of value in their products and services.

The secret of lasting success in business is to put customers first. Recognize what they need and desire and give it to them. Many people in business are in despair of wealth and fail to offer the highest quality of products and services. This is a great opportunity for those who understand what wealth really is. With the power to satisfy the customer's true needs you can guarantee your success in business.

This is not only true in business, it is also true in your career. If an employee recognizes the employer as a customer receiving a service, who is seeking to satisfy his wants, the employee will offer more value.

Career advancement will go to those who perform the best, who offer the most value to the company.

The old woman now told John of many men her husband had met through his business. Some of them lived in despair of wealth their whole lives, plodding along at the same level of knowledge and performance for years, never expecting to advance beyond their station in life. Others were ambitious and anxious to please, and quickly learned that they must offer real benefits to those with whom they dealt, in order to achieve greater successes and rewards.

When her husband had been a young man, full of idealism and hope, he had learned the principle of providing value for value, of putting the customer first. He enjoyed this advantage he held over his competition in business.

He liked what he was doing and life seemed full of promise. He could never have acquired the knowledge, vision, imagination, and willpower to do it, if he had not enjoyed what he was doing and felt hopeful about his future. He was not in despair of wealth.

It was only later when Tom could no longer find new and meaningful challenges, and he had forgotten so many of the values that had been important to him in his youth, that he lost the thread of his wealth-building journey, and succumbed to greed, power mongering, and the quick fix of ever bigger deals and more personal prestige.

Watching the life of ideas and passions grow cold and die in her husband, as he vainly pursued meaningless conquests for greater riches and glory, taught the woman the deep importance of maintaining life's priorities.

This led her to mention to Honest John one of her best ideas. Among her circle of social acquaintances, she had observed many men and women who had achieved great wealth for themselves on the basis of unusual talents. They possessed or had acquired charm, personal prestige, influence over others, or a force of attraction in their personalities, that bound others to their fate or will.

Some of them were artists, poets, or writers, more or less talented in their arts, but much more so in their wiles and charms. These individuals sought and found patronage among the wealthy, who would indulge them with money and other luxuries, mainly due to their self-presentation. They seemed to attack life with a certain self-confidence and flair that guaranteed them success, despite their apparent lack of the means to produce wealth.

Some of these people were government officials who won support with nothing more than their high-sounding ideas and gracious manners.

Some were men and women who received fine apartments, expensive clothes, and lavish spending allowances in return for the pleasures of their sparkling personalities and sex appeal. And some were business executives whose political skills managed to hide their managerial deficiencies.

But the ones the old woman remembered with fondness and secret admiration were the women who valued themselves enough not only to marry for love, but to marry for love and money. They did not value money more than love, but they valued themselves and their future enough not to settle for a man who was going to live and die poor.

And here the woman mentioned the few women she had known who had braved the world of men and established successful careers for themselves. It was their faith in themselves, their self-esteem, that made it possible to struggle and survive in a system dominated by men and the male mode of business management. They had drawn on a wealth of spiritual resources to achieve material successes and affluence.

Honest John thanked the old woman for sharing her wonderful ideas, but asked if she could share some of the more specific methods her husband had used to acquire his wealth.

"Everyone must start with what they have and who they are," she told John. "You have great wealth of which you are not even aware. Your despair of wealth is a sign of your desire to do more with your life, to be more. You have your strong body and your will to survive. You have your health. You have honesty, sincerity, and good intentions. People will always value that. You are a quick learner, and have picked up a lot of useful skills here around the farm. Also, John, I have noticed you are very good with the pigs.

"You know, the secret of making money is finding or creating value, and getting a good return on your time, effort, and money, year after year. There is a lot of value around this farm, and I cannot make much use of it on my own. I can use your help. This could be an opportunity for you. **Opportunity is a form of wealth.**

"This farm is my wealth; it represents all of my capital assets, all my physical wealth. Capital is anything that can be used to create more wealth. My fences are capital, they keep my pigs in, and allow me to raise more pigs without them running off. The corn I keep in my silo is capital, too. I can use it to feed the pigs and make them fatter, so I have more pork wealth. The corn gets used up as I give it to the pigs. That is called working capital. You have to replenish it. It is the same as cash in a business, another form of working capital. My barn and fences are called fixed assets; they are capital that does not get used up.

"And you are a kind of capital for me, too, Honest John. Your labor is a valuable commodity I can use to create more wealth on my farm. All of these forms of capital have value for making money.

"Here is how it works, John. You trade the value of your new farm skills, your honesty, your willingness to work hard, any good ideas you can come up with, and your integrity as a person, for my knowledge and advice, the use of my farm, and a share in the profits from what we can accomplish together.

"The profits are any extra wealth left over from everything we do here. We are starting out with a certain amount of land, fences, buildings, animals, corn, tools, money, ideas, skills, and happiness. After you work here a year, any extra corn, animals, and money that show up, I will split with you fifty-fifty. All the extra ideas, skills, and happiness you acquire in the deal, I will throw in for free.

"I am giving you the opportunity to stake your claim here, Honest John. Maybe you would be interested in becoming Honest Farmer John. Then you could make use of the value of assets you have found here, to create value for your own life, to build your wealth.

"And here is the final clue on the secret of making money. To get a good return on your time, effort, and money, grow corn and breed pigs just as fast as you can. Don't just work hard John, work smart. Figure out how to make the most of your time, be efficient with your effort, and get good value with your money.

"You know, I don't have a horse. That might make it a lot easier to grow corn around here. Maybe you can come up with a good idea for getting your hands on a horse."

Now Honest John felt the same thrill he had experienced months before when the old woman had first taken him in. The door to his future had been flung open once again. For the first time in his life he sensed what his purpose was, how he would build his wealth and live his life. He was in pig heaven.

Honest John took the old woman's good advice and faithfully followed the principles she had taught him. And John has thrived and prospered ever since.

Not everyone in Honest Farmer John's family turned out quite the same as he. His brother Shifty Pete, the gambler, chose a completely different road to travel. Pete was made of much the same stuff as John, full of purpose and high ideals; but he was the restless sort. He did worse than John in school, never paying attention in class, and sometimes not even being there at all. He liked to stay outside, daydream, and wander around seeking adventure and escape.

As Pete grew older he fell in with a bunch of guys who liked to gamble and carouse around at night, looking for fun and charming the ladies. Pete was not bad-looking, and he had a sense for what people like, and how to ingratiate himself. He was sharp-witted and had good gambling instincts.

He liked poker because he knew that he could win with skill as well as luck. He was careful to study his odds and pay attention to how other players reacted to pressure and how their psychology and emotions controlled them.

Shifty Pete usually came out ahead on his gambling, and also managed to turn a profit making good trades. He would win a ring, a watch, or something during a game of chance, and then sell it for a good price, or trade it for something of even greater value.

He never suffered the sort of despair of wealth that had victimized his father and brother. Pete was too sly and worldly-wise to succumb to the fate of his brother, who had nearly starved but for begging food. He always knew how to look out for himself and put his own interests first. But Pete was tortured with a restless emptiness in his soul. He was always on the go.

A time came when Shifty Pete became curious about his brother, Honest John, and looked him up on the old woman's farm.

Pete and John got to talking about all that had happened to Honest John. John told Pete of the wonderful ideas the old woman had shared with him, and Pete became interested and wanted to hear more.

When John told him that the secret of making money is to find or create value, and earn a good return on your time, effort, and money, year after year, Pete grasped the concept immediately. He knew he was getting a good return on his effort playing poker. It was easy and fun, and he usually made money at it. He was getting a pretty good return on his money too, he guessed, since he usually won. And he knew how to find value, because he could always gauge the value of the trinkets he accepted as bets, and managed to trade them for more value. He was no sucker either; he wouldn't trade unless he came out ahead on the deal. He pitied the poor saps who got desperate and excited and turned over so much of what they owned to him.

He could see that John was creating value on the farm by raising his pigs and corn. But that was not for Shifty Pete. He was not sure creating value was up his alley. Maybe there was some value to the entertainment he offered when he let people play poker with him.

There was one part of the secret of making money that troubled Pete. He could not quite figure how you get the best return on time. What exactly did that mean?

Not being the shy sort, he immediately went to the old woman, turned on the charm, and begged her to answer his question. How could he get the best return on his time. What is a return on time?

The old woman patiently explained to Pete that **time is wealth**. And time is money. When you rent a room for the night at a saloon, you might pay $40 for the privilege. That is the value of the time you spend in the room. That is the return on time that the saloon keeper earns for the room. His rate of return on one night in the room is $40.

Many forms of payment are measured by time. Wages are paid by the hour, week, month, etc. And when you borrow, or loan money, interest gets paid measured by time. A bank savings account may pay 5% interest per year for loaning the bank your money.

Shifty Pete took to the old lady's ideas about the time value of money and resolved to use them for greater gains. He began to think more clearly about where he had been headed with his penny ante gambling and trading. If he wanted the best return on his time, he was going to have to play for higher stakes.

After he left his brother John and the old woman, Shifty Pete became acutely aware of his need to up the ante and look for larger fish to fry. If he kept gambling with run-of-the-mill players, with no more than a few dollars to risk, he was never going to rake in enough winnings to make it worth his time and trouble. Somehow he had to get into the big time.

He continued to follow his usual routine, but kept on the lookout for the lucky breaks he needed to get a leg up in the world. All that he had learned from his sensible brother and the old woman had taught him to pay closer attention to what he did with his money, and to recognize the value of hanging onto as much money as he could to use for investment in his gambling and trading activities.

One night when he had found his way into a poker game with some local merchants, he managed to build up a large pot when all the other players but one folded their cards. Now Pete was sitting with a royal flush and he knew this was a golden opportunity to wring every dollar he could out of this fellow. He also noticed that his opponent had been overbetting his hands all night, and seemed desperate to make a killing in the game. Shifty Pete dug deep to draw on all his acting ability and appear even greedier and more anxious than this foolish merchant. The betting continued until finally Shifty Pete decided to give it everything he had. He reached into his money belt and pulled out all of his cash, a substantial sum. The merchant looked utterly crestfallen, and blanched at the sight of such a large bet. He kept staring at his cards, then the pile of money, then back at his cards again.

Finally the merchant cleared his throat and began to mutter, not sure of how to begin. He managed to explain that he had a large parcel of land he would like to call the bet with, there were so many acres and it was in a good location, good land. Shifty Pete smelled a great opportunity here. He agreed to the bet on the condition the merchant not only deed him the land, but give Pete the option to sell the land back for twice his bet if he did not like it.

The merchant finally agreed to the bet and laid down his king-high flush on the table. Pete showed his royal flush. It was Shifty Pete's greatest coup. A moment of great triumph. His years of honing his gambling instincts had finally paid off in one glorious game.

Afterwards Pete went over what factors had made him so successful. **Skill is wealth,** he remembered. He had been lucky to draw cards for a royal flush hand. But then he knew what cards to hold and which to discard in order to build his royal flush. He also knew how to bet and use psychology to increase his winnings from his royal flush. So his skill had combined with his luck. His skill had exploited the full value of the opportunity presented by luck. Then he remembered an old saying, "luck is when preparation meets opportunity."

Pete also realized that **knowing when to act decisively is wealth.** His success in gambling depended on patience and caution. It depended on controlling his emotions and looking out for opportunities to take bold action and reap large rewards. Pete knew to bet small and bide his time until the odds were in his favor. Then when a strong hand came his way, he could test the strength of the other players, and act boldly, taking them for all he could.

Shifty Pete examined the land he had won from the merchant. He did not know much about real estate, but he looked at many other pieces of land in the area and talked to their owners about price and quality. Eventually he decided that he now owned valuable land, so he was careful to register his claim on it with local officials.

After he filed his ownership with the county, he got to thinking about what that meant. Because he had acquired ownership of this land, he was now wealthier. He realized that **ownership is wealth.** He gambled and traded to gain ownership of greater wealth. As long as he took ownership of wealth legally, and no one could dispute his claim, it was his to keep.

Pete decided it was time to party. Off he went to the nearest high-class saloon. He ended up in a poker game where one talkative player went into great detail about trading of stocks and bonds, and how much money can be made from them. Spurred on by Pete's interest in the subject, he explained that a stock certificate gives you part ownership in a company, and that you can trade these stocks back and forth. There is really no limit to how much you can gamble in the stock market, he said, because that is where they keep just about all the money in the world.

At these words Pete's mind shifted into high gear. "This is it!" he thought. "Now I know where the action is."

Pete was ideally suited for trading on the stock market. He understood how to compare the value between two stocks and acquire more wealth by trading a stock of lesser value for a stock of greater value. He knew that since wealth is ownership, this was the perfect way to increase his ownership of greater wealth. And he would not have to twist anyone's arm to give up ownership because people were constantly offering their stocks for sale. All he had to do was assess the price and decide whether he was getting good value in the trade. He could also put his stocks up for sale and wait until the right sucker came along to pay him top dollar. How could he lose?

Shifty Pete soon found out. He lost a bundle in the stock market before he realized that it was a lot tougher to figure the odds there than in a poker game. But he knew his instincts were right, and he had the talent for it. He could control his greed and excitement as stock prices jumped up and down every day. He also knew that there was a lot of value to be found in the companies he owned shares of with his stocks. He just had to learn more about business.

Shifty Pete hunkered down and attacked it with a will. He spent months and months chatting with business people, stockbrokers, and investment bankers. He turned on the charm and bought drinks in exchange for the knowledge he needed to become a success on Wall Street.

Pete bought and sold stocks successfully, but only after learning that he had to be patient and give them time to rise in value. He borrowed money on his land so he could buy more stocks. Then he borrowed money against his stocks to build a ranch on his land and raise cattle. He traded his cattle ranch for a business in Chicago that sold medicine to pig farmers. He had talked to Honest John, who told him the medicine worked well to cure pig diseases. So Pete figured the company ought to make a lot of money. And it did.

Shifty Pete eventually started an investment banking firm and traded in whole companies, not just stocks. And he made a lot of money helping others trade their companies. In later years he marveled at the power of the teachings that had been given to his brother John and himself.

Every now and then he would turn that one sentence around in his mind and think of how he could apply it to his investing and trading: "The secret of making money is finding or creating value, and earning a good return on your time, effort, and money, year after year." That is how Honest John and his brother Shifty Pete made their fortunes.

Wealth is more than just money; it is quality of life. There are many intangibles that contribute to wealth. Honest John learned that he could become wealthy starting out with nothing. He needed to acquire some of the intangibles of life before he was able to build his wealth. He needed knowledge and skills to help him. He also needed to recognize the power of the wealth he already possessed: his longing to succeed, his courage, honesty, and natural abilities.

Honest John also needed to recognize opportunity when it came knocking. He acquired control of valuable physical assets when the old woman offered to let him work her farm. These resources gave him the raw materials to use his ideas and apply technology to building his wealth. He also had to recognize the value of the old woman's ideas, her wisdom and advice, and the value of the old farm, and the resources and opportunities hidden there. Most importantly, John had to overcome his despair of wealth and trust himself. He had to believe in and value what he could accomplish, and persist until he succeeded.

Shifty Pete, on the other hand, was cut from a different cloth than his brother. He shared the same qualities of courage and longing that served his brother so well. But he could not be tied down to the drudgery of menial tasks like Honest John. He was definitely not good with pigs.

Shifty Pete did not suffer despair of wealth, either. He was confident of his abilities. He trusted his personality and charm. He calculated his odds and took swift action when luck ran his way. These qualities were his store of wealth, the values on which he traded to achieve more wealth. He was more interested in finding wealth than creating it, but he understood the power of maximizing the return on his time, effort, and money.

There are many lessons in this simple story. It shows where wealth comes from and explains the meaning of money as a tool for storing or exchanging wealth. It shows how raw resources are transformed into more valuable forms of wealth to satisfy human wants. It demonstrates the power of ideas, and the use of technology—putting ideas into action to build wealth. And it explains how wealth is more than just money and possessions, but quality of life.

Investment in your wealth-building program will not always provide immediate benefits or obvious rewards. Look to the future and play the game for the long haul, realizing that all of your effort is a preparation for the big moments in life, the big payoffs. Sometimes your wealth will come in a steady stream, sometimes in dribs and drabs, and sometimes only in the instant you strike pay dirt. But all the while you can be accumulating not only material wealth, but a wealth of skills, ideas, and character traits that pay dividends along the way.

If there is one message I would leave you with in this book it is not to sell yourself short. Do not let despair of wealth prevent you from valuing who you are and what you can accomplish.

I have just explained the most abstract concepts of wealth-building. These concepts are so general in nature it is difficult to bring them down to earth. But in my allegorical tale of Honest John, his early struggles, and the wily ways of his brother Shifty Pete, I have laid the foundations of a practical approach to wealth-building. It may seem simple, and it is, but these basic concepts are the foundation of the most complex theories about making money. Whether you are the slow and steady type like Honest John, or fleet-footed and fancy-free like Shifty Pete, there is an approach to wealth-building and making money suited to your personality and goals.

The most important thing is that you trust yourself. Understand that you can achieve whatever wealth you desire. Recognize that the secrets of wealth are few and simple. Apply the knowledge and tools in this book and you will become wealthy.

CHAPTER THREE

The Wealth-Building Equation

Attitude + Knowledge + Skills + Effort + Resources = Power to Build Wealth

Before I explain what this formula means and how it works, let me provide a few words of introduction.

Wealth is quality of life. The **wealth-building equation** is not just a way of accumulating money, it is a way of building quality into your life. To get what you want out of life you have to have hopes and dreams, and aspire to fulfill them.

It is not enough to want a "good" life. You have to decide what that means for you personally. Some people don't know what they want out of life. They are seeking their mission, their purpose. Something always seems to be missing, but they cannot put their finger on it. They try this and that, but they end up confused and uncertain. They need to answer basic questions about what life means to them before they can take a stand and go for what they want.

I suffered this dilemma in my own life, struggling to find love and happiness, some way to satisfy my longings. I know what a long and difficult search that can be. I sought experiences of all kinds. I traveled to exotic places. I immersed myself in philosophy and religion. I attempted to meditate and unveil life's deeper meanings, its spiritual significance.

There were times when I fell into despair. I wondered what purpose life held, and whether love and happiness could ever be found. I went around in circles for years, exploring all of life's ups and downs, until I wound up in my own back yard. It all ended in simplicity for me.

I discovered that I knew everything that was important in my life by the time I was ten years old. Not in kindergarten. I did not have a clue in kindergarten (apologies to Robert Fulghum). When I was ten, I knew that life was about fun, being liked, having close friends, and relying on my family for love and intimacy. But life tripped me up when my parents got divorced. I ran into tough times. Adolescence was confusing. I got sidetracked, and it took me some time to get straightened out. Finally, after all the searching and adventures, I rediscovered the wisdom of my childhood: fun, close friends, and family. Life can be rather absurd.

Now I know what I want from life, and I have most of it. Once I found out what was important to me, I knew where to take aim. Nice home in the country. Check. My favorite sports: skiing and weight lifting. Check. A swimming pool. Check. Time to play guitar and sing. Check. Writing books. Check. Working at home and spending time with my family, priority number one. Check. Traveling to new and interesting places. Check. Meeting new and interesting people. Check. Having fun with my kids. Check. Enjoying time with my wife. Check. Continually expanding my knowledge and ideas with books. Check. Becoming independently wealthy, so I can spend all my time just the way I want. Not quite, but I am working on it.

I have lived a life of struggle, and in many ways I am still struggling. But now I know who I am and what I want. I am sharing my story with you to give an idea of the kind of focus that is useful when applying the wealth-building equation.

I am not a hunter, but I will use a hunting metaphor. You can shoot game with a gun, but you are not going to hit much if you don't know what you are aiming at. The gun is a powerful tool. But only if you shoot it in the right direction. Don't shoot at pheasant if you only like quail.

The same is true with the wealth-building equation. It is a powerful tool, but it is wasted if you aim it in the wrong direction. If you are not sure what you want out of life, you can still use the wealth-building equation. It will empower you in your search. But it is more effective when aimed with precision.

My parents were raised in poverty, and I grew up poor myself; I was never exposed to the secrets of building wealth. Standing as an onlooker to the lives of the rich, I could not understand the sources of their good fortune. I remember visiting the home of one of my buddies in grammar school. His parents were quite rich and they lived in a large home with vast rooms, live-in servants, and various luxuries that held me in thrall. These were kindly people and they always treated me very well. Whenever I visited my friend, I felt transported into a magic kingdom where peace, goodness, and riches were plentiful.

It was a complete mystery to me how they came by so much abundance. I could only imagine that they were "lucky," and some great benefactor must have been very generous to them. That anyone could create so much wealth did not seem possible. They must have "gotten it" somewhere. But from where, I had no idea.

Throughout my upbringing I experienced a quiet longing for my family to have the comfort, conveniences, and freedoms enjoyed by my friend's family. But I could never see clearly how we might acquire them.

I had few explanations for the stories of people who got rich on television or in books or movies. I saw that some got lucky and struck it rich. Some hunted and found gold. Some were discovered and became movie stars. Some invented something new and unusual that everyone wanted to buy. Eventually, I learned that "some people have a knack for business" which blessed them with the ability to make money. That was about as close as I could ever come to penetrating the mystery of creating wealth.

Once I had reached adulthood and was on my own, scratching to earn a living, I found myself floundering. I was motivated to overcome poverty and achieve wealth, but unable to find concise information to direct my efforts. Eventually I boiled down my problem to a simple question: What can I do to earn the most money in a career I would enjoy?

To be honest, at that point I was more concerned with how to make a lot of money, and not so preoccupied with whether I would enjoy the work or not. Since then I have discovered it is very hard to work at something you don't enjoy and make money at it.

I sought out wealthy people to ask what the best way to achieve wealth is. I was met with puzzlement and disbelief. They couldn't understand why I would want to try and choose a career strictly on the basis of making the most money.

Later I learned that many people approach their careers and livelihood without clear financial goals. They make a good living almost by accident. Dad was a doctor, so they become a doctor and it just so happens to be a good-paying profession. Other people carry on the tradition of a family business, which may be a lucrative one. Many people live rich or poor as if fated to do so. There is a taboo in our society against striving for money. It is all right to *have* money, but you are not supposed to try and *get* money.

I was not able to find anyone who could offer sound advice in this area. They knew how they had become wealthy, and were willing to share their own experiences, but they could not offer general advice on the *best* way to become wealthy.

The solution to my problem was not forthcoming for many years.

I continued to read and educate myself on business, investment, and personal success, but never found any single source of comprehensive wisdom on the subject. Finally, after achieving financial success myself, I realized what the formula was, the equation I had been seeking for so long.

I distilled all the various requirements for a program of wealth-building down to five essential elements. Here is the formula, and a description of what it contains:

Attitude + Knowledge + Skills + Effort + Resources
= Power to Build Wealth

My wealth-building formula is not required for becoming rich. If your great-aunt Louise leaves you $5 million, then you are rich. No strings attached.

But if you are not wealthy already, and you know I mean more than just having money, then there is no better way to achieve it than applying the wealth-building equation to your life.

You can start out flat broke, or even deeply in debt, and still become wealthy by applying my formula. It is comprehensive and takes all aspects of your financial challenge into account. But it is not a magical formula that will somehow trick the universe into bestowing riches on you. It is a practical, down-to-earth, program. A plan of action you can apply until it succeeds.

No matter where you are on your way to wealth—just starting, almost there, or long since having achieved it—this equation will continue to work for you.

Briefly, the equation works like this. You have to begin with, and maintain, the right attitude toward pursuing and building wealth. Sufficient knowledge to understand wealth and pursue a specific course of action is essential. Skills are developed by putting knowledge into practice and gaining experience to master the process. Effort is necessary to overcome obstacles and transform ideas into action, plans into reality. And finally you have to cultivate and draw upon every resource at your command and constantly work to expand the resources at your disposal.

The secret of making money is finding or creating value, and earning a good return on your time, effort, and money, year after year. To make use of this secret, it is necessary to apply the wealth-building equation to achieve the power to build wealth. Here's how to do it:

Attitude

Everything you want out of life is going to come either as a direct result of your actions, or through good fortune. Personally I like good fortune. It's so much easier. I can just sit back and relax, and let the old good fortune come rolling in.

But good fortune is not all that reliable. Most people suffer a lot of bad fortune. Considering the millions of starving children around the world, and all the misfortune you find in the lives of rich and poor alike, good fortune is in short supply. There is not enough to go around.

The alternative is to abandon passivity and act in your own best interests. To become responsible for your own life and see to it that everything, or at least most things, turn out the way you want them to. This all depends on attitude. **The foundation of the wealth-building equation is an effective attitude.** An attitude that works.

Everything you do in life, the way you react to every situation, depends on your attitude. Your attitude is formed by your beliefs, ideas, opinions, emotions, thoughts, feelings, and philosophy of life. Attitude is basic.

I don't believe in a single prescription for attitude. So when I talk about positive or negative attitudes, good ones or bad ones, I am referring to what works for you—the outcomes that you want or don't want for your life.

I used to think that I was a "lucky" person, and that generally, "good" things happened to me. It was one of the most destructive attitudes of my life. I probably inherited it from my father, who suffered a dismal childhood in the depression. His survival depended on not letting life get him down. He had a devil-may-care attitude that said, "Ah hell, it ain't so bad. Life is just a ride." So I learned to roll with the punches and wait for good luck to come my way. And I waited, and waited, and waited . . . .

Whenever times got really tough I would cheer myself up with the thought that nothing *really* bad had ever happened to me. I thought I had suffered my share of misfortune, but nothing too terrible.

I thought that perhaps I was born under a lucky star which was watching over me, until my ship came in. I just needed to hang in there and wait for what I deserved out of life.

Psychologists call this kind of attitude *denial.* It is a psychological defense mechanism, a way the mind protects itself from getting too depressed about all the things that can go wrong in life. We all need mental defenses to help us cope, but they are also a source of self-delusion. We lose track of reality and believe in fantasy instead.

This mental defense, which I was using against misfortune, helped me get through some difficult times. But overall, it worked against me. I depended on the idea of being lucky, instead of relying on my own abilities. I refused to deal with the difficult challenge of living, reassuring myself that eventually I would get my "lucky break" and strike it rich, or find happiness.

I call that a bad attitude. In one stroke it crippled my ability to control my destiny, master my own fate. It is an example of a passive attitude that allows random events to control the course of life. In many ways I was just drifting along, allowing myself to be buffeted in one direction or another according to the events around me.

A big change of attitude took place when I was seventeen and read a self-help book entitled *Psycho-Cybernetics,* by Maxwell Maltz. I learned that I could shape my own future by imagining what I wanted, then taking action to achieve it. When I held my purpose firmly in mind, I was giving instructions to my thought processes to help me achieve that purpose.

This was a simple but powerful concept for me. It dramatically changed the way I thought about myself, my life, and lady luck. Instead of waiting for good fortune, I could create it. I could picture in my mind what I wanted to accomplish, and then set out to achieve it with confidence and purpose. The mind is a powerful tool when you give it a specific task to achieve and let it loose. That is attitude.

For the first time in my life I felt powerful. I had the resources within myself, within my own mind and body, to achieve my goals. I could become who I wanted to be, and have what I wanted out of life. I have used those principles ever since.

Some people have a faith in God that empowers them. An attitude keeps them charging ahead through life, to accomplish their goals. Albert Schweitzer, the famous doctor, philosopher, and humanitarian, spent most of his life in Africa tending to the sick and needy. He held a deep compassion for the people who came to him for help. This is an attitude that made the impossible, possible. Few people have the stamina and will to endure the difficulties he was subjected to, and to attain such heights of accomplishment. But his attitude of compassion, his need to help others, made him capable of awesome self-sacrifice and service to others.

In our day, Mother Theresa helps the sick and poor of India in the same way. She is known as a human dynamo, organizing aid for the poor, establishing hospitals, raising funds to build homes, and teaching people to minister to the sick. Her accomplishments are legion. What an attitude!

You have often heard how important it is to have a "positive attitude." Me too. I thought, "Wait a minute, this isn't right. I'm getting too negative. I need a positive mental attitude." Then I would feel a little better, and nothing would happen.

What is a positive mental attitude anyway? Think good thoughts. Look on the bright side. Chin up. Steady as she goes. There are more fish in the sea. It can't be all bad. Believe in yourself. Trust in Jesus. Think positive.

There are all sorts of "feel good" phrases we use on ourselves and one another to improve our mental attitude. What I am talking about is much more than this. It is everything that guides your behavior to achieve positive results and to avoid negative results.

Every action you take has consequences which are positive or negative for you. Study the outcome of your behavior and learn to recognize what sort of results it is producing for you. This is very important, because it is your *attitude* that produces the behavior, and the behavior always produces a *result.*

There are people who will fly off the handle over just about anything. They are like a volcano waiting to blow. They have an attitude all the time, and it is "pissed off."

Such a person may alienate everyone in his life and end up alone. Or he may become a forceful leader who bullies people into accomplishment. Anger is an emotional attitude that may produce negative or positive results depending on how it is used.

Belief is another kind of attitude. Jesus said, "Whatever you believe, so shall it be." I think he meant that your view of reality is formed by what you believe.

If I believe jobs are scarce and there is no point in wasting time looking for work, then that is my reality. That is how I see my world, and I will behave accordingly. The consequence of my belief is that I will sit at home drinking beer and watching soap operas, until the morning paper arrives with the good news that it is time to look for work again. Somebody might have just quit the job I need at a company six blocks away. I could walk over there, show my qualifications, and get a job right now. But that's impossible for me, because I believe otherwise. The job does not exist in my reality. It lives in another reality—the one in which jobs are always available to those who look hard enough and persist until they succeed. My belief is an attitude that makes me helpless and poor, until I recognize it as a false, or self-limiting, belief, and act differently.

Belief is a very tricky attitude. Some people will tell you to change your beliefs so that you can accomplish more. That is fine but belief is not something you choose, despite what religion and self-help gurus tell you. You cannot choose to believe in Jesus. You have to find Jesus. You cannot choose to believe in the Buddha or Krishna. You have to discover them in your life. You can choose to follow a religion or a path in life, but you cannot believe in it until it proves itself to you.

People often fake their belief when they feel they "should" believe in an idea, or they want to believe in it. You can tell yourself you believe one thing, but deep in your heart, feel that you believe something else. To believe, you must be convinced. You cannot just decide to believe. Your beliefs must match up with everything else you know about reality. We all carry a whole system of beliefs inside ourselves, a set of ideas about what is true and what is not true.

The way to form new beliefs is to study a question until you become convinced of the answer. This book is about accumulating wealth and making money. I am providing the information necessary to understand what it means to become wealthy. I am offering new attitudes and beliefs about wealth to convince you that it is not only possible, but necessary to your life. Everybody needs money and a good quality of life. This book is about how to make that happen and should convince you to take action and achieve wealth.

Your philosophy of life is an attitude that determines what you will do with your life. If your philosophy says "money is the root of all evil," then you will be suspicious of money, and reluctant to have much of it. If you are a university researcher and believe that seeking money will bring your motives into question, you may be afraid of financial success, or unwilling to pursue it. These philosophical viewpoints control behavior and produce consequences. If you recognize the consequences of your philosophy, you can decide whether to stick to that philosophy or not. The point is to understand how your philosophy affects your behavior and your wealth-building potential.

Emotions create powerful attitudes that control you consciously and unconsciously. Fear can make you reticent and unwilling to take the risks necessary to become financially successful. Fear can also help you safeguard your money against foolish schemes. Anger can produce explosive, irrational, and self-destructive behavior. Anger can also empower you to react forcefully against difficult and frustrating circumstances. Sorrow can lead to despair of wealth and loss of will. Sorrow can also produce remorse over past mistakes and guide you to reform your ways and improve your results.

Simple-minded motivational experts sometimes warn against fear, anger, and sorrow, as if these emotions are always negative. But these emotions serve a purpose and you can use them to help you.

You cannot avoid negative emotions. They are part of what it means to be a human being. But you can get in touch with them and recognize the power they have over you, and how they affect your behavior and decision making. You can also develop strong mental attitudes that counteract the effects of self-destructive emotional attitudes.

But to use emotions to help you, you have to recognize them and how they affect you. Get in touch with your emotions. Notice their control over you. Then learn to use your emotions in positive ways.

Negative emotional attitudes about yourself affect your energy and your willpower. If you look in the mirror and feel ugly, you will quickly give up the idea of becoming a fashion model. I recently read about a twenty-six-year-old fashion model who is making over $1 million a year. I saw her picture, too. I know lots of women who are as pretty as she is, but I will bet that when most of them look in the mirror, they don't see such an attractive looking person. It is all a matter of how you feel about yourself.

It takes energy, willpower, and self-confidence to become a successful fashion model. Without a positive self-image it becomes much more difficult. Some people get that by seeking constant reassurance. It is their tool to overcome their own insecurity. How do I look? Tell me I am spectacular. Love me, stroke me, I need the attention. This is the stereotype of the glamorous actress who demands that people fawn over her to help build her self-esteem. This is usually criticized as a sign of weakness and insecurity. It may also be the secret of her success. Without it she just might not be able to maintain the self-confidence to keep going, the energy to strive.

Some people learn to convert negative emotions into positive ones, or at least to use negative emotion positively. There are ugly people who become "characters" for commercials, movies, or television. It becomes their stock in trade. Roseanne Barr, the comedienne, uses her heavy appearance and working-class personality to create comedy. She has turned emotions and qualities that make many people feel helpless about their life into a formula for success. All it took was for her to change one attitude to become wealthy, famous, and successful. Instead of thinking, "I am a fat loudmouth, nobody is ever going to like me, or reward me for who I am," she thought, "If I can make people laugh, I may become rich and famous." And she did.

Attitude is everything. It all starts there. But I am not going to tell you to change your attitude. **Understand your attitude, and it will change by itself.**

We have all been told at one time or another that we have a bad attitude and need to change. We have been shamed into believing we are failures and told to change. This is very destructive.

Noticing your attitudes and how they affect your life brings about greater awareness and the possibility of change. But many pop psychologists with a superficial approach to where attitudes come from recommend that people force change on themselves as soon as they discover a negative attitude. It is not that simple. Our attitudes are interconnected at deep levels. Their meaning is not always obvious. You have to give yourself time to understand the variety of attitudes you hold, and where they come from at these deeper levels. Fundamental change then becomes possible.

Your attitudes are your own business. But I want you to understand the effect your attitudes have on your life, because attitude is a tool for building wealth.

This book is giving you some new attitudes. Not all of them are new to you, of course. You may be familiar with most of them. But I can guarantee that if you are familiar with all of them, you don't need this book. You are already on a sure path to wealth. Because that is what this book is about—attitudes that lead to wealth.

The wealth-building attitude is simple. Once you understand what wealth is, and how to achieve it, you have the attitude you need. You must decide what wealth means to you, and whether you are willing to pay the price.

If $10 million in cash is your idea of wealth, but you are not willing to do what it takes to earn it, then the price is too high. You are not getting the value you want for your effort. You have just recalculated your wealth-building plan. You have two opposing attitudes that cancel each other out. "I will be wealthy when I have $10 million, but it requires too much effort, so I guess I will not be wealthy." These two attitudes combine to form a failed attitude.

But the wealth-building attitude does not stop there. Readjust your thinking until your wealth-building plan matches your desires *and* the price you are willing to pay.

If you don't give up on yourself, on who you are and what you want, you will continually learn how to become more, how to get more, and how to compromise less. If you reach too high, you may fall flat and end up with nothing. But if you reach too low, you are guaranteed to settle for little. Continually reach for the possible, and become what it takes to achieve it. Then raise your expectations, and reach for more.

I don't recommend striving for its own sake. Some people get high on struggling to accomplish more in life. If that is what you want to do, fine. I strive in order to achieve what is important for me, not to impress others with my accomplishments or to prove my worthiness. Striving is the means to an end: to achieve quality of life and become wealthy, on my terms.

Everybody has a desire for wealth. Everyone wants a good life. That's an attitude. Even the most self-destructive individual is acting out an urge to achieve success, to do well and find value in life, to become wealthy. Sometimes you simply have to adjust your attitude to become wealthy.

You may even discover that you are almost there already; most of what you want out of life is right in front of you and it just never occurred to you to reach out and grab it. It can be so close, and yet seem so far away.

Attitude is a powerful force and it grows from many sources—the opinions of others, how we feel, what we think, the information we receive, the biases we form, the preconceptions we hold, the model of life we choose to live by.

Attitude is choice, and it is also forced upon us by our emotions and beliefs. We can pursue a change of attitude, or create new attitudes. The willingness to broaden our knowledge and understanding of ourselves and how life works is an attitude that can make all the difference. This one attitude can allow our emotions to grow and change, and permit us to form new beliefs, new ways of dealing with ourselves and our world.

Attitude is not static, it is dynamic. It feeds on itself. We all have a thousand different attitudes that control our behavior and change as life gives us new feedback, new results.

When I discovered how wealth works, had financial successes, and realized what happiness means to me, my attitude was completely changed. My beliefs about myself, how life works, and what is possible, were transformed.

I always had the attitude that my life was important and that someday I would succeed. I also learned that success depends on effort and wanting it badly enough. Sometimes I felt the price was too high and I would give up. Sometimes I felt that I had to struggle on no matter what. I was never sure of what the outcome would be and it took a lot of trial and error before I became convinced that I could achieve my goals.

But every new success has bred a new attitude, a new belief.

I had known since I was a teenager that attitude is important. I understood the power of attitude. I also knew I could change my attitudes. Some of my worst attitudes overwhelmed me. They were a huge millstone around my neck, weighing me down for years.

These showstopping attitudes are the worst kind, the ones you really have to watch out for. A showstopping attitude can short-circuit everything. Everyone has showstopping attitudes that drag him or her down toward failure. In order to build wealth you have to deal with your showstoppers. I have already said that I am not going to tell you to change your attitudes. It is futile to observe destructive emotions and beliefs and tell yourself to change them. That does not work. It only adds another bad attitude to the problem; that is, "Gee, I have a lot of bad attitudes. I am never going to make it," or "I have just got to change these bad attitudes. I am really going to try and change these attitudes. I really must change these attitudes. Oh hell, what's the use?" These are showstopping attitudes in themselves.

The best way to deal with showstopping attitudes is to notice that they exist, recognize what a negative effect they have on your life, and use other attitudes to offset them.

Play around with attitudes to get a perspective that works. Adjust your thinking. Learn to change your behavior—just to find out what happens. Be flexible. Our attitudes are plastic. Some are easy to change, some remain fixed for a long time and suddenly are smashed down by some new insight or experience.

Here are some other examples of showstopping attitudes that can trip up your wealth-building goals:

"This is a stupid book. This guy does not know what he is talking about. He is a bullshit artist. This is not helping me. I am not getting anywhere."

The book closes. The mind closes. No action is taken. No change of attitude takes place. A showstopper.

"I am a failure, everybody knows that. I have tried, but nothing works. I give up. What is the use? I can only manage to plod along and achieve a mediocre existence. There is no point in expecting any more than that."

This is an all too familiar showstopper. Life has bruised many people to the point where they end up here. Many of us manage to keep up the brave face, but underneath, these are the messages circling around in our thoughts and feelings again and again.

"People who want to make a lot of money are just greedy, they don't care about others, they just want to exploit them. I will never become like that."

This is an interesting wealth-building showstopper, and quite popular. It is a gross generalization that lumps everybody who is trying to make a lot of money into one category, and virtually eliminates your own chances of financial success. My belief on this has already been stated. It is possible to make money without hurting others, and to actually benefit others by producing more wealth for everyone to share. Many people step on those around them in order to make their grab for money, and I am not so naive I believe we live in a world full of good intentions. There are a lot of money-grubbing, evil people striving after wealth. But I am not so foolish as to believe it has to be true for me and everyone else as well. That is a showstopping attitude.

Some things in life are not in your control and fall into the good luck or bad luck category. But most of what happens to you *is* within your control if you are willing to take charge of it. The way to take charge of it is with attitude.

Dealing with attitude is the first step to making the wealth-building equation work. For more ideas about how to work with your attitudes, see Chapter 12, "Motivation and Success."

The rest of the wealth-building equation, involving knowledge, skills, effort, and resources, depends on the attitude you bring to it. Notice your attitude about these other aspects of the wealth-building equation as I discuss them. How does your attitude affect your ability to make use of these other tools? Is this just a bunch of mumbo jumbo, or are these exciting tools, inspirational ideas, practical concepts, to put you in control of your wealth-building plan? You decide.

Knowledge

Knowledge is what we use to understand life. It explains how things work and it forms our beliefs. The less knowledge we have, the less we can understand life and what it means to us. The old saying is that "knowledge is power." It gives us more options, more ways to understand ourselves and control our circumstances. There is no limit to what knowledge can accomplish. There is a limit to what is possible, but nobody knows what that limit is. Therefore our possibilities are limitless.

This is a book of knowledge. It contains information that has the same kind of power that the design of the airplane had in its day—the power to give flight to hopes and dreams. Many people thought the Wright brothers were crazy. Eccentric bicycle makers trying to do the impossible. But today we take airplanes for granted. We are blasé about hopping on a plane and flying across the country in a few hours.

I did not have to invent the ideas in this book. Most of them have been around for a long time. Some of them have been around for thousands of years and produced wealth for ancient merchants and kings. But I have acquired this knowledge and packaged it into a high-performance toolkit for building wealth. But like any tool, if you leave it lying in the toolbox, it can never serve its purpose. It never gets a chance to perform.

Knowledge is a part of the wealth-building equation, because it gives you the power to understand and achieve wealth. Without the knowledge of who you are and what life means, you can never know what can be accomplished with your life and how much satisfaction is in store for you. **Making money and improving the quality of your life are made possible by knowledge.**

I have written a book full of useful knowledge, but I am also giving you knowledge as a principle, as a creed to live by. I know this sounds obvious. All you have to do is read the inscription on the dedication plaque at your local library to learn this truism. But when truth becomes too familiar it loses its force and its value for us.

This is an opportunity to stop and think. What do I know? What am I learning? Have I stopped learning? What do I still need to know, so that I can achieve my goals?

The pursuit of knowledge is an art. It is a unique skill that you can develop. In my naiveté, I used to want to know everything. Literally. I am a generalist so I try to maintain broad interests. But this shotgun approach to learning, stuffing my mind with trivia, was a mistake. I later targeted my learning more closely to my wealth-building goals.

Aim your knowledge at specific targets that will help you achieve your own goals. Read the books that will make a difference in your life. Associate with people who can teach you what you need to learn for success. Dedicate yourself to understanding the solutions to your problems. Use the power of knowledge to overcome challenges.

The idea of pursuing knowledge is very intimidating to some people. They have a showstopping attitude about it. The pursuit of knowledge is for intellectuals or "smart people." They may not want to be an intellectual, because they associate it with snobbery, or becoming a "brainy" type. They may also feel that they are "stupid" or not good in school. These are all fatal attitudes toward knowledge. They are also wrong.

There is no such thing as a stupid person, unless he or she has organic brain damage. Every healthy brain is brilliant and capable of learning new knowledge. But it is possible to run a program in the brain that short-circuits its intelligence. It is called the "just call me stupid and leave me alone" program. For many people it becomes too painful to make the effort to learn, or deal with the whole question of intellect or knowledge. They have had too many bad experiences with poor teachers and inadequate schooling.

Some people have that attitude only in certain areas, like math. "I am no good at math, so I won't bother with that." *Everybody* can learn math. Some people are better at it than others because of their background, upbringing, or special mental aptitudes—but every healthy brain can learn math. People who have not learned math are not suffering from a lack of intelligence. They are suffering from a lack of education. These are the kinds of people who are taught to think they are stupid and can never learn anything, when they have just never been given the chance.

Nearly every day you can read in the newspapers about the national crisis in education: most of our schools are not very good at educating people. Only a few schools succeed in offering a good education. These few schools are not only good at educating intelligent people, they are good at educating *all* people.

There are examples of inner-city teachers who have taken the toughest kinds of kids, the chronic failures, and taught them to excel. Jaime Escalante, an actual math teacher portrayed in the movie *Stand and Deliver,* taught potential high school dropouts how to do advanced mathematics.

If you want to learn something important, the hardest part about it may not be overcoming your intellectual deficiencies; the hardest part may be finding a good source of information, finding a good teacher.

Of course I recommend going to the library and using books to educate yourself. If you have the reading skills necessary to use this book, then there is no reason you cannot use many of the books offered at the library. But there is an important drawback to books. The quality of the information they contain, and how it is presented, affects how much you learn. I spent years reading academic and technical material in my profession as an information systems analyst. I used to feel pretty stupid and intimidated until I learned enough to realize what incompetent writers and thinkers these authors were. Granted, the material they were presenting was highly technical, but their understanding and presentation of the material made it much worse. It is the responsibility of the teacher to teach so that the student can learn. I came to realize that many technical writers don't understand their subject matter, which is why they present it in confusing ways. I worked with many technical writers to develop computer manuals (you computer users know what I am talking about here), and I have never seen such a mess in my life. They were always so rushed to get the material out, it is no wonder it was hard to understand and full of errors. A lot of academic material, textbooks and so forth, are written in such an incomprehensible manner.

So as you study books, don't overtax your self-esteem struggling through poorly written misinformation. If it doesn't make sense, move on! In fact, if you read material in this book that does not make sense, don't get discouraged; just skip ahead and move on.

It is not always possible to learn everything from books. Many times you need a human teacher or some other media such as seminars, audiotapes, videotapes, television, or computers to help you.

Learn what educational resources are available and use the ones that work for you.

But whatever you do, keep on learning. It keeps your mind alive and alert. The brain is just like muscle; the more you exercise it the better it works. The way the brain works to create new ideas is to draw inferences from existing ideas by making new connections. The more ideas the brain contains, the more connections become possible. The more connections you make about your life and earning potential, the greater your wealth will be. Every new piece of information multiplies the power of the mind. It thrives on stimulation, thoughts, ideas, and the effort to contemplate new concepts. Exercise your mind. THINK! That is the famous motto pasted on walls all over the IBM company. THINK!

Think about the concepts in this book, too, as steppingstones to a new way of life, in which you apply the principles of creating wealth. There is a list of suggested reading at the back of this book to help expand your knowledge. Use it!

The way to use knowledge with the wealth-building equation is to take aim and attack the knowledge that is most relevant to you and what you want to accomplish with your life. If you are pursuing a specific career, learn all you can about it. If you are starting a business, learn whatever you can about it and the particular industry you are developing products or services for. If you want to move to the country to make a home there, get magazines on country living from the library and study them for ideas. Buy books about how to search for nice areas to live.

I know people who tell me they never read nonfiction, only mystery or romance novels. This is incredible to me. I cannot believe anyone would waste the precious gift of reading, that valuable ability, on mere entertainment alone.

Read whatever you can that will add value to your mind, your skills, your capacity to increase the quality of your life and achieve your dreams.

Until you get the right perspective on learning, the right attitude, you will not strive for knowledge. So attitude is basic. But once you are in the proper frame of mind to learn, knowledge becomes the most powerful component of the wealth-building equation. Knowledge is everything.

With the right knowledge you can become a millionaire in a week. That is a literal fact. If I could give you the winning bet on a horse, the name of a stock about to skyrocket in price, the number to bet in the lottery, or the location of buried treasure, you could become rich overnight. Of course the real world does not work like that. Nobody gives away such knowledge. You have to find it. But there are other types of knowledge that work the same way. I knew people in the computer field who charged twice the consulting fee I was making, because they knew how a special computer chip worked. They had studied it and were some of a few people who really knew how it worked. There are lots of examples of people who make more money because of their specialized knowledge. Income studies have shown over and over again that earning power correlates directly with the number of years of school completed. The more you know, the more employers are willing to pay you for your work.

Finally, keep in mind that I am not saying you have to be smart. A lot of smart people are not wealthy in either the material or the spiritual sense. They may have greater intellectual capacity than the rest of us, but they don't have the knowledge that counts—the knowledge that would allow them to build wealth.

Many people who have achieved great wealth and satisfaction in life were not especially smart, certainly no smarter than the average individual. They simply had the knowledge necessary to apply the principles of wealth and to achieve their chosen goals in life. Don't worry about how "intelligent" you are. People are not stupid, unless they are suffering from brain damage. Many of us have mental blocks from attitudes that short-circuit our action, our thinking, our imagination, the expanse of our minds, but we are not stupid. We just need new attitudes to help us open up to the great possibilities of our life, and to allow us to acquire the knowledge we need for success.

Skills

For me, part of growing up and becoming a confident adult involved learning and trusting my skills. I have distinct memories of feeling inept as a child and young adult. It seemed like everybody else was faster, more intelligent, more confident, stronger, better coordinated, and more skillful.

It seemed I had only one talent as a child, my intellect, and even there I was never the best. I did well in school, but in every classroom there was always someone who scored higher and seemed smarter.

I became fairly certain I was a "no talent" individual.

My low self-esteem in this area affected me in two ways. It made me feel that I could not take on difficult challenges, because I lacked the talent to meet them. And it made me want to learn and do everything I possibly could, to compensate for my lack of ability.

What I did not understand, and what nobody taught me, is that everyone is talented. We all feel intimidated and frustrated when learning new skills, because it involves challenge and failure. But every healthy body and brain has the ability to coordinate its actions and refine them into skill. If you picture in your mind what you want to accomplish, and practice the skills necessary to achieve it, your brain will learn how to do it. All you have to do is persist in the practice and notice your mistakes, so that the brain will make refinements.

By the time I reached adulthood and had to earn a living to support myself, I felt completely inadequate to the task. I lacked the interest to pursue any particular career, and I felt incompetent to perform any useful tasks. I felt like a basket case. I could have remained helpless and incompetent for the rest of my life, but I was so desperate to survive that I attacked the problem with a will. I bounced from one job to another for several years until I landed in a profession as a general building contractor.

Here I was challenged to acquire many skills necessary for success. I needed manual skills to do carpentry and construction, handle tools, and craft the details of homes. I needed business skills to manage my employees, keep my record books, find jobs and deal with customers, and manage my financial affairs. And I needed the intellectual and emotional skills to deal with all the kinds of human problems I faced as an adult with my own business, a personal life to cope with, and a wide variety of responsibilities.

And as it turns out, I managed to acquire all the necessary skills to make a success of it. This was an exhilarating experience for me, because it taught me the most important lesson of my life. Wherever I point my interests or desires, I can learn sufficient skills to succeed, if I persist. This realization turned night into day for me. I saw all the "failures" of my childhood and early adulthood in a new light.

I had grown up thinking that skills come from talent. If you have the "natural ability" for some activity, you can perform it. I had lived under the chronic misconception as a child that I was not "creative" and had no "artistic" talents. I thought talent is something you are born with, not something you acquire.

In reality, we know that both are true. There is a genetic component to talent, and the different experiences we have in our development affect our aptitude for certain skills. But I was under the gross misconception that if I did not have talent already, I would never have it.

Every skill requires practice and refinement. No one is born with any ability but to yowl, sleep, and suckle at his mother's breast. Every other ability is acquired through effort, trial and error, success and failure, frustration and persistence.

Learning to walk and talk as a baby are extremely difficult challenges. Both are skills that require years of effort, practice, and refinement. Most children begin to talk at around two years of age and don't really begin to speak like adults until they are about twelve. Then they spend the rest of their lives refining vocabulary and usage. Talking is a very difficult skill. So are walking, running, leaping, and bounding about. Kids spend their whole childhoods in frantic play, in order to develop the foundation skills necessary to function as adults.

No one ever explained to me that as a human being, I am the most talented animal on the planet. No other animal has demonstrated the desire, the intellect, or the manual dexterity to produce the wonders of art, science, and culture that humankind has produced. We are unmatched.

If I had known this, I would not have be so blasé and discouraged about my own abilities. I would not have wasted so many years, so much precious time wishing I had talents, instead of working at and developing talents.

I am not a believer in the competition to be the "best." I find the obsession with winning that is so rampant in the American culture to be a an antisocial disease. But I do believe in being all that you *want* to be, all that you can be. And I have discovered that I can be all I want to be. If I am willing to pay the price of success, and persist at developing the necessary skills, I can accomplish whatever I want.

One of my sports is table tennis. I play in the local club. I play to win, and I love winning. I work as hard as I can to outmaneuver my opponent. And I get a great thrill out of developing my skill and watching myself improve. But we have a player in our club who was nationally ranked when he was still very active in the sport. I don't know of anyone in the club who has taken a single match off our star player. I love to play him. He has taught me a great deal, and it is fun to see how many shots I can win off him. But I don't have the time or the interest to struggle to beat him. I have other priorities in life.

The big problem for me with all this "play to win" stuff, the competitive mode of skill-building, is that for every "winner," everyone else is categorized as a "loser" and shamed. Even the winners become losers, eventually. All stars become "has-beens," and few of them accept it with calm assurance. We all want to be in the spotlight for our whole lives.

As far as I am concerned, we all should be. We cannot all share the spotlight of national acclaim, but we can live in the spotlight of our own successes. We should all recognize what geniuses we are, and get into a successful attitude. Not success in the eyes of others, although that is nice too, but success in our own eyes. The success of achieving what we want in life.

Most people have a limited idea of what they can accomplish in their life. They are taught to feel inadequate in so many different ways, to feel "average." This would not be so bad, except that we all think of average as mediocre and not very good. Average in a society that teaches that winning is everything, is far below our real potential. We feel too discouraged about our abilities.

The need for skills is very similar to the need for knowledge in the wealth-building equation. Becoming wealthy does not require you to be "smart." Likewise, it does not require you to be "talented." But it is necessary that you develop your skills. Applying skills to your wealth-building project is the only way it will succeed. How much skill will be required depends entirely on how you define wealth, how ambitious your goals are, and how difficult they are to achieve.

For some people, having a steady job, owning their own modest home, and finding enough time to relax and enjoy a little recreation will be the greatest challenge and demand all of their skill. There are plenty of people who would envy such an accomplishment.

Others will not be satisfied until they have built a business empire, own several homes around the world, achieve wide recognition and acclaim, establish several charitable foundations, and leave their mark on the world for history to remember them by.

The wealth-building equation demands only the level of skill that you define for yourself, based on your own desires and goals. The development of your abilities requires effort, practice, and some degree of self-sacrifice. That is the price you pay for acquiring them. It is up to you to decide whether your goals are worth the price that must be paid.

Skills, like knowledge, are a valuable commodity. You can trade on your skills to build wealth. Once you have decided on a career, a line of business, or a profession, target your skill-building efforts in that direction. Skills make you more effective and increase your ability to find or create wealth. They also empower you to do more with less, and to increase the rate of return on your time and effort.

Focus on what you want, what wealth means to you, and work at the skills that will make that possible in the shortest amount of time. Time is the most valuable commodity in life and we get only a limited amount of it. Learning to use time effectively is one of the most valuable skills you can cultivate.

You have to dedicate a lot of time to developing skills, but this time and effort will eventually be rewarded by much greater wealth. The refusal to cultivate necessary skills is much more expensive in the long-run than the cost of acquiring new skills.

Decide which skills interest you the most and offer the most desirable rewards. The talented actor, investor, marketing executive, carpenter, photographer, writer, politician, corporate manager, legal secretary, doctor, sign painter, plumber, has a valuable asset to use in creating wealth in exchange for money or other rewards. Some of the reward may be in the satisfaction of accomplishment. It may also be in the recognition and acclaim. Great accomplishments sometimes confer honor, privilege, and unusual influence and power over others. The accomplished composer and musician may be granted the money and stature to direct the creative talents of others in an orchestra. There are many ways in which skill may be rewarded—all of which represent forms of personal wealth. And all of which demand their price in commitment, perseverance, time and effort.

The best way to develop any skill is to seek out the training and advice of someone who has mastered it. But a skilled practitioner is not always the best teacher. And others are better at teaching skills than mastering them. Seek qualified instruction when you can.

You may find a mentor, someone who is willing to share her knowledge and experience with you and take you on as her protégé. Or you may simply study the life of someone whom you respect and wish to emulate.

With any skill there is the right way, the wrong way, and the best way. The right way to learn and master a skill is to study and use the techniques of those instructors who have spent years developing and refining them. A qualified instructor will have studied a skill to understand its mastery and to develop methods for teaching it to others in the most effective way. A good instructor will try to accelerate the learning process as much as possible. The measure of success is whether a skill produces the results intended. If a particular tennis stroke gives more players the winning edge, then that is the right stroke to use.

Really good instructors know that besides the right way and the wrong way, there is also the *best* way to exercise skill. Some people develop their skills in unorthodox ways. They are not always good at doing it the "right way," but they are very good at doing it in their own way—the way that works best for them.

Sometimes you have to decide that what works best for you is the right way, and get rid of the textbooks and ignore the experts. Just do what works, as long as you are getting the results you desire.

Make a habit of increasing your level of skill in all the wealth-building areas you are involved in. It is like improving the quality of the equipment you use to perform any task. A brilliant violinist cannot possibly produce the best music from a cheap violin. A good physician maintains and improves his skills by constantly reading and studying the latest medical journals and by attending seminars. Likewise you cannot maximize your wealth with shoddy tools. Invest in yourself. Treat yourself like the delicate and valuable instrument you are. Refine your edges; hone your skills to obtain all the wealth you deserve from life.

Effort

In one sense effort is tied with attitude as the most important part of the wealth-building equation. If you never exert any effort toward your wealth-building goals, you can never achieve them. But effort follows behind attitude, knowledge, and skills, because you can exert massive effort to achieve wealth and never succeed if you approach it with the wrong attitudes and insufficient knowledge and skill.

Effort is the most difficult and challenging part of the wealth-building equation. It is the muscle that drives the rest of the equation. Nothing can be accomplished without it.

There are many subtle aspects to effort and various pitfalls to avoid. Some people try to get by on effort alone, charging ahead with great energy, but getting few results. They forget the old saying that it is better to work smart than to work hard. You cannot just bulldoze your way through every problem or challenge. You have to approach it with the proper attitude and sufficient knowledge and skill. But acquiring and applying knowledge and skill, requires a great deal of effort. It is the price of success and cannot be avoided.

Effort has been the great nemesis of my life. It causes me more discomfort than anything. I am basically lazy by nature. I love calm, serenity, ease, and effortlessness. I want to glide through life like surfing a wave, propelled through one exciting and pleasurable experience after another, without ever being resisted and dulled by the need for effort.

Part of the problem for me has been my difficulty in visualizing my accomplishments before they happen. What is the point of exerting the effort if there is no reward, nothing to be gained? And how do I know if my efforts will pay off? I would rather relax and enjoy life now than have to work for uncertain rewards.

The only way to know if your efforts will bear fruit is to pay the price of admission and take your chances. Not exactly a great bargain. Laziness is a much better bet. At least you are more certain of your outcome. You are not going to accomplish anything, amount to much, or reap many of life's advantages, but at least your time is your own and you don't have to work hard at anything.

It is very difficult to motivate people to work if they cannot see the advantage in it. It is just too enervating to exert yourself without some gain in sight. Remember all the movies you have seen with prison bosses, drill sergeants, and slave drivers yelling orders and dishing out punishment? Nobody ever looks happy or energetic. They are all depressed and moving in slow motion. Everybody glances from one side to the other and passes a subtle message around the group with body language. The message is; "Don't anybody go any faster, or we will all have to work harder." Everybody falls into an average slow pace, moving just fast enough to keep up and avoid the lash of the whip.

You cannot beat people hard enough to make them do a good job if they hate it. There has to be a carrot, some payoff to make it worth while.

Effort requires two things: willpower and a compensating reward.

We are constantly bombarded with messages offering us rewards for expending effort. That is what the advertising industry is all about. Advertising is meant to appeal to our desires and to motivate us to make the effort to purchase products and services. We work hard for our money. We are not going to throw it away without some promise of reward.

But faced with so many fake promises, we have all grown accustomed to ignoring most of the rewards offered to us. We are rightfully suspicious of empty promises that offer no real payoffs. Finding motivation becomes difficult.

The whole point of motivation and success seminars is to convince people of the rewards they can achieve if they exert the necessary willpower. The seminars attempt to instill belief through dramatic claims for success.

From belief the necessary action should follow—the willingness to strive for success.

That is what this book is about, as well. It contains the knowledge necessary to instill belief—to show you exactly how wealth works, and how you can become wealthy. This will give you the willpower to exert the effort necessary for success. When you can visualize the reward, when you understand what wealth is, and can picture how you may achieve it, then the effort becomes worth it.

Willpower is the raw fuel behind effort. Willpower is fed by the urge to win, to get ahead, to achieve a goal, to get the prize, but it also can become a force of habit. Willpower is a habit that can be exercised and developed.

Habits are formed through repetition. The more often you repeat a task, the less difficult it seems. It becomes automatic. When you are first learning a new skill or chore, it requires effort, but after a while it becomes easier and easier.

To make willpower a habit you have to practice it. It is the most difficult habit there is to develop and maintain, but it is also the most useful one. Every time you are faced with a difficult or uncomfortable task which you believe you ought to perform, just do it.

Visualization and concentration are very powerful tools for developing the willpower habit. Despite your feelings of anxiety, resistance, self-doubt, or any other discomfort you feel, visualize yourself performing the task. Don't add any frills to your visualization, don't imagine that it is going to be fun or rewarding to do the task, simply visualize yourself performing it, like a robot, without emotion. Don't attach any emotion, negative or positive, to your performance. See it as a neutral and mechanical event. Concentrate your attention on the visualization of performing the task until you can clearly see it in your mind. Once you have it clearly in mind, don't pause. Pull the trigger, snap into action, and go do it!

Don't start this exercise by trying to get a raise out of your boss, or telling your boyfriend you don't want to see him anymore. Try it out on simple little distasteful chores that you always procrastinate about. If you hate doing the dishes and you always leave them until they stack up to the ceiling, use this exercise on them. As soon as you think of the dishes, remember this exercise and apply it, right then and there. Picture yourself in the kitchen doing the dishes. Concentrate until all other distractions and rationalizations or excuses have been replaced by the exercise. When you clearly see yourself standing at the sink scrubbing away, go there and do it.

Use the exercise at the first sign of laziness or procrastination for everything you want to do. Eventually you will not need the exercise in order to accomplish your little tasks. Your will, having become strengthened, jumps in when you need it to get you going. As you use the "visualization snap to action" technique on more difficult chores, you will gain confidence at getting things done. Then other forces come into play to help you become more action-oriented. You feel better about yourself, and chores stop reminding you of how lazy you are. Instead, they remind you of how much you are able to accomplish when you put your mind to it. Accomplishment is its own reward. There is something in human nature that produces a sense of satisfaction and well-being after completing tasks and achieving goals. Your self-confidence and self-esteem build, and these become rewarding experiences that motivate you to action and feed your willpower.

We have all had that experience. The more we procrastinate and let things go, the worse we feel about ourselves. We become infected with discouragement, despair, and the feeling of overwhelming helplessness and depression. Yuck! Get out of this muck. It takes all the fun out of laziness.

If you have ever succeeded in an exercise regimen or diet program, you have experienced what I am talking about. Getting started is the hardest part. That first effort to take action on your own behalf is the most difficult. But once you get going, a few days or weeks into your program without any slips, momentum develops. You start feeling good about yourself. You have established a routine and gotten into the habit of doing your program. Pretty soon you experience the results of your effort and the rewards it brings. You start looking and feeling better, and it all seems worth it.

The most common cause of failure in life is the refusal to take action. It is in that critical moment, that instant of choice, when you can go or stay, do it or give up. With every new endeavor that moment stands as the lion at the gate. It is like the gargoyle of a medieval church. When you start through the doorway of a new endeavor, the hideous gargoyle of fear, uncertainty, and doubt, raises its huge ugly head with glaring red eyes, and out roars the voice of challenge. "Who dares approach the doorway to success and prosperity, *you?* Worthless, good-for-nothing, helpless wretch! Be gone, before I give you what you deserve, a mouthful of dust and the scorching shame and embarrassment of your foolish presumptions."

We all want to admit to failure before it even happens. Get it over with and give up at the outset. Why face the pain of failure? Only a masochist would want to endure that.

But effort is the greatest secret of success. It contains the power to overcome despair of wealth. The one thing failure can never conquer is patience, perseverance, and effort. No matter how many times you fail, or how many rejections you endure, every time you come back to play the game, you will be stronger and smarter.

Stacy Allison, the first American woman to climb to the top of Mount Everest, after trying and failing once, said; "I had to fail to realize that self-worth isn't built upon one accomplishment. It's built through years of setting goals and reaching them."

There is a paradox in the cycle of trial and error, effort and failure. The paradox is that if you go on long enough you will feel weaker, when you are actually stronger. You cannot help but learn lessons from trying and failing. But frustration and discouragement accumulate and attack your will so that you feel weaker. You may have to build your will even stronger to come back into the game yet one more time. But finally, once you succeed (and everyone succeeds if he or she doesn't give up), you will be awesome. The old saying is that gold must be purified by fire. Golden success is purified by the effort to succeed and the burning shame of failure that must be endured in the many attempts that are required.

Of course we all know people who are overnight successes. It was easy from the start and little effort was required. They just had the knack or the good fortune to achieve success from the start. Don't you just hate those people?

I have a friend who was in drama class with Tom Cruise. She thought he was "a dweeb" and never paid much attention to him. Then his name was Thomas Cruise Mapother IV. When Cruise got his breaks and became a megastar, she was green with envy. That's human nature. We can't understand why others get all the breaks when we are trying just as hard and have just as much talent.

I recently saw an interview on *Sixty Minutes* with Jay Leno, who took over the *Tonight Show* from Johnny Carson. Leno spent ten years doing 300 shows a year in little comedy clubs all over the country before he began to achieve some recognition and fame. Leno joked that he doesn't know why he stuck with it for so long, except he did not feel qualified for any other job. Leno is now extremely wealthy, with a large garage on his Beverly Hills estate that contains his private car collection. He paid over half a million dollars for some of his cars. Leno loves them. All of his many years of effort to cultivate the attitude, knowledge, and skills that have made him a success in his profession paid off with a bonanza of returns. The rate of return on his ten years of time, and all the effort and money he put back into his career, have paid many millions of dollars in dividends. Way to go, Jay!

Effort is the nuclear weapon of success. It will blast away any obstacle that stands in front of you.

Resources

Resources are the poor cousins to the other components of the wealth-building equation—attitude, knowledge, skill, and effort. The resources component of the wealth-building equation is a grab bag of everything else you need to help build wealth. You name it: if it helps you to earn money and enhance the quality of your life, use it.

Time and good health are your most precious resources. You must guard them carefully. Make good use of your time; you have only so much of it. It's like what Will Rogers said about real estate, "They ain't making any more of it."

Making good use of your time is a matter of understanding its value and spending it wisely. Time is like cash. It is easy to squander and it requires strong self-discipline to use it well. But unlike money, time keeps running out whether you like it or not. You are always spending your time, and it is up to you whether the time is wasted, or giving you value for value. Just like spending money, you can spend your time for enjoyment, or invest it to increase your returns, or you can just waste it. There is nothing wrong with spending money for fun, as long as you don't overdo it. The same goes for time. You can afford only so much for fun—after that you start going into debt, if you don't put some time into taking care of business.

A lot of people waste time because they don't know what to do with themselves. They have no direction or purpose in life. No reason to take a positive course of action. They don't understand what a valuable resource time is and how it can be invested to pay huge dividends later on in their lives.

I have a great deal of remorse over my "misspent youth." Such an apt phrase. So much of my time went out the window, just staring at the walls. I wasn't even enjoying my laziness; I was just depressed. I look back on those years now and think of the lost treasures of time I squandered, how my despair of wealth immobilized me. I wish I'd had this book then, and those years to live over again. I could have accomplished so much for myself. If only . . . .

Jim Rohn, a success and motivation speaker, once said, "You either suffer the pain of discipline or the pain of regret." It is all spilt milk now, but I have learned my lesson and value my time above all else. And these days I don't mind the discipline, because I am having the time of my life.

Jim Rohn also gave me another credo to live by: "Don't spend casual time with casual people. Spend time with people of substance." This idea really struck me, because it immediately brought to mind all the time I have spent with people I found uninteresting and unimaginative, just gabbing away about nothing, making chitchat. I now realize most of that time was spent trying to get people to like me and offer me something more. Nowadays I spend time only with people I truly enjoy or who have something valuable to offer me: interesting knowledge or ideas, conversation to stimulate my thinking or awareness, or some other mutual benefit. I have systematically practiced a discipline of eliminating casual people from my life, people I don't really care about who just take up my time and attention and waste them for me. Who needs that?

I used to feel an obligation to be nice to people and not reject them. It was like putting up a sign over my door: "The price of admission to my life is free. My time is worthless; please help me waste more of it." Now my sign reads: "My life means a lot to me, I care about myself, and my time is valuable. The price of admission to my life is a mutually beneficial relationship that is emotionally, mentally, or materially rewarding. No soliciting."

Uninvited telephone calls and drop-in visits are terrible time wasters. I have an answering machine, and I don't answer my phone when I am busy. None of my friends are invited for drop-in visits. My life is not that casual; I have too much I want to accomplish. A friend of mine gets one drop-in visit for free; the next time he is put on notice: "Please do not drop in without calling in advance." I have a hard time disciplining myself to come out and make this request, but I have learned to do it, because it is so important.

I was talking with a friend of mine about how important it is to develop useful business contacts, people who can help you. She felt very uncomfortable with this idea because it seems so manipulative, just a way of using people for your own ends.

Unless you are Mother Theresa, always giving to others with no thought of reward, you are *always* using people. That is what people are for. If we are lonely, we seek out companionship. We are using people to keep us company. We don't really care what they get out of it, we just want to be with them so we won't be lonely. If we are looking for conversation or intellectual stimulation, or whatever it is we get out of our friendships, we look for people to provide that, we are using them for that. We try and be friendly and attractive ourselves so we will be liked, so we have something to offer others. But there is always an ulterior motive there to get something back. Not many people spend a lot of time with those they don't like, unless they are masochists. They seek out relationships that offer something in return. That is just how it is.

Some people have shallow ulterior motives, seeking only to get and not give. I don't think you can form very rewarding relationships that way, and most people will not put up with it for very long. You have to have something to offer in return. When you can create mutually beneficial relationships you exchange value for value.

There are so many valuable resources that can aid you in your wealth-building program that I could not possibly list them all. The idea is to recognize resources as a principle. Be on the lookout for resources that can aid you in achieving your goals.

Networking with other people is a valuable resource. Sometimes a friendly acquaintance, either social or business, can be an important link to opportunity. If you have a need and mention it to the people you know, they may be able to pass you along to someone else who can really help you.

If you are selling a piece of property, or trying to hire a new employee, looking for a job, or need someone who speaks Russian, you just pass the word around, and someone will pop up with an answer for you. The more people you know and are on friendly terms with, the larger your network of contacts for information and help when you need it. And you of course can provide the same sort of service in return.

Money is a very valuable resource. It can be invested to produce more money. It can buy you other resources that provide good returns on the money, such as books, courses, travel to meet someone important to your success, dress-for-success clothing, and so on. Money can also buy you time to think and develop special moneymaking projects. Money is a great resource.

But people are addicted to the idea that they cannot succeed without money—that it takes money to make money. In this respect, money is overrated. In fact, without fully developing the other components of the wealth-building equation, money will probably only bring you sorrow and despair. Most people don't know how to handle a lot of money. If they get it, they just end up losing it on poor investments or harebrained moneymaking ideas. I know this from experience because I had to learn this lesson the hard way several times.

I borrowed quite a lot of money for my construction business when I was in my early twenties. I spent the money very quickly on useless items that I thought I needed for my business. Then I spent years paying the money back.

Not long after that, while I was still paying on my debt, I had a windfall of a fair sum of money. I spent some of this on poor investments that I did not understand. The rest I spent on poorly executed business ideas.

All I got from the money was debt, guilt, shame, low self-esteem, and a kick in the rear. But maybe it was worth it after all, since it taught me a valuable lesson about having a mature attitude toward handling money. I realized after all is said and done I did not have the knowledge to use the money effectively. I had little skill in managing it, and had not made the effort to carefully analyze my use of the money to get a good return on it.

Money is dynamite. It exaggerates who you are. Parts of yourself that you can only express in mild ways without money you can show off in a big way with money. Elvis liked to take his best friends to the Cadillac dealership and buy them a new car. What a friend, huh? But how would you feel about Elvis if he then picked a flower from his garden and handed it to you saying, "Here is something special just for you." How does that compare to a Cadillac? Suddenly everything gets very distorted.

Ross Johnson, the ex-president of RJR Nabisco, once complained of a news account that claimed that he regularly tipped with $50 bills. He thought that was outrageous because he had not tipped such a small amount in years. What do you mean to people when you go around handing out money like that? I think you become less a person, and more a bank teller machine.

Money can create more problems than it solves if you don't understand it and know how to use it.

A terrible tragedy happens to a lot of older people who have never learned how to handle money. They sell their homes, collect life insurance upon the death of a spouse, or collect their pension savings, and hand it over to an expert financial adviser (which all too often means "crook"), then lose everything in poor investments.

So if you are starting your wealth-building program with little or no money, don't worry. It is not such a big deal. What you need more than money is time to develop the wealth-building equation and get it working for you. Then the money will come, and you will know what to do with it to make more money.

Vision and imagination are powerful resources to draw upon. Ephemeral and insubstantial to most people, who may never have experienced their power, they are the source of all humankind's greatest accomplishments. These resources depend on an expansive attitude. Most people feel small, so they think small. Think big! I am not talking about grand schemes that can never be accomplished. You need your imagination to expand your mind, expand your awareness, expand your thinking.

In the past my reaction to this line of conversation was always, "But I am not creative." Screeeeeeech, bonk. Halt. The whole process of my imagination would get short-circuited right there, with a showstopping attitude. Some people enjoy a creative mind without effort, without having to develop it. But that does not mean you have to be born with it. I now have a very creative and imaginative mind, and I can tell you how to develop this wonderful resource.

You need worthy goals to inspire your imagination and creative thinking. Without a purpose, without some end in mind, there is nothing to be creative about, nothing to imagine. A painter begins with a blank canvas and the intention to paint. A composer begins with a blank score and the desire to create music. An architect begins with the goal of creating a pleasing and functional building. Think big. Dream big. Dreaming is free.

Draft a simple framework for your imagination to create in. Picture this: You want a nice country home with a garden and livestock, a warm sunny kitchen, and a comfortable living room with a fireplace. It has to have a large room on the shady side of the house with windows all around looking out on pleasant scenery. Here you will do your writing for travel magazines to earn your living. Now we have set the scene, provided a purpose, a goal. But how will all of this be accomplished?

You are going to need a lot of information and ideas to stimulate your imagination and creativity. So you start subscribing to country living magazines. You study writing and read books about selling free-lance articles to travel magazines. You start looking for people who know something about what you want to do. And you spend a lot of time daydreaming about your future and what it will be like. Then your imagination goes to work and you start having visions. All sorts of pictures flash through your mind of the many different ways your life could turn out. Alternative plans form and you get ideas.

Anybody can learn to use vision and imagination. The more you do it, the better you get at it. Imagination and creativity are skills you can develop. You can make a habit of using them. That is what advertising people do every day. They practice using their imagination and creativity.

But like knowledge and skills, imagination and creativity work best when they are aimed at specific targets. I used to think that good ideas just pop out of nowhere. I thought, "Boy, I wish I would get a good idea. That could help me a lot." I didn't realize that they come from having specific goals and a clear purpose in mind.

Einstein didn't unravel the mysteries of the universe because he was sitting around minding his own business when all of a sudden these incredible ideas popped into his head. He wanted to explore the secrets of the universe. That was his goal, his passion. All of his brilliant insights and creative revelations were the result of studying a lot of information and ideas provided by others, then using them to pursue his own purpose. He spent years daydreaming about his chosen pursuits, allowing his imagination to work from the knowledge and information he had previously acquired. He was aiming his creativity and imagination at a specific target—the secrets of the universe.

That is the stated purpose of Stephen Hawking, our modern-day Einstein. He has said that his goal is to unravel all the principles of physics before he dies. An ambitious goal he may never achieve, it has certainly spurred his imagination.

I can give you a whole shopping list of resources that will add power to the wealth-building equation. They will give you ideas for many more that you can add yourself.

Free time, peace and quiet, a rich uncle, a prime location for business, valuable contacts, reliable transportation, a personal computer, good books, knowledgable acquaintances, land, friendship, a clear mind, a simplified existence, efficient methods, a program for success, better organization, a long walk to think, good tools, special skills, useful ideas, rest and relaxation, an automatic dishwasher, enriching experiences, hard lessons learned. You get the idea.

Develop your resources and use them effectively to serve your wealth-building plan.

Here are the four most important ideas in this book:

- Wealth is quality of life, not just money (but hey, we all love cash).
- Any reasonably normal and healthy individual can achieve wealth, once they know what it is and understand how it works. Actually a lot of wealthy people are not particularly normal or healthy at all. They just happen to know how to become wealthy.
- The secret of making money is finding or creating value, and earning a good return on your time, effort, and money, year after year.
- The wealth-building equation provides all the tools you need to achieve wealth. And here it is again:

Attitude + Knowledge + Skills + Effort + Resources

= Power to Build Wealth

Here are some lists of words that help key on various meanings within the wealth equation:

Attitude	**Knowledge**	**Skills**	**Effort**	**Resources**
Posture	Ideas	Apprenticeship	Practice	Money
Mood	Education	Experience	Patience	Contacts
Will	Information	Practice	Character	Time
Character	Data	Technique	Physical work	Assets
Disposition	Study	Talent	Persistence	Capabilities
Stance	Facts			Ideas and talents

By combining all the most important concepts of this book, then studying and applying them as I have described, you will become wealthy. I guarantee it. That is, *if*—if you take this information seriously and put out the effort to apply it to your life.

This book contains many useful tools, but it is up to you to open the toolkit and put them to work. Refer back to this book from time to time and it will give you many years of good use. The fundamental principles in this book have been in use for thousands of years. They never wear out. They are never outdated. They are timeless.

CHAPTER FOUR

Surviving Debt

I once worked as a bill collector. This is a terrible confession to make, almost as bad as having to admit working for the Internal Revenue Service. They would not have had me anyway. I wasn't cruel and heartless enough.

The bill collecting job only lasted a couple of months. I just didn't have the stomach for kicking people when they're down.

I learned some valuable lessons about debt, though.

I discovered that it is not illegal to be in debt. It does not make you a criminal or a bad person. I talked to all kinds of people, in every imaginable circumstance, who had wound up in debt. Some were irresponsible, it is true, but many had just run into some bad luck and fallen behind. I also found out that there is not a whole lot a bill collector can do to you, especially if you are broke and don't own much. And if you go bankrupt, there is nothing a bill collector can do. I was taught that if people would just send me a few dollars a month, without skipping any payments, then I wouldn't have to bug them again. I had people sending me $10 a month on $500 worth of debt. That was not a problem. In fact they could have sent me $10 a month on $5,000 worth of debt, and I would not have hassled them if I did not think they had any money. But if they refused to send me money, and they owed a lot, I was told to be ruthless.

In California bill collectors are governed by the State Department of Consumer Affairs. It is against the law for them to harass you over the telephone. If they call you, and you don't want them to call again, you simply say; "Please do not call me again, or I'll report you to Consumer Affairs." Voilà, no more nasty phone calls.

I was pretty nasty, too. You should have heard the terrible things I would say. But if my debtors mentioned the Consumer Affairs Board, I would roll over and purr like a kitten.

In other states like New York, collection agencies may still continue to call. But they are *not* allowed to harass you. If your creditors are calling you, try to get them to stop. Give them some incentive to leave you in peace. Getting your creditors off your back will give you the peace of mind you need to get on with your life and pursue your wealth-building program.

If your creditors are hassling you because you have fallen behind on your payments, you may need my "Debt Restructuring Plan" described in "Resources." If you use the "Debt Restructuring Plan" and arrange to make smaller, regular payments to your creditors, you can use your payments as leverage to get them to stop calling you. Make your payments for several months, then ask them not to call any more. If they call again, politely ask to speak with their supervisor. Explain that you have been making payments but will stop if they continue calling.

Supervisors don't want to hear about problems; they want their employees to handle them. So if you talk to a supervisor, your bill collector may be reluctant to call you again. He doesn't want you phoning the boss and getting him in trouble.

Whenever you talk to your creditors or bill collectors, be sure to get the full names of the individuals you talk with. People who are being nasty on the phone don't like to be identified, especially if you use their name to complain about them.

You should also know what agencies in your state regulate bill collectors. They have information booklets describing the rules that apply to bill collectors there. Learn the rules and use them to give you leverage to get bill collectors to leave you alone.

Being in debt is one of life's most discouraging experiences. At least it was for me. A few years after fleeing my job as a bill collector, I found myself in debt. I used to fantasize that if I could get out of debt, I would be free and happy again for the rest of my life. No such luck. But I *am* happy not to be in debt anymore. I know I never want to get into debt again. I'm glad to be free of all the pressure and worry of that obligation hanging over me.

I read an interview with Sam Walton the other day. He was the richest man in America before his death in 1992. He lived with the burden of debt for many years, because he borrowed so much to keep opening up his Wal-Mart stores. It was one of the biggest days of his life when he sold stock in his company and finally paid off all of his debts.

Going into debt is saving and investing in reverse. Instead of building your future you are squandering it. None of us go into debt because we like the idea of squandering our future. But like a bad habit, it is easier to give in to the moment than to think about the long-term consequences. Sometimes you have to indulge your bad habits until you get sick of them. I've heard people say that about recovering from alcoholism. Sometimes the best thing that can happen to an alcoholic is to hit bottom. When he feels bad enough about himself and his life, he just won't ever want to drink again.

Debt is like investing in reverse because you have to pay interest on it.

When you invest, you *collect* interest on your investment. When you borrow money, you *pay* interest. When you invest, your money is working for you. When you borrow, you are working to make money for someone else.

Sometimes debt is a necessary part of living. I have a mortgage on my house, and I have to keep up those payments. But that is different than borrowing to consume. The money I borrowed to buy my house is backed up by the house. Unless the value of my house drops suddenly, I can always sell the house and pay off the mortgage.

Sometimes people get into debt because they are not being careful enough about managing their money. Maybe they expect a big refund on their tax return, so they go out and buy a new television. Then they get a big surprise when the tax refund does not come through, and they owe Uncle Sam instead.

Businesses use debt to make money. If the borrowed money can be invested to earn more than enough to pay the interest on the debt, and eventually pay back the original amount, then it may be worth it. But here again people get into a bind, because of unrealistic expectations about the investment risks involved. You can't just look at what the investment is *supposed* to do, if it works out. You have to look at what would happen if it does *not* work out.

In this day and age though, going into debt is as easy as falling off a log. I get an offer in the mail almost every day to apply for another credit card. I could go many thousands of dollars in debt with no trouble at all. In fact, the more money you make, and the better your credit rating, the larger the temptation grows.

So just getting out of debt is not the whole answer, you have to *stay* out of debt. Like dieting, you have to make a habit of self-restraint. You have to eat, but if you eat too much, you get fat.

It's the same with debt. You have to spend money, but if you spend too much, you get behind and have to catch up. It is hard enough just to stay even. And once you are trying to catch up, the cards are stacked against you, because you are paying interest. If you owe on credit cards, you are paying killer interest rates. If I could invest all of my money at the interest rates banks charge on credit cards, I would get out of the stock market.

If you are already in debt, you may feel that you have lost the game of wealth before you have even begun. Many people feel overwhelmed by their debt problems and cannot see a way out of them.

If you are in debt now, this book is for you! The most important thing you need to understand when you are in debt is how money works and how to make more of it. The best chance you have of getting out of debt and staying out is by studying the material in this book and applying it to your life.

You need to know that there is nothing shameful about going into debt. Lots of upstanding citizens do it. John B. Connally, ex-governor of Texas, thought he was a very wealthy man, but went bankrupt a few years ago. Willie Nelson owed so much money to the Internal Revenue Service that he dedicated an entire musical tour to paying it off.

I know it feels bad to be in debt because I have been there. I also know you don't exactly feel like bragging about it. But you are not alone, many people fall into debt. The number of people who stay out of debt almost equals, but not quite, the number of people who eat right, get regular exercise, and brush after every meal. My wife qualifies. I don't. So don't feel guilty about it.

Here is what you do.

First and foremost, **stop going deeper in debt!** Debt is a downward spiral that just gets you in deeper and deeper over your head.

If you have a serious problem with debt, and feel that you cannot control your spending habits, contact your local chapter of Debtors Anonymous. You may find the help you need from a supportive group of people who understand your problems.

If you can handle it on your own, then do it. Spend less than you earn every month. It is simple. I repeat, **spend less than you earn every month.**

Now this may require a major adjustment to your lifestyle. If you took on too big a mortgage and you are on the fast track to bankruptcy, sell now. Don't kid yourself if you are in over your head. Start dealing with it before the roof collapses. If you have set up a lifestyle that you cannot afford, cut your losses and get out from under it as fast as you can. If you are making your car payment but slipping behind on the mortgage, or vice versa, something has to give. If hanging on to your racquetball membership is blowing your budget every month, something has to give. You get the picture.

Let's assume that you have gained control over your debts and arranged to pay them off, however slowly. It takes $50 a month for 20 months to pay off $1,000 in debts. Just over eight years to pay off $5,000 at $50 a month. Over thirty years to pay off $20,000 at $50 a month. Forever—right?

Or maybe you owe $50,000, or $150,000. It does not matter, and here is why. Once you get your debt payments under control, and you stop going deeper in debt, you can start working on *increasing* your earnings and building wealth.

Eventually, when you make enough money, you can pay all your debts in one lump sum.

You don't believe me—right? Just a fantasy?

No, this is for real. And part of what I'm talking about is helping to get the right attitude going. Get control of your spending so you are not going deeper in debt. Get a handle on the debts you presently have. Get in the habit of saving, which we will soon talk about. And get your wealth-building program working for you.

If you are in a really bad fix—if you owe many thousands of dollars—you need to consider filing bankruptcy.

If you own expensive assets (a nice car, expensive jewelry, antique furniture, valuable paintings, land, etc.), your creditors have the right to file a claim against them. They can go to court and get a judgment against you. Then they can have the judge call you into court and have you explain under oath what you own. You would have to reveal all the things you have that are valuable, unless you want to risk perjuring yourself. Bad idea. It could mean jail.

It is not illegal to be in debt. But it *is* illegal to lie in court.

After the judge makes you tell your creditors what you own, he can give them the right to take it. Your creditors could then go to the sheriff's office and have someone sent around to collect your things. They can also get at your bank account, garnish your wages, etc.

Bankruptcy avoids all that. It also ruins your credit.

There are several kinds of bankruptcy and I won't try to explain all that here. Once you file bankruptcy, though, your creditors are out of luck. They can no longer hassle you directly. They have to work with the bankruptcy court to collect whatever it decides to give them. When you go bankrupt, the court takes some of your assets and divides them between your creditors; some assets you are allowed to keep. After that, your creditors cannot bother you any more. Period.

That means you can make more money and buy new possessions, and the creditors cannot take them. **Once you go bankrupt, your old creditors have no more claim against you.**

But any new creditors do, so don't go out and get into debt again. You can go bankrupt only every six years, but I don't think you want to make a habit of it.

Another reason why you may want to file for bankruptcy if you owe a *lot* of money, even if you don't have any assets now, is so your creditors cannot go after your future assets.

Let us say you are not wealthy now. You have some personal belongings and a decent job. But that is all. You owe $10,000 on your credit cards and other loans. You follow the "Debt Restructuring Plan" in "Resources" and get your creditors on the program. They are not going to hassle you any more. You are free to go about your business and get your wealth-building plan in gear.

But if you owe $100,000, and start making some money and acquiring some assets in a few years, your creditors might take notice and forget about your repayment plan. They will go to court for a judgment and swoop down on your assets. If you don't want that to happen, and have them ruin everything you are trying to build, you may as well get the bad news over with now and go bankrupt.

There are two important reasons why you may not want to go bankrupt. Number one is that you are an honest person and want to pay back the money you borrowed. You borrowed it in good faith and never meant to cheat anyone, and you still intend to pay it back. Number two is that if you go bankrupt, it ruins your credit rating. When a bankruptcy goes on your credit record, it becomes very hard to get a car loan, a mortgage, a credit card, or other forms of credit, for many years. At least one credit reporting agency I know of reports a bankruptcy for ten years after it occurs. That is a long time to have to pay cash for any new car you want to buy, or to have to call on friends and family to cosign a loan for you.

I cannot tell you whether you should file bankruptcy. That is a personal decision only you can make. I would strongly urge you to avoid bankruptcy on anything less than $20,000. It is just not worth it. You can handle a lot more debt than $20,000 with the "Debt Restructuring Plan."

As long as you can pacify your creditors you can get on with your business of building wealth. However, there is one creditor you cannot pacify—the IRS.

If you owe the Internal Revenue Service money, your problems are more serious. The IRS is merciless, and you cannot escape with a bankruptcy. Do everything in your power to pay them off first. Other creditors can be dealt with by filing bankruptcy as a last-ditch measure. But the IRS never goes away.

Whatever you do with the IRS, do *not* tell them what you own, unless they drag you into court. Honest citizens go in to straighten out their debts with the IRS and get screwed. I heard about one just the other day. A friend of mine is an honest businessman, a sincere and well-meaning person, and a nice guy. He bought a business that had debt problems. Part of the deal was that my friend take over the business' debts. Some of the debts were to the IRS, so my friend went in to straighten them out. The IRS asked him for his bank account number. Boom! The next thing he knows, they've cleaned it out.

If you owe the IRS money, don't go in and tell them, "I own a classic Thunderbird automobile, a little piece of land, and a nice Rolex watch." They will grab them.

If you cannot pay off the IRS outright, then show them the budget you used in the "Debt Restructuring Plan" with your other creditors and plead poverty. Assure them you don't own *anything*. They will agree to a monthly payment plan. But try to pay them off faster than your other creditors; they are the worst.

As you slowly pay off your debts you will want to start thinking about repairing your credit rating. This can take years, but don't neglect it.

Eventually you will want to have good credit again, because credit is a form of wealth.

To repair your credit rating, you have to pay off all of your debts and maintain a history of making payments to your creditors on time. That is the main thing creditors look for when they consider making a loan. You must show the ability to make payments on your debts, without missing payments and being late. The "Debt Restructuring Plan" I have provided in "Resources" is perfect for establishing a history of making payments on your debts. Once your debts are paid off, lenders can look at your credit history and see that you have faithfully made payments on your debts for years, and therefore are a good credit risk.

It is important that you know what information is being provided to creditors about you. Get copies of your credit report from the major credit reporting agencies. TRW and TransUnion are the major ones, but there are others as well. If you are turned down for credit, the creditor is required to tell you which credit reporting agency it used to get your credit report. You should then contact that credit reporting agency because it is required by law to give you a copy of your credit report for free. If you have not been turned down for credit because of a report it has provided, you can still get a copy of your credit report from it for a small fee.

Once you have a copy of your credit report, make sure it does not contain any errors. If it does contain errors, write back to the credit reporting agency and explain the error and request that it be corrected. They make mistakes all the time, and can accidentally add someone else's credit problems to your report!

You can also write short explanations about your credit that can be included on your credit report. If you had a dispute with a merchant, refused to pay your bill, and it was reported as bad credit, you can give your side of the story.

Keep an eye on your credit rating by getting copies of your credit reports from time to time. And do what you can to improve it. Talk to your creditors and ask them to remove derogatory information from your credit report. Sometimes they will report you for making late payments. If you call them and explain that your payment is on the way, and request that they not report it as late, they will sometimes do that for you.

Once you have tamed your creditors, it is time to start your savings program.

I've got to be kidding right? You are buried in debt, and I am talking about a savings program. Well, I am actually serious.

If you are going to spend less than you earn, what are you going to do with the money you don't spend? No, the answer is not give it to your creditors. Whatever you don't spend, you are going to save.

Budgeting and saving are not my idea of an ambitious way to accumulate wealth. Actually I take that back. For most people, budgeting and saving is an ambitious idea. But pinching pennies is not the way to amass a fortune. The main focus of wealth-building should be *earning*. If you don't earn, there is not much you can save.

Getting in the habit of saving part of what you earn is a first step to wealth-building and an essential discipline. You have to learn restraint of appetite to accumulate investment capital. Don't wait; start today.

Think of it this way. Ten percent of all you earn is yours to keep. And that is what you do. Keep it. Invest it. And let it work for you for the rest of your life.

The less you earn, the harder it is to keep a big chunk. And since this chapter is about debt, which you are trying to pay off, I won't hold you to ten percent, or five, or two. But save *something* every month. It gets you acting and thinking in the right direction. It is not just symbolic either. It is a way of life.

Life accumulates to the positive or negative. The debt spiral is a downward cycle of life. **Saving and investing is a positive, life-affirming cycle.** It shows you care about yourself and believe you deserve a good life. Continuously going deeper in debt is a form of despair. It is a way of giving up on yourself and is ultimately self-destructive.

Getting into the habit of saving is like regular dental checkups. It's a pain, but in the long-run, you save your teeth and avoid gum disease.

I was discussing this concept with a friend, and he said, "Why bother? I could get hit by a truck tomorrow, and all my saving would be wasted. I want to live while I can."

Well, I have no problem with that. I want to live while I can too. And I hope to live until I am ninety. There is an old man in me, just waiting to happen. And that old man does not want to rely on a bankrupted social security system, or a fragile health care system to look after him.

There are many misconceptions about old people. One of them is that they become stupid and useless, and don't feel anything anymore. Well, someday you may look like an old bag of bones, but you are liable to feel like a real live loving, caring, longing, aching, yearning, remembering, imagining, hopeful human being—a person who still wants a good life, who wants to live for today, but who may not be quite agile enough to earn a good living anymore.

There is a necessary balance to achieve between today's enjoyment and tomorrow's. You get blind drunk today, and tomorrow you pay with a hangover. You blow a wad at the mall today, and tomorrow you owe the debt, with interest.

But the great thing about saving and investing is that it pays a bonus when you catch up to it. If you save $10 today, in five years at 5% you get to spend $12.76.

All right, I know, $2.76, big deal! But it *is* a big deal when life accumulates to the positive. You get to feel better about yourself. You are looking out for yourself. The money is there not just for a fling, but also if you *really* need it, for the proverbial rainy day. You are not getting deeper in debt, you are getting richer. And finally you will have more fun with the extra money.

Make an agreement with yourself on how much you will save as a percentage of what you earn. Let's say one percent, just to go easy on you. Every time you get money, mail a check off to your savings account. One percent of all you earn is yours to keep. You get a check for $127, one percent equals $1.27. That is not enough to bother with a check, so dig in your pocket and count out $1.50 and throw it in the cookie jar. Every time you go to the bank, dump the cookie jar in your savings account.

Be sure you have a special savings account to accumulate your funds. This is not a fund to dip into to pay for Susie's dental work, or to pay off the debt on the T.V. from Christmas past. This is a "sacred" account that you use to build your wealth. Think of it as a shrine to future happiness and never use it casually. When you have $500 or so saved up, open a "money market" account where you can earn better interest.

Let me emphasize: Pay yourself and your creditors first. When you get your paycheck, get in the habit of writing out checks to all your creditors and your savings account first thing. Don't wait until the end of the month when you are broke and think. "Gee, well I promise myself I will pay the creditors twice as much next month." That does not fly.

Now that we have got your debts handled, I want you to start making some money.

But one more time:

- Stop going deeper into debt. Spend less than you earn. Get into this essential habit.
- Work out an agreement with your creditors to pay an amount you can afford every month. Never miss your payments.
- Start saving. You are saving and investing, not spending and wasting your future.

Spending less than you earn and staying out of debt is basic to building wealth. It becomes easier as you earn more with which to meet your needs. But before you earn more, you can gain security, self-confidence, discipline, and good habits, upon which to build your fortune. It feels very good to have spending and debts under control. Try it and you'll see. Saving is not just about having money for "a rainy day." It is about positive action toward getting more out of life, instead of depleting your life. It means taking care of yourself and feeling good about yourself. It is one of the best things you can do to give substance to your program of wealth-building. Not just because you accumulate money, but because you accumulate the power to act in your own best interests.

CHAPTER FIVE

Your Career

"You know, someday you have got to think about a career." You may have often heard these words from your parents, spoken through a cloud of concern and anxiety for your future.

I hesitated to use the word "Career" in the title for this chapter, because of what it means to most people. Perhaps a better title would have been "Your Job," since the majority of us work at a job to earn a living, and try not to think a whole lot about how our "careers" are going.

Having a career, in the usual sense of the word, implies advancing up a ladder of successful achievement in a particular line of endeavor. From a successful career we hope to derive not only salary increases, but greater prestige, recognition, self-esteem, responsibility, and personal satisfaction, all of which are worthwhile career goals and forms of wealth to be treasured.

How we approach our jobs often results in frustration and apathy. We don't feel empowered in our work life to produce valuable goods or services for others in return for a fair living and a dignified existence. Many times we end up consumed by the rat race, slogging through a demeaning existence as a "wage slave."

As a teenager, I could feel myself being propelled from my childhood existence, where I depended on my parents to look after me, into the world of adulthood and self-sufficiency. I resisted the transition, kicking and screaming all the way. I had watched my parents struggling to support me my whole childhood. And I spent my teenage years living in poverty with them, wondering what sort of future any of us would have. By the time I graduated from high school I was jobless, broke, and homeless, with "no direction home," as Bob Dylan sang.

At that point, I was consumed with despair of wealth, confronted by only two visible options: live free and starve (which I did for a couple of years), or shackle myself to the yoke of industrial production and become a wage slave.

I grew up in the working-class world of blue-collar liberalism. We all knew that the rich get richer and the poor get poorer. The fat cats scramble over poor working-class slobs to get ahead, intimidating and exploiting them to supply the labor and sweat from which they amass their wealth. I would have no part of that game. My dignity demanded that I fight against such a fate until I conquered it—or die trying.

All too often though, my stomach overruled my idealism and pride. I would work at menial jobs just to eat and survive, becoming increasingly bitter toward a cruel world which would not allow me the dignity of living life on my own terms. Where is it written that I have to work for pay to justify my existence? I was intimately familiar with the resentment that comes of working a job for barely enough money to eat, sleep, shelter myself, and show up for another day's work.

As I thought about writing this chapter, I remembered how empty-headed and automatic my assumptions were in those days. "Who" was forcing me to work this way? Why did I have to demean myself in order to survive? I pictured myself standing in the woods with no modern implements of any kind at hand. How would I survive except by gnawing the bark off trees, or smacking bunny rabbits with heavy stones?

Every convenience and comfort of our modern world is the product of human ingenuity and hard work. I could choose to suffer the humiliation of nature's own demands for survival, or work for a "boss," and survive in the modern way. Either way, it was up to me to decide how to survive and enjoy life in a world that does not really care. Mother Nature has never extended her hand to me in a kind gesture of loving forgiveness to nurture me and soothe my troubled soul or my aching back. Certainly the modern industrial economic complex has offered me no succor. There are just not that many free handouts, and the ones that do exist charge a high price in self-esteem and loss of identity.

The ultimate despair of wealth is wishing you could move back in with Mom and Dad. Eat home-cooked meals prepared and served like clockwork, have your laundry done for free, and watch TV and drink beer without worrying about when the rent is due. A gentle, womblike existence.

Unfortunately, what a lot of people do with their jobs is not much different. They move from home with Mom and Dad to "home" with the company and all the gang they work with. They end up palling around with friends and fighting political battles with disagreeable fellow employees, the sibling rivalry of the workplace. They depend on the paycheck as they used to depend on home-cooked meals; they shirk their chores and fear the day Mom storms in to demand they clean their room once and for all. They live the impostor's lie, hoping never to be found out. Their "loyalty to the company" is a sham, something they joke about during Friday afternoon beer busts after work.

There has got to be a way other than working just to survive, replacing "Mom and Dad" with the "boss and the company," living in apathy and despair of wealth. And of course there is. Many people are energetic and dedicated in their careers. They settle into a chosen path and derive sufficient rewards from their work to justify the necessary sacrifices. They see their future stretching forward in a logical progression of greater achievement and remuneration. These are the lucky few who are not living the quiet desperation of the majority, a majority who have not been as fortunate in their adaptation to job and career.

But even these more successful people often fail to fully appreciate what it means to take responsibility for one's life enterprise and practice entrepreneurship.

Once we reach adulthood, life hands us the keys to whatever career vehicle is at hand and says, "It's all yours; hop in and drive." We stare at the keys, the old jalopy we may have been saddled with, gaze at the long road stretching out before us, fumble around for the instruction manual and a road map, and in no time find ourselves muttering, "I can't believe this. How am I supposed to drive this thing?"

Statistics show that most people never do master the damn thing. They just go along for the ride, careening through employment on a hope and a prayer, expecting that it will all work out somehow, but usually pooping out at the end, broke. They become dependent on social security and, if they are lucky, a small fixed income from some other source. But as likely as not, they will find themselves working after retirement at some sort of job to help make ends meet.

The greatest revelation for me as a working adult has been the realization that I have to manage my life enterprise as an entrepreneur. I cannot give over responsibility for the quality of my existence to some authority greater than myself. It's like relying on Mom to pick up my dirty laundry and cook my meals. No government agency, employer, or any other authority, can take responsibility for my life. It might be nice if they did, but ultimately all the nuts and bolts of providing for my own well-being falls on my shoulders alone.

This is good news and bad news. Because you have the freedom to choose your own destiny and shape your future, nobody can force you to live a life that does not suit your individuality and unique needs. On the other hand, the responsibility for your future depends solely on your choices, your ambitions, your desires, your drive for success. You make it or break it on your own merit. That can be pretty scary.

After the Great Depression of the 1930s, a lot of people took blue-collar jobs in big companies and clung to them for dear life, punching a clock for a lifetime to collect a pension and a secure retirement. For the most part, this strategy worked. America was the leading economic power in the world; our large industrial base was second to none. We exported a substantial portion of the world's manufactured goods, and were able to provide secure lifetime employment for millions of our workers.

But the economic balance of power has now shifted. The economic fortunes of the United States have not declined, as so many pessimistic economists and futurists are now claiming. We are still competitive, and likely to maintain and improve our overall standard of living for our people. But we cannot assure ourselves of complete world dominance in many industries where we previously owned the world market.

This means that you cannot expect today's companies, large or small, to provide lifetime employment and a secure future. The old approach of relying on union work and large employers to provide secure wages and retirement benefits is now a sucker's bet. As large companies struggle against global competition, their financial well-being is under constant threat, and many promised pension benefits rest on a precarious future. Just because the company you work for has assured you of a comfortable retirement doesn't mean the money is going to be there when you need it.

Among the nightmares that accompanied the scandal surrounding Robert Maxwell's mysterious death and the unraveling of his business empire was the revelation that he had raped companies of their pension funds, so that employees no longer had money for their retirement.

Many companies provide pension benefits on a "pay as you go" basis. They don't have the pension money saved up; they have to make the payments to retirees out of current earnings. If the company runs into problems, how can they keep up their payments?

In today's world it is naive to rely on the government or big business to provide for your retirement and old age.

Your life enterprise is your own business. It is your responsibility to attend to it and see that it is successful. Nobody but you cares enough about your own interests to look after them and maximize the quality of your life. When life hands you the keys to an old jalopy—demeaning work for low pay, hopes of job security and maybe a pension for retirement—throw the keys back and shop for better transportation.

Whether you choose to work as an employee or to start your own business enterprise, **you should conduct your life enterprise as a wealth-building program in which you succeed through self-interest and self-reliance.** Give up childlike dependency on government, big business, or the generosity of others. Using the information in this book, you can find your own direction and succeed on your own terms.

Here is how:

Treat your career as an exchange of value for value. The job market trades human talent for wages in order to produce goods and services. You are out competing in the work force against other job applicants for various employment opportunities: good working conditions, satisfying work, top pay, status, recognition, responsibility, and whatever job perks turn you on. In exchange you are willing to offer your skills, knowledge, experience, and time for the rewards of a particular job. To compete successfully, you must operate like a business selling its wares. You are an entrepreneur, offering a service to employers, in exchange for benefits that will enhance your life enterprise.

The measure of your success will be in the amount of money you earn, how much you enjoy your work, and to what extent your work furthers your overall goals.

You should treat employers the same way you would customers in a business. Because you value their patronage, you offer your customers the best quality of goods and services at an attractive price. It always pays to treat your customers well, cheerfully answering their complaints with friendly and accommodating service. But when customers step beyond the bounds of common decency and human respect, sometimes you have to throw the bums out. The same goes for employers. To earn the best profit for your services, you expect to offer your employer the best possible product, including service with a smile. But that does not mean subjecting yourself to disrespectful and inhumane treatment. Hold your head up and demand respect in a mutually beneficial exchange of value for value.

To accomplish this you cannot come begging. You must develop your worth in the marketplace and plan for career survival and success, the same way any entrepreneur would plan for business survival and success. It is important to continually use your imagination to consider how to translate who you are, what you want out of life, and what skills you have or could acquire, into meaningful and lucrative employment. What are your resources, abilities, goals, aptitudes and ambitions? What is your long-term plan of attack and model for success? A profession is not just a job with a salary. It is a direction in life that has a thousand alternative courses to follow.

Too often when we fall into despair of wealth, and despair of meaning in our jobs, we become slackers. We sacrifice our self-esteem and show resentment toward indifferent bosses by coasting in our jobs. If you had your own business and just slid along, offering bad products and poor service, you would not be surprised to find that you were not earning a profit. The same goes for jobs. You have to be motivated toward an adequate reward for your efforts, or you just won't produce. If you always take the short view—devaluing yourself and what you are capable of, and just taking whatever job comes to hand—you will lose.

Take the long view instead. See yourself not just for who you are or what your current capabilities are, but who you can become. Visualize yourself constantly accumulating knowledge, experience, and skills. Get the best return on your time and effort, not just by hoping to make more money, but by investing your time and effort to increase your knowledge and skill, making you worth more.

The best way to earn an adequate reward is to make yourself indispensable to potential employers based on your qualifications, and then market your skills to the highest bidder. Shop for market opportunities, for skills that can be sold on a lucrative basis.

Fashion designers are often passionate about their work, seeking to create a work of art, a fashion statement, along with recognition for their achievements—and lots of money besides. Few people enter this profession under the naive assumption that success will come easy. They know that there is a lot of competition in the field, and to succeed big they are going to have to stand apart, offering something different and special. They work hard to develop creative designs, establish new fashion trends, and achieve the ultimate in professional accomplishment—their own successful fashion label. This may require many years of subsuming their ambitions under the umbrella of employment and apprenticeship with an established clothing company. But in the long-run, it is their own life enterprise, their own entrepreneurship they are cultivating. Under these circumstances they must balance short-term sacrifices and gains against long-term goals and the ultimate prize.

Taking responsibility for your life enterprise, earning a good return on your time and effort, requires planning your career and taking the long view. You don't start out with a little knowledge, skill, and experience, and immediately command all the rewards your chosen career path may offer. You sacrifice in the short term, invest in your skills and experience, aiming for long-term rewards.

But don't compromise too much. If you need a job to survive, you may fall into the trap of sacrificing personal freedom, fulfillment, and the opportunity for meaning and accomplishment in life, just to get a job and a weekly paycheck. Instead, make *creative* compromises all along the way. Weigh your choices, the advantages and disadvantages of each career decision, to figure out how you can maintain forward progress in your life enterprise, improving the quality of it, and building future wealth.

As an employee never think of yourself as a prisoner, checking in with your parole officer to earn time off on the weekends for good behavior, and collecting your paycheck as meager compensation, drawn from society's compassion for your plight. An employer is not a parent who has the right to oversee your goals and accomplishments, pass judgment on your future, and relegate you to low pay and low status.

A friend of mine, who is a wise investor and financial planner, recently told me that he thinks the best thing that can happen to some people is to lose their jobs. He gave the example of someone he knows who got fired from his job and decided he would never let that happen again. This person started his own business, made much more money and was happier working for himself. Getting fired was the catalyst to starting a whole new life. Changing jobs can be a time of crisis that forces you to reevaluate your career goals and seek better opportunities.

I started as a carpenter in high school. I got my contractor's license in California by the time I was 23. When I ran construction crews, I hired guys twice my age to work for half of what I was making. I couldn't figure it out. And I didn't have the nerve to ask either. "You dummy, you know more about this stuff than I do, why are you working for me?"

Actually, they were not dumb. And they did know more than I. But they didn't have the same motivation, the drive to succeed. I still can't figure it out, though. With a little extra effort, a little courage and boost to their self-confidence, they could have done what I was doing, instead of taking orders from some young greenhorn. They would have been the boss, in charge of their own show.

I wonder if these men had fully considered the situation they had allowed themselves to fall into. Despair of wealth had cast them into menial roles in life, when they could have had so much more. My construction crew just wanted to drink beer at the end of the day and forget their problems, until the next day's work forced them back to the grind. This deadly form of apathy can go on for years, charging a high price for the refusal to seek out new ways to improve skills and earn a higher return on time and effort.

Picture the president of a large corporation. She flies around in a corporate jet, takes time off for golf every other day, earns a million-dollar salary, has an office the size of a basketball court, and commands the respect of thousands of people. She likes almost everything about her job because it contains so many valuable perks. She enjoys high self-esteem due to the status and recognition given her. She is the boss and manages her own time. She is in control. She makes lots of money, lives a freewheeling and exciting lifestyle, and in general enjoys her work and takes satisfaction in it.

One day our corporate president gets a phone call from the board of directors of another corporation. Would she be interested in heading their larger and more prestigious corporation at twice her current salary, say $2 million a year?

This happens all the time. Corporations hire new presidents from outside the company, for huge salaries. Lee Iacocca was hired to run Chrysler Motors after he got fired from Ford. Why would a person get offered an incredibly high-paying job like that? Why don't they call you or me and offer us the job?

The difference is that such a person has established his or her worth in the eyes of others. They have built a valuable reputation. What you receive in compensation for what you do depends on the perception of your worth in the eyes of others. The corporate president has spent time developing and demonstrating abilities and establishing credibility.

If you are in your own business, you must establish a good reputation for the value of your products or services, rather than your own personal credibility. But as an employee, you are constantly faced with the necessity of maintaining your credibility or worth in the eyes of your current employer, or some new employer. Usually that means laying down a consistent history of past performance and achievement in the jobs you have held. You present this on your résumé when you go for your next job or promotion.

You may be able to sell yourself into new and better employment by convincing an employer that you have qualities and skills necessary to attack a new level of challenge. Many employers will hire solely on the basis of self-confidence and personal presentation.

Despair of wealth often results from people's low self-esteem, the feeling that they have little to offer in an exchange of value. If this is your problem you need to attack it directly. It is hard for others to recognize your worth if you don't see it yourself. Your feelings of worthlessness can cause you to act them out and make them a reality.

Self-improvement is one of your most important wealth-building tools. But I am not talking about making yourself a better person. If you are mean, nasty, and selfish now, and you like it that way, by all means remain mean, nasty, and selfish. I have no problem with that. When I say self-improvement, I am speaking strictly in terms of accumulating wealth, or making money—getting the best return on your time and effort. I am talking about becoming a well-oiled machine of wealth production. Self-improvement is the pragmatic response to how the world works. The more you have to offer, the more you can expect in return.

So don't confuse low self-esteem regarding who you are as a person, with low self-esteem regarding what you can accomplish in your career. They are often mixed together in people's minds and emotions, but they are two separate things. No matter who you are or how you feel about yourself as a person, you can improve yourself and earn more money. You may not be popular and never get invited to parties, but you may still be the best, and highest-paid, microwave technician in town.

I once worked with a guy who was a manic-depressive nerd who whined and screamed all day on the job. I am not exaggerating when I say this guy was weird and obnoxious. But he was tolerated on the job because he was the most brilliant computer programmer in the company.

All people can improve their marketable skills, no matter who they are or where they start from. It is simply a matter of wanting to, and putting out the necessary effort. You have to find the best market for your skills and experience, and demand the best price you can get.

I know a couple of popular business success authors who don't recommend requesting raises. They think it is too "selfish" or "self-interested" to ask for more money. If you care only about money, then you may not be willing to do your best in the job.

I disagree with their attitude and their approach. They are living in a fairyland where bosses care and are always looking out for their employees' best interests.

The company you are working for is selling in the marketplace where supply and demand rules the price of goods and services. It doesn't think "Gee, the customer will think we are not doing our best if we try to charge more." Your company will charge whatever the market will bear for its products. Why shouldn't you do the same? **Your employer is your customer.** You give him the best service you can to keep him coming back for more, and you charge him the highest price he will pay. If your price is too high, he can shop elsewhere in the market for a better deal. You are not greedy, selfish, or antisocial if you want more money. You are just a capitalist, like the company you work for.

If you forgo a wage increase for six months because your conscience tells you that the boss should decide when you deserve a raise, then you have a very expensive conscience. You could lose a lot of money during your career waiting for your bosses to show their generosity.

Plan your career for the long haul. Think about how much you want to earn over a lifetime. Think about how you will continually upgrade your earning power, by increasing your knowledge, skills, and experience, trading on them for higher salaries and bonuses. The cash income part of the career equation is very important and you should not ignore it. **Sacrifice short-term income only if it furthers your long-term goals.**

The career puzzle contains three components: finding satisfaction in your work, building more marketable skills, and making enough money.

You can find satisfaction in your work in several ways. You may follow your heart's desire and insist on work that is enjoyable and meaningful. You may succeed at work that you don't especially enjoy, but that brings you satisfaction because you do it well. Striving to succeed at work that is not satisfying in the short term may lead to better opportunities down the road.

Someday you may even wish to start your own business. In the interim you can acquire skills and establish a track record of accomplishment. This will provide you with the reputation and credibility to obtain financing for your business.

Ongoing career planning should set you up for a lifetime of lucrative employment or business accomplishments. Build your skills for future opportunities. Broaden your knowledge and experience as much as you can, so that you have more career options.

Making money in your career is a fairly simple equation. It requires that you have the honesty and courage to demand what you want. Depending on the market for your skills and experience, you may only be able to increase your pay a little at a time. But don't kid yourself. If you are in a low-paying profession, unless you just love what you are doing, get out of there!

Many people suffer a serious conflict between doing what they want to do, what they might enjoy as a career, and earning the money they need. There are several considerations to this issue.

Whether you have a specific career goal in mind or just want "satisfying work," you must direct your career goals toward doing what you like. Sometimes this will require making short-term compromises, as in the example of the fashion designer. You may have to compromise your goals in the short term, accepting positions not worthy of the satisfactions you hope to attain in the long-run.

You may have to work at your chosen career as a sideline for some years, as many writers, painters, and musicians do. In some cases, it may take many years before the big break comes. A friend of mine worked as a musician in small venues for years while doing carpentry and other jobs to support himself. He was past forty when his second album hit big, and subsequently grossed over eight million dollars. He has now been doing what he loves for years, owns his own house, and is financially secure. But he had to keep his ultimate goal in mind and continue developing it, in order to make his dream a reality.

Another aspect of enjoying your work is avoiding difficult work environments. A lot of the aggravation at work can come from bosses and associates who are disrespectful, obnoxious, or just no fun to be around. Look for companies where you like the layout, people seem friendly, and the work is interesting. Find a position where you will be appreciated and allowed to exercise your abilities with the maximum freedom and support. Finding such a situation can add to the quality of your work life, to say nothing of your health and general disposition.

If you love art but need to earn a living as well, naturally it would be appealing to combine art with work. You can go into commercial art, working in advertising or graphic design. If you are concerned about subverting your artistic talents to commercial interests, do the art you love, but learn to promote it successfully. A substantial aspect of the success of any artistic endeavor is the power of promotion. Either study and learn how to promote yourself or seek out a talented promoter, convince him of the value of your work, and encourage him to promote it.

Sometimes the solution to getting everything you want out of life—a career you enjoy and lots of money besides—is to combine the elements of your wish list, and then see where they fit into the world puzzle. Many people live under the mistaken notion that they cannot do what they want to do because it is "not commercial." Look at it another way. There are almost 250 million Americans, enough to buy just about every imaginable product or service. Selling what you love to do is a matter of finding or creating your market.

I had a friend years ago who was a hippy ne'er-do-well. He never had held a job for long and was uncertain of his direction in life. He was pretty eccentric. One day we were chatting and he told me of his latest scheme for earning a living. He wanted to sell herbal remedies for pets. I thought that was an off-the-wall idea, and a wave of pity washed over me as I contemplated the sad fate of my friend, grasping after straws to survive. But he was unstoppable, and very excited about his idea. Think of all the good it would do for cats and dogs! He studied herbal medicine and put together various concoctions. Years later I was browsing the health food store shelves when suddenly I saw "HerbalAnimal," the brand name my friend had chosen for his products. He had sold what I thought was a weird idea, because that was where his interest and enthusiasm led him.

I know people who sell "chain saw carvings," large sculptures which they carve from logs using a chain saw.

A guy in my town, Izzi Tooinsky, "The Mayor of the 21st Century," makes a living as an expert juggler and storyteller. He stands in the street, offering humorous anecdotes and juggling knives, swords, hatchets, hats, and flaming torches. He passes his hat around the crowd, sells his storytelling cassettes, and offers a clipboard for people to sign up on his mailing list. He also performs on stage around the world. He enjoys what he is doing and runs a tidy little business besides.

What these people have done is added up their criteria for a fun way to make money, and found a market for it in the real world.

I have done that myself.

I made a list of how I want to live and make money. What could I do that would allow me to have a nice house in the country, work at home, be my own boss, spend time with my family, and do work I enjoy while providing a valuable service to others? Once I had specified my criteria for a satisfying and lucrative career, I had a target to aim at to focus my skills and talents in the proper direction.

Ready, aim, fire. I am writing this book at home, working close to my family. I feel very satisfied to produce something that will help others. I am marketing my skills, ideas, and talents to you, my reader, who have offered me your kind patronage.

A friend of mine is a writer and loves the arts. She also enjoys travel. Her ideal career is to get writing assignments to cover performing arts events, and produce feature articles for magazines who will pay her travel expenses. This matches her personal and financial needs in several ways. Getting her travel expenses covered is money in the bank, free travel which she enjoys. Plus she attends art events, which she also likes doing. She writes, which pleases her, and she earns a living. Thus she has managed a pragmatic approach to earning her living, as well as doing what she loves.

Don't just accept that you have chosen a low-paying career out of the love of doing it and cannot hope for financial success. You can have your cake and eat it too. Develop the attitude that you can do what you want and make money as well. With this attitude, you will constantly be looking for ways to generate income from your favorite interests.

Consider Andy Warhol, the famous leader of the pop art movement of the 1960s. He started out as a commercial artist, but later became a pop icon. Warhol was a self-promoter who did and said weird things, and made lots of money besides. He didn't accept the idea that because he was strange he could not make money. He combined his love of art, poetry, and absurdity with his love of money and happenings. And he was extremely successful.

Warhol also supported what might be considered the first punk rock band, the Velvet Underground, with Lou Reed as its star performer. Reed is another iconoclastic individual who has made it big. After going solo, Reed made albums of dark, brooding music, instead of the more commercially successful "pop" music. But he stayed true to his roots, and over the years survived and prospered.

A job is a temporary means of employment, but a career is a lifetime event. It is important that you understand the difference in this distinction so you can plan your career and survive your job.

One job, or one position in a company, should be only a way station along the path of your whole career. You might take a job just for the income to tide you over while you are studying for your future career. We have all heard of people doing this to get through college, or while they are getting their acting career off the ground. I often hear that half the waiters or waitresses in New York and Los Angeles are actors or actresses.

I recently returned from a cruise to South America during which I met a number of the performers providing shipboard entertainment. It turns out that many of them combine work and play by signing up to perform on cruise ships, where they can travel and see the world while earning a wage besides. One young dancer confided that dancing and singing on the ship was a lot of fun, and offered a chance to experience the diversity and richness of life for a while, before settling down in New York, where she hopes to establish her stage career.

To be successful in your career over the long-run, you have to think ahead and aim in a trajectory that includes all of your goals. If you plan to grow and change, allowing your talents and ideas to accumulate, giving you greater career leverage, your life will become more flexible, and more opportunities will be open to you.

Consider all the things you want out of your career—increasing pay, better working conditions, more prestige and job satisfaction, doing more of what you enjoy, exercising more power and responsibility, acquiring skills to start a business, etc. Make a list of everything you want out of your career and plan to get them. Decide what compromises you are willing to make in order to achieve your career goals. Then be true to yourself and persist in acquiring the skills, experience, and credibility that will support your career goals.

Remember wealth is quality of life. And your career is one of the biggest parts of your life. So you have to decide how to get the most benefit from it, including money, satisfaction, and enjoyment.

The financial aspects of career planning involve marketing your skills for the highest rate of pay, targeting your career goals to where the most money is. But earning money is not enough. You also have to save and invest it to accumulate wealth and let that money work for you to create more money. Then you have more freedom to choose a career that may not pay as well, but offers more personal satisfaction. Jacqueline Kennedy Onassis, the wealthy wife of former president John F. Kennedy, and shipping magnate Aristotle Onassis, works as a book editor. She obviously doesn't do it for the money, but her wealth gives her the freedom to pursue a satisfying career that does not depend on money.

Another financial aspect of managing your career is insulating yourself from unemployment. If you have enough money and other financial resources at your disposal, you will not always be standing at the brink of poverty and debt. You have more flexibility to change jobs without worrying about falling behind financially if the next job is not quick in coming.

That is what entrepreneurship is about, managing your life enterprise on a sound financial and wealth-building basis, running it like a business. Build up personal and financial assets to free you from dependence on others, and you are not at the mercy of big business and government or the winds of economic fate. You take responsibility for your own life and control your own destiny.

All of the principles of wealth-building contained in the wealth-building equation apply to your career. Use them as essential tools for building career success. Maximize your earnings and savings and use the chapters on investment to put your money to work for you.

The way you go about planning and pursuing your career will have a major impact on your wealth-building success. Do not treat your career lightly. Take the time to consider how to maximize the return on the time and effort you devote to your career. Eventually, all the effort you put into making a success of your career will pay you back many times over.

CHAPTER SIX

Your Own Business

Aside from striking it rich through sheer luck, there are five fundamental routes to making a lot of money. You can rise to a high-paying position in a corporation, become a successful salesperson earning large commissions, earn a share of profits from promoting business deals, or become a star and get paid for your talent or fame as a writer, actor, singer, athlete, artist, or media personality. Or you can start your own business.

Starting a business is one of the best ways to make money and achieve financial independence. More people have become rich starting their own businesses than in any other way. It is also an opportunity to achieve creative freedom and greater control over your life. You become your own boss and can decide how to invest your time and resources to not only make the most money, but pursue a business adventure that provides challenge, excitement, and a better quality of life.

The purpose of business is to produce wealth. By creating and selling goods and services of value to human beings, a business makes new wealth available. A business is a machine of wealth production, and the money it earns is its reward for bringing new wealth into existence. When you start your own business your first thoughts should be about what wealth is and what it means to you.

For me, business has to mean something more than making money. If you want a lot of money, you can dedicate yourself to becoming a robot for business profits. But that is not wealth, that is poverty. I am in business to become wealthy, not just to make money. I want to enrich the quality of my life with my business.

Capitalism is a way of creating greater wealth for yourself by creating greater wealth for others. I don't mean this in a moral sense, as in "it is better to give than to receive." I mean that by producing something that others value, you will be able to barter for the things *you* want.

I always include three people in the business equation: myself, my employees, and my customers. The most efficient way to succeed in business is to make all three happy. Customers will pay for goods and services that enhance the quality of their lives. Employees will work for what enhances the quality of their lives. And you can do business for whatever enhances the quality of your life.

The original business was the business of personal survival. In pioneer days, the U.S. Government gave away large tracts of land to settlers. A pioneer family with a horse, a wagon, a gun, and a few simple tools could march off into the wilderness and stake their claim on a bountiful existence. With the right piece of land, in the right setting with natural resources and plentiful game, they could build a rich life. That is why people risked so much to do it. And they did it all for themselves; strictly out of self-interest. They didn't have to produce wealth for others. They could create nearly all the wealth they needed from their own land, trading only for the few basic commodities of civilization they could not make themselves. Everything else they raised, harvested, or manufactured by themselves, for themselves. They created new wealth and achieved an abundant quality of life.

That is what capitalism is all about—drawing on ideas and technology to create wealth which enhances the quality of your life. You start and run a business to build wealth for yourself. The rest of the business equation, which comes from adding employees and customers, applies when you invite employees to share your wealth-building vision, and you invite customers to trade *their* wealth for the wealth *you* have created.

The business of personal survival is the main concern behind most people's decision to work as an employee or be a business owner. We work to earn a living, otherwise most of us would be doing something else with our time. But if working and doing business are only a way to survive and nothing more, you may be "working for a dying" instead of "working for a living." Consider how your business could enhance both your personal, as well as your financial, well-being. In your own business you can be the boss, determine the success or failure of the business on your own merits, reap all the rewards (if the business is successful), try out any idea you want, take more control of your life, gain self-respect and pride in creating something of your own, and accomplish things you may never have thought possible.

There is another way to view the whole challenge of starting a business. **You are already in business for yourself.** Whether you work for an employer, or are your own boss, you have to maintain your income and make ends meet. So there is no way to get out of the game. It is just a matter of how you play it.

If you look up the word "entrepreneur" in the dictionary, you will discover that it comes from the French word *entreprendre,* which means "to undertake." Webster's Dictionary defines entrepreneur as "one who organizes, manages, and assumes the risks of a business or enterprise."

When you think about it, being an entrepreneur is what life is all about. We all have to "organize, manage, and assume the risks" of our life enterprise.

Most of us don't think of ourselves as "entrepreneurs." We imagine some special blessing or charm that casts its spell on the entrepreneur and gives him or her the power to invent new products and services that we could never have conceived. When you read about entrepreneurship in the news, you are left with an uneasy feeling about the mystical quality of business success, and the brilliance and daring of the entrepreneur. You are led to believe that entrepreneurs are a breed apart, gifted souls on a special mission. Nothing could be further from the truth.

We all have the power to organize, manage, and assume the risks of a business or enterprise. It is an ironic misfortune to assume that we have to invent the next "self-developing camera," or an entirely new mode of personal transportation, before we can succeed as "entrepreneurs."

Most successful and wealthy entrepreneurs start very ordinary businesses, make money, and enjoy personal satisfaction accomplishing what most of us would not be very interested in reading about in the news. This is why we never hear about them. There have never been very many IBMs, Xeroxes, Microsofts, McDonald's, Ford Motor Companies, Coca-Colas, or the other unique success stories we read about, and there never will be. It is natural for the more fascinating and unusual stories to be reported in the news, and for the rest to be ignored.

On the other hand Harvey Mackay, author of the best-selling book, *Swim With the Sharks Without Being Eaten Alive,* runs an envelope company. How ordinary. But Harvey likes what he is doing, and has a very lively and exciting time doing it.

There is a secret to wealth that is easily overlooked because it is so obvious. Wealth is ownership. Whatever resources you legally control are part of your wealth. Whenever you build up or acquire a business, it does not matter how smart or talented you are, the main characteristic of your business success is that you own the company!

As you build your business, you are also building the prestige of your company to attract talented people to work for you. As the owner of the company you stand to benefit the most. It is through your ownership of a company that you have power to control its destiny and yours.

Business is one of my favorite subjects, and I am constantly studying and learning more about it. But I did not always feel that way. I used to think of business as oppressive, musty, boring. Business people wore suits and ties and spoke in grave tones about recent sales trends and profit outlooks.

After doing business for many years I finally realized that I *was* a "businessman." I never thought of myself that way before because I never really understood what business was supposed to be about. I assumed that business was reserved for sober-minded individuals who understood the arcane science of netting another one cent of profit from every dollar in sales, or some such thing. It was all vague to me.

Now that I know much more about business, I've learned that the business of "doing business" is vital, exciting, and as dependent on imagination as cogitation.

By thinking of your own enterprise as something more than "working at a business," you will begin to imagine new possibilities for yourself. Your business can free you from the drudgery of working for a living. Creating a business can offer not only the most viable means for amassing a personal fortune, it can also be a fulfilling experience of accomplishment and creativity.

When you work at a job, your freedom is limited. Somebody else tells you how to spend your time. It can be like living at home and having your parents run your life. But when you have your own business *you* get to call the shots. It is not always fun and games, but at least you are in charge of your life. I love the freedom of being in business for myself and deciding how to make the best use of my time.

You take a risk when you go into business for yourself because you no longer have someone else to worry about where the money for your paycheck comes from. You have to make sure the money keeps rolling in yourself. That is an important reason why many people don't start their own business. They don't want the responsibility of making sure the business is successful and profitable. They like the security of a steady paycheck, and for some people that makes good sense.

But employers don't risk being in business and putting their money on the line for nothing. In most cases employees pay their employers to take that risk for them. If you have your own business, *you* get to take home the profits of the business. When you work for someone else, you get the same pay, no matter how profitable the business is.

Large businesses can employ many people at fair wages. Some of those companies offer satisfying jobs and the benefits of a steady paycheck. But the security of working for someone else can be an illusion. Our economy is going through dramatic changes, causing many people to lose their jobs unexpectedly.

Nobody can fire you from your own business. As long as you can make a go of it, you have a dependable income that no one can take away from you. In that sense, you may have more security in your own business than you would in a job.

Another reason to quit a job and start your own business is to make more money. Many employees never make enough money from their jobs to satisfy more than their basic needs. They struggle for just enough to get by. Being in business is a constant creative opportunity to earn more profits. Every business has necessary expenses, including the cost of paying your own salary. But after all these costs are covered, you can always find new ways of adding value to the business to increase your profits.

I was born and raised poor. I spent so many years living in poverty that I learned to increase my sense of comfort and well-being by needing less. I studied Buddhism and the ascetic life, learning to view the trappings of material existence as distractions from the satisfactions of the spirit. As a senior in high school I lived on one meal a day. I was my present height of 6'1", but I weighed only 115 pounds. I had no home, no medical insurance, no job, no savings, few capital assets, hardly more than the clothes on my back, and uncertain future prospects.

The day I graduated from high school, I remember feeling particularly prosperous. I was free of school. I had my own pickup truck, which was my "home." I had just received my food stamps. I had a few dollars in my pocket, and I was off to visit my sister at her cabin in the woods. To me this was heaven. But looking back, I can't believe I endured such poverty.

Today I am a healthy 165 pounds. I live in a large house on three acres of land in a Victorian-style country village. My car, motorcycle, and travel trailer are paid for. I have no debts, am fully insured, and my kitchen contains all the latest modern conveniences. I work at home in an electronic office full of computers and telecommunications equipment. I have plenty of toys to entertain myself and family, and recently returned from a cruise to South America. I love it and wouldn't give it up for anything. In the words of Pearl Bailey, "Honey, money can't buy you happiness, but let me tell ya', I been rich and poor. And rich is better."

When I graduated from high school I knew how to get by on very little. My despair of material wealth forced me to seek spiritual wealth. But spirituality did not fill my belly, satisfy my physical needs, or provide material freedom or security. My poverty enslaved me in a limited material existence.

I wanted to have material comforts. I wanted to do things, go places, enjoy life. My own business is what helped make that possible. Working for someone else always bound me to his needs and to his schedule. Working for myself freed me to create my own vision, using my time as I saw fit to design a lifestyle of my own choosing.

The profit motive has earned me advantages greater than just surviving. I have more security, personal freedom, and opportunities for individual expression. The wealth I create through my business endeavors gives a deeper meaning to my life than scratching for a living from day to day ever could.

I have often marveled at the lives of mega-rich business tycoons. What keeps them going after they have made their first $10 million? Surely they don't need more money. They could batten down the hatches, put their money in safe investments, and live well for the rest of their lives. Obviously there is more to it than money; there is a creativity and stimulation in doing business which they must find exciting and fun.

Few jobs give you the elbow room to really take initiative, expand your thinking and imagination, and be creative. But your own business always gives you that opportunity. It is yours to do with as you please, as long as you can make money at it. By starting your own business, you can make money, control the quality of your life, and run your own show.

A lot has been written about the risks of starting a business, and how common it is for businesses to fail. I have started several businesses. Of all the businesses that I started, only one ended in debt. All the others survived for a time, paid me a living or contributed to my income, then died a natural death when I lost interest in them or chose to pursue better opportunities.

In viewing my early business career you might think me a failure, or at least slow to get the point. Why not just give up and get a job? On several occasions that is just what I did. But although I did suffer many disappointments along the way, I earned hundreds of thousands of dollars from these businesses, and with every business I gained new and invaluable experience. Government statistics and outside observers might report a long string of failures. But from my perspective, I have enjoyed one long career of growing, learning, earning, and succeeding.

At the end of it all I have no debts, plenty of money and investments, a home and other assets, and the skills and motivation to make money anywhere, anytime.

Weighing the pros and cons of going into business should be the first step in deciding whether to give it a go. The result of this exercise may cause you to become more enthusiastic about going into business, discourage you from the idea altogether, or help you to pick a better business than you originally had in mind.

Here is how to do it:

Sit down and list all of the considerations involved in starting a business. Make a list of two columns with the headings “Advantages” and “Disadvantages,” and write down every reason why you might want to go into business, and vice versa. Consider all the factors that favor or don’t favor a business venture, such as money, time, interest, skills, contacts, ideas, health, family needs, etc.

Now make a second list of all the businesses you might choose to start. Use your creativity and imagination. Let your mind wander freely. Get wild. Think of becoming a safari leader in Africa; starting your own advertising agency; setting up an import business and buying odds and ends from all over the world; becoming a piano tuner; making handcrafted wooden toys; buying an airplane and giving bird’s-eye tours of natural wonders; becoming a chimney sweep. The possibilities are endless.

Keep your lists handy as you read through the rest of this chapter. Feel free to add to them and, as you consider starting a business, you may discover that 1) you are not cut out to be in business at all, 2) this is not the right time to start a business, but it is a good time to prepare for it, or 3) you are going to start the business you've always dreamed of.

Before you get too serious about giving up a reliable source of income and jumping into a business, get serious about building knowledge and skills. What do you need to know to run a business? Where do your talents lie? What do you need to learn to increase your chances of success? Go back to the wealth-building equation and think about your attitudes, knowledge, skills, effort, and resources. Consider how these wealth-building tools apply to starting your own business. What would you create? What kind of activities do you want to be involved in? How could you make money at that? Would you enjoy doing it?

Spending time in your local library will be very helpful at this point. You will find there is plenty of information available on how to start and run a business. At the library make a large stack of books about starting a business: 101 businesses you can start for nothing, accounting made simple, finance, business management, economics, marketing and advertising. Everything you can find on business. Now look at all those books, read their titles, and think about them for a minute.

Does anyone know everything about what is in those books? Do Ross Perot, Steve Jobs, Donald Trump, Bill Gates, Ted Turner, David Rockefeller, William Randolph Hearst, David Geffen, Carl Icahn, Estée Lauder, Henry Kravis, and Gene Autry know most of what is in these books? No, they don't. These are among the richest people in America, but they don't know everything about business. Rockefeller and Hearst inherited their wealth, but the others all built their own fortunes in business. Jobs, Geffen, Autry, Lauder, and Gates never finished college or received formal business training. The point is you don't have to know everything about business to become wealthy.

How much of what is in these books do you need to know? That all depends on what you want to accomplish. I never went to college, but I have studied economics, accounting, business finance, investing, business management, computer science, the construction business, business law, personal finance, real estate, and many other disciplines. I did this because I have become a nut for business and investing. But Michael Dell, who is now a 27-year-old member of the *Forbes 400* richest Americans, had not studied all these books before he founded Dell Computing at the age of 18.

Most people who are successful in business and have never received a formal business education don't bother getting one. What for? They know how to make money. They are already doing it. Many people are successful in business who have never learned the first thing about accounting, economics, management science, or marketing.

There is a true story of an old patriarch of a large and successful business in New York. His son and some young managers came to him with a new business plan, trying to convince him that by modernizing his business practices he could increase his profits. He told them to go look in the storeroom on the 10th floor of his building, where they would find an old wooden vegetable cart. He said; "That is all I had when I started this business. Now look around you. Everything else is profit, so don't tell me how to run my business."

His son and employees may have been right about how to improve business profits. But the old guy knew how to make money, and whether they had a better idea or not, he did not need them. What he had done had worked just fine.

So why bother studying that big pile of books in the library?

The reason is that these books provide a framework, a snapshot, of a whole world of ideas and opportunities, technologies and tools. By getting a glimpse of this world, the terminology that is used, the structure around it, you gain entrance to it. You become baptized into it. It is an initiation rite that gives you membership. You don't have to wait for someone to invite you into that world; it already belongs to you. It is sitting at your local library waiting for you to open the door and step in.

As you evaluate your prospects for starting a business and turn to various resources for information and advice, keep in mind that it is useful to listen to advice, and then throw it away. We all want to sound like an authority when we give advice, especially the "experts." It is easy to sound like an expert. But no one has a crystal ball that shows what the future will bring, who will succeed and who will fail, or which ideas are good and which are not.

During the nineteenth century, the head of the U.S. Patent Office recommended that the government close it down, since everything useful had already been invented.

Only you can finally decide on the merits of your ideas and efforts. Whether your ideas and efforts succeed depends more on how far you are willing to take them than on what the experts have to say. More important than anyone else's opinion or advice is your willingness to strive, create, and succeed. No book can or will tell you whether you can succeed, or exactly how any business enterprise should operate.

It is true that the better educated you are, and the more experience you have, the more likely you are to succeed. It is also true that some of the most unexpected and surprising business success stories describe people who lack the "proper training" and don't know that what they are attempting is "impossible."

Steve Jobs, founder of Apple Computer, is a college dropout who had no business training before starting Apple. Bill Gates, founder of Microsoft, the largest computer software firm in the world, is also a college dropout, who had no formal business training prior to founding Microsoft. If these individuals had listened to the "experts" about their chances of success, they would never have started in business.

You don't have to be an expert to succeed in business. You don't even have to know everything about what you are doing. In business *nobody* has all the answers. You are much more likely to succeed if you are willing to admit that you don't know everything about how to run a business. Then when you need to know something, you are free to ask somebody who does know. When Henry Ford was once asked how he ran specific details of his corporation he said, "I don't have to know all of that, I pay other people to know that."

Although there are many different areas of skill and knowledge necessary for business success, you don't have to do it all yourself. When you own a business you can have almost every one of its chores done by someone else. You can hire competent employees or outside services to do just about anything.

When you manage a business, the question always comes up: "Am I doing this job right, or am I making mistakes?" And the answer is the same for everyone—of course you are making "mistakes." You can always find ways to improve your performance, and you can always look back and recognize some "wrong" decisions. It is not always necessary to get it right. It *is* necessary to perform to a level that maintains the survival of the business. Sometimes the most you can hope for is that the bottom line ends up in the black, and you get another run at improving your performance.

Keep in mind that no small business ever does it all correctly. There are always details falling through the cracks, chores demanding attention but left undone. It may help you to realize that you cannot do it all, and therefore you should continually focus on priorities. What are the areas of the business that are essential to maintain on track?

For most businesses, keeping a close eye on the money is essential for survival. In other businesses, focusing on the right form of advertising or sales approach will make or break the business. Service businesses often require a special emphasis on customer relations and good will. Manufacturing businesses may depend on productivity and quality control for their success.

There are few hard-and-fast rules as to the essential ingredients for business success, despite what the experts say. Going into business is similar to marriage or child rearing. Somehow you manage, and no amount of books or professional advice ever solves all of your problems.

Most of my businesses involved little financial risk, were started on a shoestring budget, and made money from the start. However if you leap into a business with your life savings, enthusiastic about the promise of freedom and riches, but naive about the risks and difficulties, you are liable to end up unhappy and broke. You can spend a lot of money on a business before you figure out how to make a profit from it.

There is a popular term nowadays called "other people's money" or "OPM." The idea behind this phrase is that it is so easy to lose money in business, you should never invest your own money. You should use—that's right—"other people's money." This cynical viewpoint toward business investment is not a particularly valuable business maxim. But it offers one clue to success in business. Be very careful about risking your money. Spend cash on your business only when the money you put into the business will help you make even more money.

The reason most commonly cited for the failure of new business start-ups is lack of management expertise, including the skill of managing money. Obviously the more expert you are at managing a business, the less likely you are to fail in a new venture. Nevertheless it points to the central challenge of entrepreneurs, which is to acquire and coordinate all the skills necessary to achieve success. If you carefully evaluate what going into business means for you, what details are involved in starting and running a successful business, and what factors are liable to cause failure, you will greatly increase your odds of business success.

You might minimize the initial costs of starting the business by doing everything yourself, exchanging your time for some of the money you need. But that is the other half of the problem. You don't have any time because you are too busy working to make money, and to make more money you would need more time, which you don't have because it is all spent making the money you are earning now.

The time problem is tough and there are no easy solutions. The money problem on the other hand, is not as important as you might think. The average person, without the business experience or training necessary, will probably blow most of the money he invests in a new business.

You start with nothing but good intentions, the best laid plans, and fifteen grand from Uncle Bob. In no time you are trying to figure out how to explain to dear Uncle Bob, and all your friends, just how you managed to burn through $15,000 in three months flat, starting a window washing business.

Money is not always the answer to starting a business, although every business needs a little money to get started, and some businesses could not be started without a lot of it. Success in business depends on the time, effort, creativity, and commitment you are willing to dedicate. Outside money tends to be an illusory tool to grease the wheels, but more often than not it just burns a hole in your pocket. Time, on the other hand, is crucial to starting a new business, and you never have enough of it.

The only way to get the time you need is to make it. Making time for your business has to become a habit. It is not easy, and it never gets easier.

If you say "every day from 7 to 8 p.m. I will work on the business," and at 7:15 a friend calls, or you feel tired, or some other emergency or distraction comes up, there goes the biz. You have to be working at the business all of the time. You think about the business when you are brushing your teeth. You carry a notebook and make notes while you eat or are riding the bus to work. You make phone calls while you jog around the living room. Whatever it takes. I get most of my inspiration in the shower. Often you can find me dripping on my computer keyboard, while I get my latest brainstorms on record.

Get into the mind-set that you are in business and business goes on 24 hours a day. This is tough, especially if you have children or other family obligations and you are trying to switch between hard-driving entrepreneur and patient, loving parent or partner. That is one good reason to make a lot of progress in your career or business early, before you settle into other responsibilities. But if it is too late, then you may have to bite the bullet.

Since you never have enough time to do everything for a new business, you should continuously remind yourself to look for ways to:

- get better organized
- get more accomplished in less time
- work harder
- work smarter

Make a habit out of doing business 24 hours a day. When you go to sleep at night, plant ideas for your unconscious to work on (no joke, this actually works). When you get up in the morning, think about the business and keep a notebook close at hand.

This is where the wealth-building equation, and the secret of making money, can help you again. Use them to take stock of your situation. Where do your attitudes, knowledge, skills, effort, and resources fit into your present situation? And how can you get the best return on your time, effort, and money? How do you find or create more value?

You could decide to start your new business gradually, as a sideline to what you are currently doing. Get additional education or experience if necessary. Set up the licensing, bank accounts, brochures, advertising, suppliers. Do your planning and market studies, figure out who your first customers might be, try to pre-solve as many problems as possible. Prepare thoroughly and minimize the risk of failure in every way you can. And then go for it.

This is how many people succeed in their own business. They spend some years apprenticing in an industry, working in various areas of responsibility to learn how the business works. In the meantime they save up their money or make business contacts for financing, network with suppliers and customers in the business, and look for friends or associates who might join in a new venture. Once they have established sufficient knowledge, skill, and resources to increase their likelihood of success in their own venture, they go ahead with it.

Fortunately, the first and most difficult phase of a business does not last forever. Once you are successful and grow a little bit, you should be able to off-load some of the work and responsibility onto employees or outside services. And many of the things you do to start a business have to be done only once. As long as you still have a job or other source of income, you may be able to spread the initial work of getting the business off the ground over a reasonable period of time.

In my family nobody had any useful financial advice to offer, but I can picture many families where some old grandmother or grandfather advises: "If you want to succeed in life, you have to save your money, work hard, and persist." It turns out this is pretty good stuff. These three maxims are the key ingredients of success applied by thousands of immigrants to America in achieving a level of prosperity not possible in their native land. Despite language barriers, cultural confusion, and lack of education these determined, hard-working, thrifty individuals have proven the value of these basic principles over and over again. America was built by such people, beginning with the founding mothers and fathers.

Many of the problems inherent in small business ventures can be overcome by the brute strength of these simple techniques. Much of what seems difficult in the beginning becomes manageable and even trivial over time, once you have persisted, acquired greater experience, sorted out the trouble areas, and learned to carefully manage your money.

In the short-run, the difficulties can seem insurmountable. In the long-run, you may find yourself wondering what all the fuss was about. Visit with as many older successful business people as you can, and ask them what it was like getting started, and how they managed it. You will end up hearing the same story over and over again. "Oh, it was hell in the beginning, I never thought we would make it, but, I don't know, we just kept at it and gradually things got better."

Generalizing about what it may be like to start your own business can be dangerous. It is nice to know that if you run into a lot of difficulties, you are not alone. Many have come before you and surmounted similar problems. No one can predict what your unique experience will be like. If you hear a lot of horror stories about how difficult starting your own business can be, you may end up with the wrong idea—a showstopping attitude. Better to strike a balance between realism and optimistic enthusiasm. Look around at all the successful small businesses there are and realize their owners were not just "luckier" than you; they probably started out just about the way you will.

We hear a lot in the news about business competition. Competition is a fact of life in a free enterprise system. That's as it should be. Competition improves and refines the quality of available goods and services.

Many people worry about starting their own business because they feel there is already too much competition to face in order to succeed. This is probably true if you decided to go out and start a new automobile company or television manufacturing business, or introduce a new kind of refrigerator. Big business in America is facing worldwide manufacturing competition on all fronts. But the situation is different for most small American businesses. Americans have a unique heritage from which to draw upon. We are a melting pot of ingenuity, creativity, non-traditionalism, and originality. We also have a free enterprise system, and a diverse, flexible, economic structure that can support an endless variety of business enterprises.

One natural assumption to make about competition is that everyone is carving up the same pie. In a small town of 10,000 people, two ice cream stores have to share the same population to carve out ice cream profits. But thinking of it another way, ice cream consumption is not static. How much ice cream does each person eat? One cone a month? Two? Three? If people eat more ice cream because they like your flavors so much, the pie you are competing for gets larger.

In my town there are two copy shops right across the street from one another. One is large and busy, has many employees, and is always full of customers. You have to take a number to get service there. The other shop is quiet and friendly, with only two young employees who have worked there for several years. That is where I get my copies done because they are cheaper, and I don't have to wait in line. I asked them how they do with such strong competition nearby. They said, "We do fine. Some people like us, and other people seem to like them."

What is more important than competition is the fact that every business has its own unique characteristics and ways of doing business that set it apart. If you apply the wealth-building equation in your approach to business, you will have no trouble competing, or creating a unique and standout business.

I subscribe to *Forbes*, a business magazine. Every issue is full of business profiles, descriptions of how companies get started, and the ideas that compel people to go into business for themselves. Time and again, they describe enterprising individuals who see new ways of doing things, or choose to express something unique about themselves in their business life. They look at a business or industry from a different perspective to see how they can provide a better product or service, or they follow their interests and find other people, customers, who share those same interests.

Forbes ran a story about Sub Pop, a small alternative music record company out of Seattle, Washington. Jonathan Poneman and Bruce Pavitt got together and decided to start producing records because they loved the music of the offbeat bands they followed as aficionados of the local Seattle music scene. Jonathan's mother thought he was crazy. He and Pavitt used up their combined $19,000 in savings in three months. Now, several years later, with over $1 million in annual sales, the company is successful. And Poneman and Pavitt don't compete with major record companies. They sign joint deals with them to share profits.

But you don't have to come up with an original business idea to start your own business. Maybe you have always wanted to own your own shoe store. There are millions of shoe stores in the world. Why start another shoe store? Maybe there are no shoe stores conveniently located in some part of your town. Or maybe there aren't any that specialize in high-fashion ladies' shoes, in work shoes, etc. You don't have to invent a better mousetrap. All you have to do is find a need and fill it.

You don't need to pick a business just because you are convinced it will make money. You can create a business that brings personal satisfaction, is interesting and exciting, is in alignment with your overall wealth-building goals, *and* makes money.

Thousands of little market niches are waiting to be filled. At the checkout counter at hardware stores, toy stores, or just about any store, there are little knickknacks called impulse purchase items. You buy them on the spur of the moment because they are cheap and look interesting or useful. For every one of those items, someone somewhere has a little business churning them out and selling them all over the country.

My kids have an *Uncle Milton's Ant Farm,* and I had an *Uncle Milton's Ant Farm* when I was a kid too. Uncle Milton created a business to last a lifetime. I get the impression from reading his instruction booklet that Uncle Milton really had a thing for ants. He found an exciting and fascinating way to make money which no one else cared about. How many people compete in the ant farm business? Not many. You don't necessarily have to be the "best" in business. You can simply be unique.

In my town there is a boutique called "Tanglewood Forest" where the owners make and sell limited-edition fantasy dolls. The store is like another world. Tree elves, wizards, flower fairies, and witches hang from the trees, stand on grassy mounds and fill the store with an aura of magic. I have never seen a shop like this before. It is the creation of Marci Wolfe-Bushart and her husband. It is their way of sharing the value of their individuality with others and creating quality of life for themselves.

Apply the secret of making money—finding or creating value, and getting a good return on your time, effort, and money, year after year.

What sort of business would take advantage your skills, offer the most return for your efforts, and make the most money over time? The wealth-building equation and the secret of making money contain puzzle pieces which you need to arrange and rearrange in your mind. This helps you exploit their wealth-building potential by applying them to the specifics of your life.

Here is an exercise you can do for this:

At the top of separate pieces of paper write the following words: attitude, knowledge, skills, effort, resources, value, time, and money.

Now spread the papers out on a large tabletop and begin writing your ideas about each of the words. Start anywhere you like and jump back and forth as the ideas start coming. How do you want to spend your time? How much time do you have? How much money do you have? What value do you have to offer for money? Where can you find or create more value? How can you convert your time and skills into something of value to make money? What valuable products or services could you offer? What resources are available? How could you increase your skills? What attitudes affect your thinking about your own business?

All the topics overlap. Don't worry if you find yourself writing about time and effort on the "money" sheet. Shuffle the papers around and jump from one to the other, as your ideas shift direction. Create new categories, if you need to. You are brainstorming to get ideas about who you are, what you are capable of, how you can become more capable, where you can get more money, how you can improve the quality of your life and start a profitable and fun business. You will also find new ways to understand how your attitudes, knowledge, skills, effort, resources, value, time, and money work together to build wealth.

If you put enough effort into this exercise, a picture will form, giving direction to your thoughts about your own business. You will plant seeds which will sprout and grow in your unconscious as well. Repeat this exercise from time to time to bring your business ideas into sharper focus. A successful enterprise feeds on inspiration, creativity, and imagination. This is how it always begins, with a spark of an idea in the mind of an individual.

When I first visited Apple computer in 1976, it was a tiny little business in Steve Jobs' garage where the Apple I computer was being assembled at the rate of about 10 per month. By 1992, Apple Computer had annual sales of over $6 billion and employed over 14,000 people who produced millions of computers.

Although Apple is one of the more famous examples of small business success we read about, there are thousands of successful new small businesses cropping up every day. Almost all the large companies of today began life as a small business, dreamed up by an enterprising individual.

General Electric was once owned by Thomas Edison. Westinghouse became successful marketing the inventions of Nikola Tesla. Nabisco was founded by Adolphus Green, who invented and marketed Oreos, Fig Newtons, and Animal Crackers. Henry Ford started with nothing and went broke several times before becoming one of the richest men in the world. Alexander Graham Bell founded AT&T, despite attempts to arrest him for trying to swindle people into investing in an "impossible and useless invention"—the telephone. Hewlett-Packard was founded by two engineers with a few hundred dollars in a garage in the 1950s. Ross Perot founded EDS in the 1960s with several thousand dollars in savings. Edwin Land founded Polaroid in the 1930s, and eventually invented the self-developing Polaroid Land camera.

And the list goes on. These are examples from among America's 500 largest companies which have annual sales ranging from $1.5 billion for the smallest of them, to $123 billion in the case of General Motors.

There are over seven million small businesses in America, most of which were founded on a shoestring by enterprising individuals seeking independence, wealth, freedom, or the opportunity to create something new and different. Small business is an important part of American life. And big businesses depend on small businesses to provide them with goods and services. By joining the ranks of small business owners, you are gaining membership in the most vital part of our economy, contributing to the overall health and wealth of our nation.

A lot of people get turned off to business because they know only about the boring parts. Or they know only what they read in business magazines or newspapers, which discuss the dry statistics of business, or the economic bad news. But once you discover what it means to be in charge of your own enterprise, with unlimited creative possibilities and opportunities for wealth-building, business is no longer just "business." It is a way of life, combining the goals and dreams of a full life with the means to make it all possible. You do what you want, and you create the wealth or resources to do it at the same time. What a gas!

As long as you make more money than you spend in a business, it will survive, and you will stay in business. This is the most important thing you need to know about having your own business. If you follow a few simple government rules, pay your taxes, and don't do anything illegal, you can make a business out of just about anything you can imagine. You can market anything of value, which people cannot easily get for free, and profit from it. If you sell it at a price greater than it costs to produce, including your pay for doing it, you are in business.

Of the many challenges you will face in starting a business, one of the most basic is deciding what form of wealth you want to create, what goods you want to trade, or what product or service you want to produce.

To solve this challenge you have to answer a few simple questions for yourself. What can you do, or what would you like to learn to produce a product or service? What would you enjoy doing that would be both a fun business and a rewarding way to spend your time? What product or service would sell the best? What do other people value or want that you would be willing to provide?

Every business needs products or services for which it can charge money. And it needs a group of customers willing to purchase those products or services. This is where most people get stuck. They are not sure what products or services they would like to offer, and they are not sure who would buy them.

Choosing what you want to sell is a personal decision that only you can make. To choose a product or service you can do your own market research. You don't have to hire someone to gather statistics and do a demographic analysis for you. You start by picking a business idea, like making custom guitars. Then you think about who would buy them, how much they would pay, and you start making phone calls and asking around. You call music stores and ask if they would sell custom guitars for you. When they tell you they don't know what you are talking about, you ask for the manager or owner, or the name of a guitar store or special guitar dealer. You are trying to get the lay of the land, who does what, where, and when in the guitar business. Some people will not know how to answer your questions at all, but they will give you a name or another phone number. Eventually you will come across people who know a lot and love to talk about it. You will learn all kinds of things you never expected about the custom guitar business.

Once you get an idea for a business and want to know whom you would sell your products to, start asking around until you get enough information to get a feel for the marketplace. There are basic questions you can ask yourself about your customers. Who are they? Where do they live? How much money do they have? Where will they look for my product (in the phone book, newspaper ads, word of mouth, at a store, etc.)? How many of these people are there in my area, or in the world in general?

You don't have to answer all these questions before you start your business; they are just a way to help you think about whom you are going to sell to.

Once you decide what you are going to sell and whom you are going to sell it to, you have to decide *how* you are going to sell it. Most people don't like to do sales and are afraid of starting their own business because they don't want to ask people to buy from them.

Good salesmanship is an important part of any business, but it is not as difficult as you might think. Good salesmanship mainly involves being friendly, helpful, informative, and providing good service. If people need or want your product or service, you won't have to convince them to buy it. As long as you are helpful and friendly and provide a good product, they will buy from you gladly, and tell all their friends about you too.

In fact you would be surprised how easy it is to succeed in business just by offering common decency to your customers. Customers will come flocking to your business because you provide a good product or service, accompanied by concern and understanding for your customers. Most people are so used to being abused or "fleeced" by businesses, they are surprised and delighted when they are treated with courtesy and respect.

When businesses treat me well, they have a customer for life.

There are many ways to let people know about your business. You can tell your friends and acquaintances and put out the word. Take out a small ad in the yellow pages of the phone book. Put up fliers on bulletin boards. Open a store in a good location where people will notice you. Or call on people who might need your products and services and let them know what you have to offer. One or more of these may be the only advertising you need.

Once you get past deciding what you want to sell and whom you want to sell it to, you only have a few more obstacles to overcome. You must decide how to efficiently produce your products or services and how to keep track of the money.

Efficiently producing a product or service can be attacked effectively using the wealth-building equation. Unless you are going into a business or profession that requires extensive knowledge and training, most businesses can be run with common sense and a little attention to the details.

Keeping track of the money can easily be handled by hiring a bookkeeping service that spends a couple of hours a week with your checkbook, keeping your accounting up-to-date. Your accountant may even do this service for you, as well as giving you tax and accounting advice, and preparing reports that summarize the financial condition of your business. Your main financial responsibility to the business may be only to study and understand the reports your accountant provides you. You don't have to understand accounting to do this; just be sure to hire a good accountant.

Sit down with your accountant once a month and ask a few simple questions: How much money am I earning? How much money am I spending? Am I earning more than I am spending? How much money do I have? What areas of my business are earning the most money? What areas of my business are spending the most money? How does the current financial performance of my business compare with its past performance?

These are all questions a good accountant should be able to answer easily and simply. If she can't, get another accountant. To stay in business you must earn more money than you spend. If you don't know whether you are earning a profit, you cannot ensure your business survival. Don't let bad bookkeeping or a bad accountant ruin your business. Get good advice and make sure you understand the basics of your business financial situation.

Applying the secret of making money to your business is pretty straightforward. Keep it in mind as you conduct business. Create or find more value in the ways you produce your products or services. Increase the efficiency with which you use your time, effort, and money, to increase your returns.

Always be looking for ways to increase sales of your product and reduce costs. Cost cutting in business is a mundane chore that will make your business more profitable, as long as it does not reduce your ability to produce a good product and sell it. There is no trick to it: just think about ways of doing it and put out the effort. The combination of increasing your sales while reducing your costs will always result in maximizing your profits.

To succeed in business you need a product or service to sell, someone to sell it to, an efficient means of producing the product or service, and a method of keeping track of your money and measuring your financial success.

Choosing which business to start when you are not already inspired can put you in a quandary. I can recall on several occasions leafing through the phone book yellow pages from A to Z. This? Nope. This? Nope. This? Nope . . . .

If you already have a business idea to try out, you are in luck, you have the foundation upon which to build your business empire.

If you don't know exactly what goods or services to choose, don't let that stop you from taking action. If you begin research on one idea and it doesn't work out, that's OK. You haven't lost your shirt yet; you're still in the research phase. The idea is to get the juices flowing, the wheels turning, and the creative energies flowing. Don't just stare at the phone book trying to think of the world's greatest business. Take action. Start getting your business organized. Make plans, even if you don't know exactly what you are going to end up doing.

You may discover that what you originally wanted to do is already being done quite effectively by someone else, someone you would have to compete with to survive in business. This does not have to slow you down, but it may force you to reevaluate your thinking and your plans along the way.

Perhaps you had thought of opening a dress shop but there already are several of them around your town. Maybe you should open your shop in a different town nearby, or maybe you discover that nobody has opened an accessories shop yet (scarves, belts, jewelry, etc.). You might change your mind about the kind of retail business to open, and start a hardware store instead. You may think about it some more and decide that your upscale neighborhood needs a little specialty garden tools boutique.

The basic idea has not changed. You want to run a little store, but you have shifted your thinking around on where the best opportunities lie.

Once you decide that being in business for yourself offers the most opportunities for personal wealth and satisfaction, you can spend a long time laying the foundations for your success. You don't have to jump into it right away. You can explore many available options, including starting a business from scratch, buying an existing business, investing in a franchise, or perhaps even doing a joint venture with your present employer.

With a lot of time on your hands, and little money or borrowing power, you may choose to start a business from scratch. Or perhaps you have a unique idea or an existing profession that is best marketed through your own new venture. The benefits of starting a business from scratch include making all the choices about what the business does, how it is organized, where it is located, and what products or services it sells.

Buying an existing business can offer some reassurance that it has an established track record and base of customers, and will continue to do as well in the future as in the past. If you decide you are interested in buying an existing business, you have several ways of finding one that suits your needs. You can look in the classified section of your local newspaper, the *Wall Street Journal*, or business magazines, under "Business Opportunities." You can call upon the services of a business brokerage. A business broker is similar to a real estate broker, but aids in the buying and selling of businesses. Be careful, though. Business brokerage is an industry rampant with charlatans and incompetents. To locate a legitimate broker see *Resources*. Or you can ask your friends and acquaintances if they know of anyone with a business for sale.

When buying an existing business, there are several essential precautions to take. First and foremost, be sure not to pay too much—get good value for your money. Investigate the business thoroughly. You can bet the seller is not going to give you all the bad news, so you are going to have to dig up the problems yourself.

Use an accountant to help you audit the books of the business, and be sure he knows how to uncover any financial sleight of hand being used to disguise the true debts and earnings.

Talk to the existing employees, customers and suppliers of the business, and make sure they are happy with it. Try to get them to discuss any problems they have experienced, or any suggestions they might have for how the business could be improved.

Do market research on the business to determine if there is any reason why it may not do as well in the future as it has in the past. You may discover that there is more opportunity in the business than the present owner realizes, and with a few improvements in its management you could make it more profitable.

In determining the value of the business to you, consider what it can afford to pay you as a fair market salary. And be sure to deduct that as an expense of the business before determining its net profit. Then figure out how quickly the profits will repay any initial and ongoing investment in the business, and compare that with what you could earn from other investment opportunities available to you.

Another way to start a business is to buy a franchise. A good franchise offers a formula for success, as well as valuable services from the franchisor including training, ongoing help and advice, cooperative advertising programs, efficient supply of inventory, and various other benefits.

There are thousands of franchise businesses available to choose from, but most of them are not worth considering. People create franchises to sell as a business; they seldom create a good business for the franchise buyer. *Success* magazine provides an annual list of their 100 favorite franchises. You may want to review their recommendations.

There is a legitimate purpose for creating viable franchises. When a business is growing fast, opening successful new business locations, but cannot raise enough money to maintain its growth rate, it may choose to sell franchises. Ray Kroc sold franchises to expand the McDonald's hamburger chain, and many purchasers of a McDonald's franchise are glad he did.

If you are considering a franchise opportunity, you will want to look at it from two angles, the business itself and the franchise agreement.

To examine the business it is better to completely ignore what the franchise salesperson has to say. In no time someone with good sales ability will have your heart racing and your mouth watering for the "greatest business opportunity of the century." Instead, get the financial projections and the description of the business operations. Go to several of the franchise outlets, talk to their owners, and compare what the franchise literature says with what franchise owners have to say about the performance of the business.

The business could be very good, but if the franchise agreement gives away too much of the profits to the franchisor instead of to you, or places too many restrictions on your freedom to manage the business in your own way or to sell the business, it may be a bad investment. Other franchisees can help you understand and appreciate the shortcomings of the franchise agreement. It would also pay to let an attorney review the agreement and point out problems.

Investing in the right franchise can be a great way of going into business for yourself at a minimum of risk, without having to reinvent the wheel, and with a lot of built-in training and support you could not get in any other business.

A good way to get started in business with little money, in your spare time, is to sign up with a multilevel marketing program.

Before you quickly pass on this idea let me explain.

If you have already been involved with a multilevel marketing program, you probably have a five-year supply of soap out in the garage, boxes of full-color brochures you might as well have thrown out ages ago, along with nauseating memories of mass rallies where everyone jumps around trying to get excited about door-to-door sales.

If you have not been involved in multilevel marketing programs, you may at least be familiar with some of the countless news stories decrying multilevel marketing programs as scams that delude people into believing in instant riches and pyramid schemes.

It is true that, like franchising, most multilevel marketing programs are not worth the trouble. But there are some honest and reputable companies that market their products using multilevel distribution organizations.

The most famous and successful MLM company is Amway. Mike Wallace did a report on Amway for the *60 Minutes* news program, and came up with nothing bad to say about the company or its founders, Richard DeVos and Jay Van Andel. He did run across some complaints about certain dishonest participants in the program. But with hundreds of thousands of small distributors, it would be impossible for Amway to police them all.

I have participated in a couple of different MLM programs, and I am very enthusiastic about them. I must confess though that I did rather poorly, because at the time I lacked the sales ability required. Despite what MLM companies and their distributors will tell you, sales ability is really at the heart of success in MLM. There are some techniques you can apply that minimize the amount of cold calling and door-to-door sales work you have to do, but it is still sales.

If you are a people person, enthusiastic and energetic, and have developed or feel you could develop your sales skills, then I would strongly recommend investigating opportunities in MLM. The important advantages to becoming an MLM distributor are the low start-up costs, the quality of the sales brochures you are provided with, the appeal of the products you choose to sell, and the potential for a huge income by building a large MLM organization.

Looking around the company where you currently work, you may find joint venture opportunities to explore with your present employer. A good idea for a new business, product, or service might be of interest to them. Take it high up in the company and pitch it. Sell yourself and your idea as one package, offering to manage the project for a share of the profits. If your employer will not do a joint venture with you, then consider taking your ideas and talents to other companies in your industry to find a willing partner.

Reading the latest books and magazine articles on business and management could lead you to believe it requires phenomenal brilliance, insight, rapid decision making, and hard work to succeed in business today.

But if the thought of all that pressure and competition just makes you nervous, consider this: you can find some nice, sleepy, old-fashioned business somewhere, and run it for years without worrying about how fast the rest of the world is changing.

I get my hair cut at a barber shop with one of those candy cane striped barber poles in front. My barber keeps a television blaring in the corner and gossips about the usual bits of small-town news. If I had walked out of the barber shop I patronized when I was ten, and into the one I now visit, I would find hardly a clue that thirty years of technological innovation, and world transforming change had intervened. That is just the way my barber and his patrons like it.

My barber probably does not really want to know anything more about making money than what he is already doing. He likes meandering into his little shop every day, turning on the television, and browsing through the newspaper, until his first customer shows. By his standards he may be a richer man than I am.

I have covered many difficult aspects of starting a business, and it may sound discouraging. You may be thinking that someone would have to be crazy to start a business. Your friends may have been telling you this already. That is probably what you have been telling yourself every time you think of starting a business: "I am not the business type." "I don't have enough money." "Where would I find the time?" "I would probably fall flat on my face, be worse off than when I started, and feel like a fool."

Once again, speaking from experience, I can say all of the above is true. You do have to be a little bit crazy to start a business, because you cannot really know how it is going to turn out. You have to take it on faith. And faith is kind of a nutty thing. It is hard to trust yourself until you have succeeded. And you cannot succeed until you trust yourself, or at least give yourself a chance.

A friend of mine was once employed as an international trader. In fact he earned the nickname, "World Trader," because he was always wheeling and dealing on a grand scale, always full of big ideas and grand schemes. Eventually he formed his own company and brought in a bunch of friends and relatives to invest. For months he generated a lot of commotion around who would invest what and how the huge profits would be divided up. His idea was to form a cooperative venture with a number of deep-sea fishermen in the American Northwest. He would trade their fish around the world seeking the best prices. It may have been a brilliant idea, who knows? But between the bad weather, a boat that sank, and bickering fishermen, things did not go well. People lost their money and "World Trader" became the world's biggest failure. At least he felt like one. Though not the humble type, World Trader slunk around hangdog for weeks.

Then he got a call from a business group. Would he be interested in heading a new business venture trading on the international fish market? In fact he would be doing a venture quite similar to the one he had just bombed at. Naturally World Trader was flattered and thrilled at the prospect of improving his fortunes. Nevertheless he was compelled to ask these people why they had chosen him, after he had just failed so miserably.

They expressed their confidence that, having learned the wrong way to do the business, he would not repeat the same mistakes. Despite his failure they were impressed with his abilities, and felt certain he would succeed. And that is exactly what he did. He made a leap of faith, hoping for the best, and finally achieved the wealth and success he desired.

The magic of being in business for yourself comes when you realize your unlimited potential. First you have to acquire the self-confidence to risk being in your own business. Then the rest of the wealth-building equation comes into play. You seek out the knowledge that applies most directly to your business idea, your goals, and what you want to accomplish. You pursue the skills necessary to achieve it. You put out the necessary effort. And you study and organize the resources available to you, or that you must acquire, to make your vision a reality. Finally you realize that you can do it. You get other people to share your vision and work with you so that your enterprise grows. Now you own a company and are in charge of your own destiny. You can go anywhere or do anything with your own business. The sky is the limit.

CHAPTER SEVEN

Investment Strategies

Investing is generally thought of as putting money into specific financial investments—such as the stock market, real estate, or a business—and getting money back with a profit.

Most people think about investing only when they have some money saved up. It does not occur to them that other forms of their wealth—time, effort, knowledge, ideas, skills, technology, etc.—can be invested in the same way as money.

We have all heard of "investing in a good education," and we understand it to mean that spending money to go to a good college, and putting in time and effort to get everything possible out of a college experience, will provide financial and personal benefits for the rest of our lives. Your investment strategies should include an understanding of how to invest all of your resources for greater wealth. Doing this requires some thought. Although the principles of investing are simple and straightforward, it can be difficult to decide how to apply them to your own life.

My own understanding of earning, investing, and wealth-building was simplified when I discovered the secret of making money. There were always pieces of the puzzle that guided my thinking and action (most of us have some idea of what investing and wealth-building are about), but putting it all together in a single clear picture in my mind was difficult. Because all the various approaches to making money and wealth-building are muddled up among so many books and sources of information, it took me many years to sort it out in my own mind.

The secret of making money is really an investment equation. **Finding or creating value, and earning a good return on your time, effort, and money, year after year is the secret of investment success.** And the people who have built large fortunes during their lifetime have all applied this secret.

The way I discovered the secret of making money was by studying textbooks on economics, investment, the stock market, business books, and the lives of wealthy and successful individuals. I also relied on my own experiences as an entrepreneur and investor. The secret of making money is a distillation of all the business and investment principles I have ever learned, boiled down to one sentence, a concentrated "magic potion" for making money. Combined with the wealth-building equation, it provides a powerful tool for making money and achieving quality of life.

Thomas J. Watson Sr. took charge of IBM when it was a small company on the verge of bankruptcy and built it into one of the largest and most successful companies in America. He brought with him 19 years of experience at National Cash Register, where he had risen to second in command. He also brought his vision of what IBM could become. And he applied ideas and technology to create the wealth that IBM represented by the time of his death.

Watson applied the secret of making money every step of the way. It was the tabulating machines that IBM built which attracted him to the company in the first place. He saw the value in them. He created more value by immediately getting a loan for research to improve the tabulating machines. And he earned a good return on his time, effort, and money year after year, by building IBM into a huge company. The "good return" was the growth of the company and its profits that occurred consistently, year after year. Personally, Watson stayed in debt for many years because he kept borrowing money to buy more IBM stock. He invested everything he had in IBM: his time, his enthusiasm, his creativity, his imagination, his money (including money he did not have), and a tremendous amount of effort. He lived well and had fine homes, housekeepers, chauffeurs, fancy cars, and European vacations during most of the time he ran IBM. But it was not until he was nearly sixty years old that Watson earned enough to pay off all of his debts and become fabulously wealthy.

Let's compare Watson to one of his employees, someone who worked on the assembly line at IBM, who put in just as much time and effort as Watson. Such an enterprising assembly worker may have applied the secret of making money, found or created value in selecting better techniques or materials for building tabulating machines, and earned a good return on the time, effort, and money that went into his work. But the difference between the money earned by the assembly worker and the money earned by Thomas J. Watson Sr. is in the scope of their vision. The assembly worker saw himself as a hardworking individual earning an honest wage. Watson saw himself as the head of a magnificent enterprise which he could build into a major force of industry. From his past as the son of a poor farmer and his own early beginnings as a sewing machine peddler, Watson's vision of himself as a man of wealth and stature empowered him to build one of America's most successful companies.

Thomas J. Watson's life exemplifies the power of the wealth-building equation, which gives you the ability to expand your vision of yourself and what wealth means to you. A simple comfortable life can satisfy many people. Others must achieve a higher rate of return to attain a satisfying life. It is all relative in terms of how you see yourself, what you need from life, and what you think you can accomplish.

The strategy of investing that I recommend is integrated with all the parts of your life, career, business, and financial wealth. It involves a program of investing in yourself first, building your earning power. Then you begin to accumulate your financial resources and other assets and put them to work building wealth. It is a lifetime program of earning, saving, investing, and spending. This approach is exemplified in the life of Thomas J. Watson and in the lives of many other super successful wealth-builders.

Donald Trump offers an example of someone who applied the secret of making money. Trained at the Wharton School of business, and the son of a wealthy homebuilder, Trump started out in business with his father. He worked for several years learning the business and accumulating investment capital of his own. He also joined some of the more prestigious business clubs in New York City and devoted much of his time to socializing and developing useful business contacts. Trump recognized value in New York City real estate at a time when many other investors saw only a city whose best days were over and had fallen into decline and decay. He pestered officials to give him a low down payment, a low price, and good financing terms on a large tract of rundown waterfront property previously owned by railroad companies. He got a good return on this investment by developing and selling the property at a substantial profit. Trump made other shrewd buys in New York real estate and created value by renovating old hotels and by building posh condominiums for the rich.

One of Donald Trump's more successful deals occurred when he bought a large estate in West Palm Beach, Florida. This classic old property was worth many millions, including the value of furniture and art it contained, but the owners of the estate had little luck selling it for the price they were asking. Trump made several offers over the course of a couple of years, always offering less money each time. Finally, the owners let it go to Trump at a bargain price—a perfect example of investing for value.

In fact, it was this story that switched on the light in my head about the importance of investing for value. I could visualize the part of the land, the furniture, paintings, and other things Trump had paid for with his money. The rest of the land, paintings, and furniture had signs on them saying "This stuff goes for free." Like a bolt of lightning I suddenly got it. Wealth comes from finding or creating value.

Eventually Trump's successes may have led to overconfidence. He invested a lot of money in Atlantic City casino properties, as well as a small airlines, and more New York hotels. When the gambling business became overbuilt and overcompetitive, and real estate prices fell, Trump was caught in the squeeze. He now had a lot of debt from the heavy borrowing he had done to buy expensive properties. He justified the high prices he paid for his investments by calling them "trophy" properties, one of a kind items that he believed he could sell for premium prices. He had lost sight of finding or creating value and getting a good return on his money. Trump was able to think big, to envision a large role for himself in life as did Thomas J. Watson Sr. But Trump may have lost perspective and succumbed to grandiosity about himself and his accomplishments, instead of keeping in touch with where the real values were.

It is useful to think of investment strategies in one of three ways: you are either lending money at interest, buying a share of a business, or speculating on assets.

When you loan your money at interest, you are letting someone else use your money, in return for paying rent on it.

Owning a share of a business means putting your money into a machine of wealth production, to produce more money than you put in. A business exists to produce new goods and services. Your money helps it buy equipment, advertising, labor, etc. In return you get a share of the profits.

Speculating on assets means buying low and selling high. You buy things for bargain prices and sell them at a profit; for example, finding good buys in real estate and selling at full market value. Or buying stocks or bonds when their price is low and selling when their price is high. Or buying wholesale in a business and selling at retail.

The primary purpose of any investment usually falls into one of these three categories. Categorizing investments in this way helps to focus your expectations about how the investment should behave. If you are lending money at interest you would focus on the creditworthiness of the borrower and the rate of interest your investment would yield. If you are buying ownership in a business you would be concerned with the health of the business and its future profitability. If you are speculating on assets you will focus on when, why, and how much you expect the asset to go up in price, so that you can sell it at a profit.

It is useful to consider how businesses make investment decisions. You can draw a parallel between what a business is trying to accomplish by building up wealth and earning cash profits and what you as an individual entrepreneur are trying to accomplish by following the wealth-building program I recommend. I think of people and businesses as similar in many ways. You are trying to manage your life enterprise for maximum wealth, maximum quality of life, and a business is trying to manage its enterprises for maximum wealth as well.

Investors in a business are looking for one thing—the maximum return or profit on the money they invest. In most businesses investment decisions are made in the finance department. It is the financial officer's job to decide how to spend the money of the business and earn the largest increases on that money in the shortest amount of time.

The two most important concepts that the finance department uses to decide on the best investment are *risk* and *rate of return.* Considering risk is necessary when deciding whether the investment will be successful or not. The rate of return measures the financial value of the investment.

Risk is a tricky subject which is seldom explained well in investment literature because it is so difficult to understand or measure. I don't think I have ever read an explanation of risk that made sense to me. But an understanding of risk is crucial to understanding investments, so here goes.

Imagine a carnival game in which you can have three balls for ten dollars. If you can toss any of the three balls in a bucket you will receive one hundred dollars. That is ten times your money, a very good return on investment for a few minutes' work. But would you accept this proposition? Maybe, or maybe not, depending on the risks involved.

The first question that comes to mind is where you have to stand in relation to the bucket when you throw the balls. If you are allowed to stand close to the bucket, you would be certain of tossing at least one of the balls into it. This would be a sure bet. But what if you were required to stand five feet away? Now the proposition becomes trickier and you have to consider whether you have the skill to win.

At five feet the game may still not involve much risk, but suppose that you are required to stand 25 feet away. Unless you are skilled at tossing games, and know how good you are, you may have a difficult time assessing the risk. Three tosses at 25 feet may not be enough to win the one-hundred-dollar prize, in which case you lose all of your money. Now the risk is much greater. There is a large reward for taking the risk, but you lose your investment if you fail.

So far you could have simply assessed the risk using intuition and good judgment. Standing close to the bucket, or at five feet away, you can clearly see the investment opportunity and judge your odds of success using common sense. But standing 25 feet away, it becomes necessary to apply some mathematical analysis to help in the decision. If you get three throws for ten dollars, you could buy a lot more throws and still make a profit on your investment. You could buy 30 throws for a hundred dollars and still break even on your investment if you succeed in just one of 30 tosses. By investing in more throws you can increase your odds of success. By combining common-sense judgment and some mathematical analysis, you can come to a fairly definite idea of your prospects for success, standing 25 feet away.

If you have to stand 100 feet away the whole picture changes dramatically. Your judgment would probably tell you that no amount of reward could justify the risk of losing your money attempting to hit the bucket at that distance. But what if you were given the chance to practice, and compile statistics on how often you could find the bucket? If you spent a lot of time improving your skill, and developed a mathematical record of your of successes, you might discover that you could consistently earn a profit at this game. Then, even at 100 feet away, the rewards might justify the risks because you had acquired sufficient knowledge to assess the conditions surrounding the game and judge your likelihood of success.

The best way to cope with investment risks is to understand what your investment targets are and how to reach them. Whether you rely on common sense or mathematical methods, the key factor is whether you understand how the investment works to produce a profit.

Businesses may aim at distant investment targets if their knowledge, skill, and experience indicate they can overcome the risks involved.

Notice that the above example of assessing investment risk describes a game of chance. There is no wealth-building involved. The value of the game is in the entertainment, or the opportunity to transfer wealth from someone else to you. Whoever offers you this game of chance must assess the odds of your winning against his opportunity to profit from your losses. Since the game involves both skill and luck, certain individuals may have greater opportunities for success than others. Whoever puts on the game must set it up so that the odds come out in his favor.

When you assess investment risk it is important to consider who is controlling the game and whether your profits are the result of the creation of new wealth, or merely involve the transfer of wealth from less skillful players of the game to more skillful players. The stock market, for example, can reward investors from the profits of businesses that create wealth, or from skillful playing of the market itself.

Measuring the rate of return on an investment requires calculating how much profit you earn on the amount of money you invest, within a given period of time. If you put $100 into a bank savings account and it pays you $5 interest on it at the end of a year, then you have earned a 5% annual rate of return on your investment. This is a simple example in which it is easy to calculate your rate of return. In other cases when you move money in and out of an investment in differing amounts and time intervals, it becomes more complicated to calculate your rate of return.

Combining risk assessment (one crucial factor in investment) with the rate of return offered by the investment (the other crucial factor in investment) has its limits as a method for determining the value of investments. If you took a poll of business students to discover how many want to go into finance, you would find most of them yawning and growing weary at the mere suggestion. There are thick textbooks that describe all sorts of statistical methods for measuring risk and assessing the potential rate of return on investments. All of this math can be useful, as we saw in our simple example of the game above. But sometimes the math goes out the window as people judge their investments based on events and common sense.

The front page of the *Wall Street Journal* on September 10, 1992, announced: "Sweden sharply raised a key lending rate to 75% in an effort to repulse a run on the nation's currency." Later in the article it stated that this 75% interest rate was up from 24% the day before, and up from 16% two days before. When I first read the article I was confused. I thought they must mean that they had increased the interest rate *by* 75%. But it turns out they had increased it *to* 75%! The Governor of the Swedish central bank, Bengt Dennis, is quoted as saying: "We wanted to show investors our muscle." Obviously there is more than just mathematics at work here. World events and human psychology often overwhelm the rationality of mathematics and create new equations. Where is the risk assessment of increasing an interest rate from 16% to 75% within a few days, and what is the rate of return for Sweden? Nobody knows. It is a judgment call, a bold maneuver to contend with extraordinary events.

The insurance industry routinely applies mathematical models to investing. Insurance companies keep detailed records on the statistical probability of all sorts of disasters, to determine how often they are likely to have to pay out on claims. They know how often cars get into accidents, how long people live, how likely you are to trip and break your leg, etc. But when hurricane Andrew wiped out a huge section of South Florida in 1992, insurance statistics must have been thrown severely out of whack. The same goes for the 1992 Los Angeles riots, and the San Francisco earthquake of 1989, and the 1991 Oakland fire. Mathematics cannot predict these events or fully account for their effects on your investments.

Under real-life circumstances investing is an exciting game of survival, of weighing the risks and the rewards. The mathematical nuts and bolts are only one part of the game, and not necessarily even an important part, because success depends on many other factors that may outweigh cold mathematical analysis.

There is a common misconception passed along in most discussions of risk and reward: the greater the risk you are willing to take, the more money you can make. It is usually said that if you are young and adventurous you can afford more risk and therefore can make more money. This is a foolish idea. The greater the risk, the more likely you are to *lose* money. Losing your money is not the way to "achieve a higher rate of return." You should make every effort to reduce investment risks while maximizing your rate of return, no matter how old you are.

When the finance department of a business decides what to invest in, it could just put the money in the stock market and leave it at that—simple and straightforward. In that case it would be betting on the fortunes of other businesses instead of its own. Or it could explore the opportunities within its own business, and decide it can make more money doing what it knows how to do best.

The finance department must assess the risk and the rate of return, but the final judgment of where to invest is only loosely based on these two factors. The rest of the company gets in on the action as well. The research department may like the idea of developing a new kind of computer. The sales department may like the idea of selling it. The manufacturing department may *not* like the idea of making it. The finance department wants to know how much all this is going to cost, how likely the project is to succeed, and how much money is going to be made on it. Then the research people tell everyone what a wonderful computer it will be, and that the research costs will be minimal. The sales department loves the concept and enthusiastically spouts huge sales numbers based on the need it sees in the marketplace. The manufacturing department sees nothing but problems: great costs in setting up the necessary equipment to manufacture these revolutionary computers, and many difficulties in maintaining the quality of the product when applying such new technology. The finance department wants only the numbers. Just the facts, please.

That's more or less how a business decides to invest its assets. It works the same way in your life when you assess your skills, your future, the value of your ideas, the power of your vision, and the risks involved in new endeavors. To some extent it is mathematical and logical, but on other levels it is intuitive and judgmental.

Comparing the way a business runs to how you manage your life is interesting on another level. Businesses pay people to bring organization and discipline, as well as inspiration and enthusiasm, to an enterprise to make it successful. The way we function in our business lives is often much more organized and practical than the way we operate in our personal lives. Recognizing that the science of business is really the science of wealth and success, you can study business to acquire effective formulas for your personal life.

It is typical for people to live with a "split personality" when it comes to money and personal well-being. They work or do business in order to earn enough money to live on, then they go home and spend their time and money seeking well-being. When they work or do business they divorce themselves from most of the sources of their well-being. When they set work and business aside they don't think too much about how their total wealth and well-being are intertwined. This split personality is evident in most of what you read about money and investments. There is little said about where wealth comes from or how to earn a lot of money while you have a good time. Most investment and personal finance books focus on what to do with your money once you have it, how to make it grow to make more money. They don't have much to say about wealth as quality of life and how to combine making money with building wealth and achieving personal well-being.

B. C. Forbes, founder of *Forbes* magazine, hit the nail on the head back in 1917 when he wrote, "Business was originated to produce happiness, not pile up millions. Are we in danger of forgetting this? Too often talking with so-called 'successful' men I cannot but feel that they are making business an end and aim in itself, that they regard the multiplying of their millions and the extension of their works as the be-all and end-all of life, life [*sic*] itself."

Early in my career, my fixation on money short-circuited my thinking about where wealth comes from and what money really is. If you wait to have money before you think about investing, you will never understand investing, or where money really comes from.

The basic principle of investing is to spend your wealth, in order to get greater wealth, or quality of life, in return.

This is easiest to understand when applied to money alone. We don't hand money over to someone else and risk losing it, or forgo the opportunity to spend it on ourselves, without good reason. We put money in a bank savings account, and let the bank loan the money out, so we can collect interest on our savings and earn a profit on the money we loaned. We invest money in a business, expecting the business to make enough profits to pay back our money, and then some. We put money into the stock market expecting to get more money back.

I use the phrase "spend wealth" to describe investing because we often "use up" one form of wealth, converting it to another form of wealth, in the hopes of greater eventual gains. When we use up time, effort or ideas, investing them for money or business arrangements, we hope these will eventually produce greater wealth.

Investing in a business may only involve spending your money, and letting others do all the work, or you may also be investing your time and effort. It is important to let all these interchangeable concepts of wealth and investing simmer around in your head. If you already have plenty of money, or other financial assets, you need only to understand how to invest them for greater wealth. But if most of your wealth is still latent in your ambitions, knowledge, skills, business contacts, sales ability, imagination, ideas, time, or other less tangible resources, then you need to think about how you will invest them. How will you convert them into money or other more tangible forms of wealth, such as a home, cars, ownership in businesses, nice clothes, financial assets, art, fine furniture, beautiful surroundings, or whatever has lasting value for you?

Good resource management influences how much wealth you own or can spend. Think of money as one form of your wealth. It can be combined with other forms to create more wealth. Many business tycoons increase their wealth in this way. They sell off one business that they have built up into a valuable asset and they buy another business where they see future value.

If you think about what you own, whom you know, what your skills are, where you live, what opportunities exist around you, how much money you have, how you spend your time, you can evaluate how your wealth-building resources are being used to create more wealth. You may realize you are wasting time and attention by fooling around with your personal computer. Or you own a boat you never use, which could provide money for investment. Or you own a home which is demanding too much time and work. Or the cash you have sitting in a savings account would grow faster in the stock market. Or the piece of land your parents gave you could be traded in for a better investment. Or you could follow through on that business idea you have been toying with.

Try to turn all of your assets, both tangible and intangible, into productivity tools for wealth. Anything you own or do should either directly add to the quality of your life, or it should be working to improve the future quality of your life. If not, it should be eliminated from your life.

If you have the good fortune to receive unexpected gifts of money or other assets, consider the opportunity they provide for adding leverage to your wealth-building program. I have been fortunate to receive several generous sums of money from my extended family. These gifts greatly increased my investment opportunities and accelerated my wealth-building progress. A friend of mine once received an unexpected inheritance. He quickly bought himself an expensive car and lived extravagantly for a while. He felt this might be his only chance to taste "the good life." Too bad, that money might have been the steppingstone to lifelong wealth.

Think of your wealth as a power generating plant. It won't do anything for you if you don't put it to work. It needs a source of energy to convert to electricity. Whenever possible, you want to place your wealth in the middle of a flow of energy that drives your power plant to produce more wealth for you.

If you are in a low-paying job, put yourself into a high-paying job. If your money is in a bank savings account, put it someplace that earns more interest. If you have boats, cars, trailers, homes, or toys that are sitting around not being used and storing your money in unproductive ways, sell them and put the money to work. If you have contacts that could help you succeed, don't be shy; use them. If you have books sitting around with important wealth-building information in them, read them.

Don't leave your wealth-building power plant sitting around rusting. Keep it busy.

When my family and I were living in Mexico a couple of years ago we decided to purchase a car to use for the several months we would be there. I knew that buying a new car and reselling it when we left could be an expensive proposition, so I went to the Mexican used-car dealership looking for a bargain. I saw nothing that interested me except a brand-new

Volkswagen Beetle (yes, a "Bug"; they still make them in Mexico) with only a couple of thousand miles on it. The dealer was asking 13.5 million pesos for it, claiming this was an excellent bargain. His story was that a business friend had gotten into a bind and needed to unload the car. I checked with the Volkswagen dealership in Querétaro and discovered that the new ones go for 18 million pesos, or 15 million on sale. I also checked the Mexico City classified ads for used Volkswagens and saw nothing this new for less than 13 million. So I offered 12.5 million pesos and he took it. We drove our shiny new adventure-mobile all around central Mexico for several months. It even survived getting backed into by a tour bus, although a new hood and body work were required to restore it. To maintain my investment I had to "hire" a policeman to collect for the damage from the bus driver before he drove off. Before we left Mexico, I sold the car for exactly what I paid for it. In effect, we got to use a nearly new car for several months at no charge. By converting my cash into a car, then back into cash, I was able to use my wealth to produce "free" transportation.

To manage a lifetime program of wealth-building, continually re-investing your assets to accumulate greater wealth, your investment strategies must focus on how to increase your earnings and savings, maximize your investment returns, and control your spending.

Many authorities place a heavy emphasis on saving. They don't say much about earning, as if it does not matter how much you earn. I have exactly the opposite attitude. There is little chance of saving anything if you are earning low wages. You would have to live like a monk to save much out of a $10,000-per-year income. But people who make only that much are told that if they ever want to have money, they will have to learn how to save. That does not make sense.

To save a substantial amount of money, you need substantial earnings to save from. And to make a lot of money investing, you need to start out with a large sum of money. You are going to get rich investing only *after* you have built up substantial savings from your earnings. **First concentrate on building up your earning power, and earning and saving a lot of money. Then you can make a lot of money investing.**

Because of despair of wealth, people become easy prey for all sorts of foolish schemes for getting rich quick. There is nothing wrong with getting rich quick. Sometimes it happens when everything falls into place on an exciting business idea, or when someone becomes an overnight success in movies or as a pop singer. But if you are desperate to make it happen, you are liable to subject yourself to fantasy and disappointment, repeating a vicious cycle that will keep you discouraged and poor.

Every day I get a new phony magazine in the mail, the latest technique in direct-mail marketing to fool you into reading about a sales offer. The offers I get are full of claims about how fast you can get rich investing, starting with little or no money. These are all scams, because there is no surefire way for people to get rich quick investing. It just doesn't happen. I have studied a lot of these offers and it sends chills up my spine to think how fast they are losing money for people.

The secret to investing for wealth is not making a killing at some get-rich scheme: gambling, striking oil, picking the winning lottery ticket, or getting the right angle on the stock market. The secret to investing for wealth is first earning more, then saving more, then investing shrewdly—with safety and a high rate of return—and finally letting your money work for you.

Saving is a habit that builds on itself. As you begin to improve your earning power you should be saving continuously. I pointed out in "Surviving Debt" that to stay out of debt you must spend less than you earn. Once you spend less than you earn, there is a little left over to save. Don't let the small amount you are saving discourage you. The purpose of getting into the habit of saving is not just to build up a large nest egg. It will keep you out of debt, establish a positive discipline for taking care of yourself, and pay off big later on, when you are earning more.

Compounding is the single most powerful financial principle for investing money. Understanding the principle of compounding is crucial to amassing wealth through investment. You don't have to understand the mathematics of compound interest, but you do need to understand how compounding operates over a lifetime to accelerate wealth accumulation. Compounding occurs when you invest your money to earn a profit, then reinvest the original amount and the profits.

Suppose you invest $100 at 10% a year. At the end of the year you get your $100 plus 10% or $10. Now you have $110. You reinvest this at 10% and the next year you get your $110 back, plus $11. Now you have $121.

The most important ingredients of compounding your money are how long you let your money compound and how high a percentage you earn on your money. These are even more important than how much you invest. Watch this.

By letting $100 compound for 25 years at 10%, you will end up with $1,083.

By letting $200 compound for 25 years at 10%, you will end up with $2,166. Twice as much.

If you double the amount you invest, you will double the amount you end up with. Makes sense—right?

But if you invest $100 for 50 years at 10%, you will end up with $11,739. More than 10 times as much as investing it for 25 years!

In this example, by doubling *the length of time* you invest your money, you don't just double how much you earn, you increase how much you earn by more than 10 times.

Now check this out.

If you invest $100 for 25 years compounding at 20%, you end up with $9,539. More than eight times as much as investing it at 10% for 25 years!

By doubling the *rate of return* on your money from 10% to 20%, you don't just double how much you earn, you increase how much you earn by more than eight times.

To summarize:

1) Save as much money as you can, as soon as you can, for investing. Let your money work for you, instead of you working for your money.

2) The sooner you start saving your money and letting it compound to make more money, the more money you will end up with.

3) Earn the highest rate of return you can safely get on your money. Think of 9% as not just a little better than 8%. It is a *lot* better. Over 25 years, one more percent of return per year will earn you 25% more money in the end, if you are letting it compound. And 25% is the difference between $1,000,000, and $1,250,000. A quarter of a million dollars!

The secret of compounding is to save as much money as you can, for as long as you can, and let your money compound at the highest rate of interest, or investment return, as you can safely get.

I say the highest rate of interest *or investment return,* because your investment return may not be from interest on a loan or bond. It might be profit you get from investing in a business, stocks, or real estate. Regardless of the source of the money, the rate at which money compounds is a crucial factor relative to how fast money works to increase wealth. Similarly, the rate at which other capital assets are turned over at a profit affects the rate of return on those assets. This applies in real estate when you buy a property at a discount price and turn around and sell it for a profit. The quicker you sell it, the quicker you can repeat the process and the higher the rate of return you will get on your money. It is the speed at which this turnover takes place, as well as the margin of profit on the money invested, that determines the overall rate of return.

For example, if you buy a house every year for $100,000, and sell it at the end of the year for $110,000, your rate of return is 10% a year. But if you buy and sell such houses only every two years, your rate of return drops to 4.9% a year (not 5%, half of 10%, because of the mathematics of compounding).

Percentages are an important concept in understanding investing. When I started learning about investing, almost twenty years ago, I had difficulty understanding what percentages meant. I knew they were a measure of what I was getting back for investing, but they always sounded paltry to me. What good is saving at 5%? Getting 20% does not sound that much better. I thought something like a 1,000%, or 10,000% would be a nice way to make my investments grow. I mean, how fast can you get rich on

$100 or $1,000, investing at 20%? But as you can see from the explanation of compounding, even 1% can make a big difference in the long-run.

If you are in despair of wealth, desperate to overcome your financial difficulties, you may have difficulty accepting realistic investment goals.

Investing for wealth takes years. Seldom does anyone strike it rich investing. Investing requires patience. But with the power of compounding you can become very rich. Warren Buffet, one of the richest men in America, made all his money investing in the stock market over the last 35 years. In 1992, according to *Forbes* magazine, he was worth over $4 billion.

Here is how you let your money compound when you invest. In a bank account it is easy. You just leave the money in the bank. When the bank pays interest, they put it into your account, and then your interest earns interest. In a stock mutual fund, you request that they reinvest all interest and dividends for you. Then the mutual fund just keeps reinvesting all the money they make for you in the stock market. If you own bonds that collect interest, when the interest is paid to you, you reinvest it. When you earn profits in a business, you reinvest in the business to produce more profits.

Compounding always works this way. When you make money investing, you just reinvest it, and your money is compounding on itself.

You don't need a lot of math to be a good investor. If you study investment books you may find some difficult formulas. Don't worry about them. You can make lots of money and invest successfully by having a good handle on addition, subtraction, multiplication, and division. No higher math is needed, except an understanding of calculating percentages. You can use an inexpensive calculator to do compound interest calculations, figure loan payments, and make other investment calculations easily.

Controlling spending is a skill that involves understanding the value of shopping for bargains, spending as a way of investing in yourself and the quality of your life, and dealing with negative attitudes that cause you to spend unnecessarily.

Shopping for bargains is similar to investing for a high rate of return on your money. Saving 20% on a purchase is like investing your money for a 20% return. You are putting a portion of your money back in your pocket which you can save and invest. But when you shop for bargains you have to consider the amount of effort required in relation to what you save. Saving 25% on a 75¢ soft drink is not worth the trouble. But when you are filling a whole shopping basket full of bargain-priced groceries, saving 25% may mean $25 off a $100 grocery bill. Then your savings are worth the effort and really add up. When it comes to a really big-ticket item like a new car, television set, refrigerator, or a home, shopping for bargains becomes especially important.

Not buying something in the first place is the best bargain shopping technique I know. It provides a 100% rate of savings—a very good investment. I was talking with a friend about the principles in this book and she asked whether I thought it was O.K. to spend $5 on jewelry from street vendors, when she really cannot afford it. She said these little splurges give her pleasure, but she has to take a lot of kidding from her friends about how she spends money. I explained that it does not matter what you spend your money on. The whole point of spending money is to enjoy life. What matters is that you keep your spending in perspective. Weigh your expenditures against your overall wealth-building goals. I suggested that she set aside a certain amount every month for "mad money" to do with as she pleases—just for fun and entertainment. The rest of her money should be dedicated to necessities and her savings program.

How much money you choose to spend or not to spend depends on how much you earn, the standard of living you have established for yourself, and how quickly you want to build up savings to invest and work for you.

If you form good habits of saving and spending before you earn a lot of money, you will be much better off. Most people find that as they earn more, they spend more. Wayne Newton earns $250,000 a week as the highest paid entertainer in Las Vegas. But he filed bankruptcy on $11 million in debts despite his high income. If you establish a modest but comfortable lifestyle, and keep your spending under control as your earnings grow, you will end up with large surpluses of money for saving and investing.

Many people are out of control in the way they spend money because they are in despair of wealth and desperate for a shopping fix—like a drug. When you are poor and in debt, or your life feels empty even though you earn a lot of money, spending money becomes a way of consoling yourself—like drinking alcohol to soothe your troubles. Some people need psychological counseling to overcome such emotional despair. But a lot of the problem comes from not understanding how money and wealth-building work. When you don't see the value in shopping for bargains, saving your money, and investing for the future to accumulate wealth, you live carelessly, spending your money as fast as it comes in. When you understand that good saving and spending habits build a sense of self-control, self-confidence, and self-esteem, and put into motion a positive momentum for accumulating wealth, then you discover a magic potion, an elixir for financial success and personal well-being.

If we all knew the future in advance, investing would be easy. If we knew where and how to invest our time, effort, and money for the best return, we would all be rich. But there is no such certainty to investing.

When everybody knows the safest and surest way to make money, all compete to do it. When a lot of people compete to have something, they drive the price up, and the opportunity for a profit on it is reduced.

Think of it this way. If you can buy oranges for 10¢ and sell them for a dollar, you can make 10 times your money investing in oranges. But if someone else discovers your investment secret, he or she will start buying and selling oranges the same way you do. When enough people are buying oranges where you do, this demand will drive the price up and reduce the profitability of selling them. Also with more people selling oranges, there is more competition for customers. Now all of you orange investors are going to start reducing your prices to get people to buy *your* oranges instead of somebody else's. You may end up buying oranges for 60¢, and selling them for 62¢. What originally was a great investment has now become an ordinary investment. In fact, it has become an uncertain investment, because if your cost of oranges goes up just two cents, you will no longer make a profit. Once the profit on an investment becomes marginal, it loses its attraction, and the competition in it stabilizes. It reaches an equilibrium in the amount of return it offers in relation to the money, effort and investment risk involved.

This is how all investments work—stocks, bonds, real estate, businesses—everything. When people find a good investment, they will flock to it, driving the price of the investment up, until it does not offer such a good profit anymore. Then it is no longer a sure thing, because the margin of profit becomes so thin.

Good investments become average and uncertain investments, once everybody knows about them. Because people compete to invest, they make investments uncertain or risky.

There are many different types of investments available, and so many complicated concepts associated with them that it is nearly impossible to understand what they all are and what you are getting for your money.

When you look at a conventional list of investments—including annuities, bonds, collectibles, common stocks, convertible securities, foreign stocks and bonds, futures contracts on commodities, futures contracts on interest rates, government agency securities, life insurance, limited partnerships, money market funds, mortgage-backed securities, municipal securities, mutual funds, option contracts, precious metals, real estate, savings accounts, treasury securities, unit investment trusts, zero-coupon securities, etc.—you may find yourself overwhelmed by the complexity and terminology.

Most people either give up on the whole idea, throwing up their hands in frustration and just sticking their money in the bank, or they let some salesperson talk them into an investment, because the sales pitch sounds good and the company seems large and respectable. Don't let some "expert" tell you what to do with your money, without ever understanding the reasoning behind the investment. If you don't feel confident that you understand an investment, don't invest.

The best investments for the average individual are explained in detail in this book, and here they are: yourself, the quality of your life, your career, your own business, the stock market, and real estate. Invest in yourself first, understanding your attitudes, getting an education, and acquiring skills. Increase your knowledge about investment strategies with your wealth-building goals as your target. Invest in your career to achieve maximum income and personal satisfaction. Invest your money, creativity, sweat, and imagination in starting your own business, which is the best vehicle around for becoming wealthy. Investing in the stock market is similar to investing in your own business, but it requires that you already have some financial capital built up. Among financial investments, owning shares of stock has proven the most reliable and profitable over the long term. Real estate provides a vehicle for both personal shelter and security, as well as a way of building wealth. You may find other areas of investing you wish to explore in detail, but do it only if you can educate yourself to both their advantages and pitfalls.

Most business and investment opportunities are bad deals! In order to get the best investments you have to shop hard until you find a good deal.

In business, this means you must be willing to invest your time and effort until you find a quality product or service you can provide at a good price. In the stock market, this means shopping for the best performing mutual fund, not just the first one that comes along. See Chapter Eight, "The Stock Market," for details. In real estate this means working hard to find undervalued properties that offer better investment opportunities.

I have often heard professional investors complain that individuals spend no more time and effort investing thousands of dollars in the stock market than they do shopping for a new pair of shoes.

Bad deals are a dime a dozen. Educate yourself until you know what you are doing, shop and compare value, and hold out for the good deals.

The secret of making money is finding or creating value . . . .

A friend of mine, Michael Conlen, is a metal sculptor. His specialty is glass-top coffee tables. He hunts up interesting metal parts from junkyards and abandoned factories and buys them to create works of art. He invests his time, energy, money, and artistic vision to find and create value. He uses ideas and technology to build new wealth, ornate coffee tables, that have both practical and artistic value.

My sister-in-law buys and sells antiques. She travels all over the Northeast, shopping garage sales and antique auctions to find bargains. If the seller of an antique does not recognize the quality, uniqueness, or historical importance of what he is selling, he may let it go at a bargain price. She is finding value during her shopping excursions. But she can also create value in two ways: one is to refurbish the antique to improve its quality, the other is to study and promote its value. The more she studies antiques—their history, origins, and craftsmanship—the more she can add to their value when she sells them to her customers. When she explains to a customer why a particular piece is worth more money, she is adding to its value in the eyes of her customer. She is also adding to its value in the eyes of future owners of it as well, because the story will get passed along from owner to owner.

Here is a simple approach to planning your investments of time, effort, and money, and all of your other wealth-building assets. Block out your investment program on a monthly basis. You pay most of your bills by the month, and you should be able to measure your income more or less on a monthly basis. If you have financial investments, such as stock brokerage accounts, you will probably get your statements once a month. Consider how your investments are shaping up. Are you getting wealthier? Are your investments paying off? What are the results of your investments? How fast are you getting results?

Think about how to get more money in exchange for your time, either this month, next month, or in 12 months. If there is not enough money, what is the problem? Do you need to work harder? Do you need more knowledge and skills? Do you need to shop for a better job where your knowledge and skills will be rewarded with higher pay? Do you need to work up more courage and ask for a raise?

Think about how you are investing your time every month. Did you buy a house that requires a lot of yard work? Are you making the best use of your time, or squandering it? Every month evaluate how you use your money. Consider what you spent it on. Was it worth it?

Taxes are among our largest expenses. Anything you can do to reduce your taxes can have a big effect on your net income and savings. When you do your taxes each year, be sure to spend time with your tax preparer asking questions about each item on your tax return. Don't just drop off your paperwork, pick up your return and write a check. Sit down and ask questions about all of the tax matters that apply to your situation. If you are used to going to a quickie tax preparer, shop around for someone who is willing to talk about your tax needs. It may not cost much more, and could pay for itself in what you learn about how to save on your taxes.

Our tax laws are a mess, and have only become more complicated in recent years. You can expect to be confused about your taxes. Accountants and tax attorneys themselves are confused about the tax laws and must continually update their education. Don't let this intimidate you. Ask questions and learn as much as you can. Your tax preparer has no stake in finding deductions for you. Since the law holds your tax preparer responsible for any mistakes she may make on your return, it is in her best interest to be cautious. You, on the other hand, have nothing to lose by being aggressive about taking deductions, as long as you stay within the boundaries of the law. The more you know, the more you save. The better your understanding of the tax laws, the more effectively you can plan your financial strategies for reducing taxes.

To help reduce or eliminate taxes on your investments, use tax-deferred, or tax-exempt, retirement programs. If your employer provides a 401(k) or similar retirement program, set aside as much money for it as you can. If you are self-employed, talk to your accountant about setting up Keogh or SEP-IRA programs for yourself. Put as much as you qualify for into an IRA account. You greatly increase your rate of return from compounding when you use these programs, because your investment profits are not taxed until much later.

Money is only a temporary store of wealth. Sometimes it is good to have a lot of cash, because you can buy real estate, stocks, businesses, and other expensive assets cheaply when the economy goes sour and prices are low. At other times you don't want to own or lend cash, because its value is being eroded by inflation, and your wealth will grow better elsewhere.

Think of money as a kind of wealth which is more or less valuable under varying circumstances. If stock or real estate prices become too high, you might sell stock or real estate to get cash. If stock or real estate prices fall, it is a good time to have cash to buy at bargain prices. These opportunities were abundant during the Great Depression, when money was valuable and you could buy stocks and real estate cheaply. When stock prices took a big dive in the fall of 1987 and the fall of 1990, cheap stocks were available. Right now in the early 1990s, real estate prices have fallen all over the country. This would be a good time to buy real estate.

Successful investment strategies to make money require thoughtful consideration. Develop better investment judgment by learning as much as you can about investing. Many people believe that because of its complexity, investing should be left to experts. This is a form of despair of wealth, a way of giving up responsibility for your life and expecting experts to do what you are not willing to do for yourself. Few investments turn out more than a mediocre performance when left to the "experts." There *are* a few people who are selling good, sound investment advice. But if you don't know enough about investing to appreciate the quality of their advice, how will you find them?

Fear is one of the worst attitudes you can have toward investing. Uncertainty creates fear, which leads to panic and rash investment decisions. Learn to live with uncertainty in your investments, and control your fear with sound thinking. You can reduce uncertainty by shopping for good investments that make sense and that you can understand. Fear is largely the result of ignorance. Dispel ignorance and fear by educating yourself.

The best attitude you can have toward investment is realistic optimism. Trust in yourself and believe in your future. Understand that America has a long history of economic success, and there is nothing on the horizon to discourage you from believing in America's future economic prosperity.

A positive attitude toward investing will also help you control your spending, stay out of debt, and increase your savings. If you are in despair of wealth, and don't trust your capacity to earn, save, and invest, you will be casual with your money, not earning enough, and always spending too much. But if you understand your power to build wealth, you will have a positive attitude toward money and will manage it effectively.

Remember, the secret to financial success is to increase your earning power, increase your rate of savings, invest carefully for a high rate of return over as long a period as possible, and control your spending. Simple. As long as you are willing to do it.

There are over one million millionaires in this country. What have they got that you don't have? Maybe somewhere around one million dollars. Except for that, what do they amount to? Think of that. Over one million people like yourself, but worth at least a million dollars. If you apply the wealth-building principles in this book, isn't there some way you can match some of them? I think you can. I encourage you to believe in yourself. Set that million-dollar goal for yourself and do it.

CHAPTER EIGHT

The Stock Market

In my early twenties, when I was first trying to establish a career direction for myself—basically trying to figure out how to strike it rich—I picked up a few books on investing and the stock market. I thought their advice sounded pretty good. Buy low, sell high. Hey, what a concept! That made a lot of sense. If you buy stock at a low price and sell it at a high price, you make money. All you have to do is buy it when the price is low, and wait for it to go up.

Now I was starting to get a handle on this thing. Here was a strategy I could follow to get rich. I liked that.

Then I discovered a little more sophistication was required. There were "price resistance levels." I had to watch the stock price, and when it settled down at one level for a while, that meant it was consolidating for its next move. Then it would "break out" and suddenly jump up in price. This is where they lost me. I didn't feel very confident about recognizing these price fluctuations, and knowing when low was low, and high was high.

About the same time I was listening to cassette tapes from an investment seminar. One of the experts mentioned the name of a stock he thought was bound to skyrocket in price. Aha! A hot tip. I figured since he was the expert, he wouldn't recommend a stock that was *not* going to go up in price. So I jumped into the stock market and bought $250 worth of "US Antimony." Ten years later I sold "US Antimony" for about $8. Less than my broker charged me to get rid of it.

By the time I sold this terrible investment, I had made many thousands of dollars in the stock market. After "US Antimony" had become almost worthless, I hung on to it for a while to remind me how *not* to invest in the stock market. It was my first and last hot tip.

Over the years I studied the stock market, I learned that my original education on the subject was pretty worthless. The first books I read, written by well-known authors and still published to this day, were junk. A recipe for disaster. Luckily I had enough skepticism not to follow their advice all the way down the road to ruin. Unfortunately there are more bad books on the stock market than good ones. These books are written either by people who don't understand how to invest successfully in the stock market, or by charlatans who hope to convince people to buy their books with promises of an easy path to stock market riches.

I apologize for not offering any "secret techniques" for "striking it rich" in the stock market. There are none. There are many schemes that you can read about in numerous books and newsletters. You may hear friends enthuse about someone who made a lot of money in the stock market using "a new system." But the stock market will be a good investment for you only if you can manage to steer clear of "hot tips" and fast-buck approaches.

My first attempts to understand and invest in the stock market took place around 1980. I read stock market books and newsletters, and listened to cassette tapes of "experts" discussing "little-known methods." Applying what I learned I succeeded only in wasting money, time, and my enthusiasm for the stock market. I was so discouraged, it was not until 1987 that I felt the urge to give it another go. I dug out my old stock market books (all of them bad), subscribed to some investment magazines, and began to study carefully how to get in on the booming stock market. Finally in August, with the market peaking at all-time highs, I put all my retirement savings into a leading mutual fund. Two months later disaster struck—the great October crash of 1987. I watched with despair as my life's savings shriveled in value.

I had made the most common mistake of beginning stock market investors—getting in at the point of maximum enthusiasm, just before the market peaks. I will show you how to avoid making this same mistake yourself.

Fortunately I had sufficient common sense to realize it wouldn't do any good to sell. Good advice from friends kept me from getting out at the point of maximum despair. I held on to my mutual fund shares and, as the stock market recovered in 1988, I made my money back.

During this same time I was talking with a friend who is an investment adviser about my stock market troubles. He suggested I attend the course he teaches at UCLA on stock market investing. It was lively, interesting, and renewed my enthusiasm for the stock market. It also helped clarify some of my confusion toward it. I learned why most people lose money in the stock market. But most important was the reading list of stock market books included with the course materials. This is the best list of stock market books I have ever seen (see "Resources" for my suggested reading list). I learned many of the secrets of stock market investing from these books.

By gaining an in-depth knowledge of stock market investing, I found out why my early attempts failed. I have done very well in the stock market since then, building up a substantial portion of my wealth from it. I discovered that investing in the stock market can be exciting and fun, as well as a way to make a lot of money. But you must follow a successful approach that does not depend on "magical thinking."

Most people in despair of wealth find it difficult to face reality head-on. They get into magical thinking about their money, hoping that by discovering a secret technique, their money problems will be solved. That is how so many people fall prey to investment gurus who convince them to try their special brand of magic for getting rich in the stock market. This "magical thinking" is an ineffective attitude that comes from despair of wealth.

I offer a simple, fail-safe approach that anyone can follow to invest in mutual funds. You don't have to be a stock market wizard to earn high investment returns in the stock market. Mutual funds can provide you with professional management that will invest your money for good returns.

For people like myself, who want to put in the effort to get that extra investment edge by becoming a stock market enthusiast, I've given a detailed overview of how the stock market works, and how to successfully invest in individual stocks.

Whether you follow the simpler approach of investing in mutual funds, or the more detailed approach of buying individual stocks, investing in the stock market can be an exciting, rewarding, and safe way to build wealth. The stock market is a fundamental building block for establishing and maintaining financial success.

There is no more convenient and effective way to invest your wealth than in the stock market; that is why so many American institutions invest most of their capital in stocks and bonds.

There are several common misperceptions about what the stock market is. Many people think the stock market operates like a financial gambling casino where everyone places bets, and wins or loses on the roll of the dice. For this reason they either avoid investing in stocks, or they do it casually in the hopes of getting lucky. If you treat the stock market like a gambling casino, you will invest your money as a gambler and lose it, as most gamblers do. A lot of people love the excitement of gambling in the stock market, and it can be fun. But it is not how you make money.

Some people think of the stock market as a complex financial machine that will pay you a lot of money if you analyze it with the right mathematical formula or computer program. This is not how the stock market works. Large stock brokerage firms, using expensive computer systems, and buying and selling huge amounts of stocks, have been able to skim a small amount of money out of the stock market for some years. But their techniques are not available to individual investors. In order to be successful in the stock market, you must apply judgment and experience, which cannot be replaced with computers or mathematical formulas.

Finally, many people think of the stock market as a game of psychology, an attempt to read the minds of other investors and achieve an investment advantage by anticipating their investment moves. They imagine that understanding mass psychology will lead to shrewd conclusions about stock market behavior that will yield quick investment profits. Although there is some psychology involved in stock market investing, it is not a magic force for amassing stock market wealth.

All three of these notions about the stock market contain a grain of truth, just enough to get you in trouble. These misconceptions about the stock market lead to either losing money by attempting to make a fast buck, or making no money at all, because you are afraid of the stock market.

The stock market can be a safe and reliable investment, if you understand how to use it. As long as business and the economy do well over the long run, the stock market will do well over the long run. Given the long history of business and economic success in America, it makes sense to trust our economy and invest in it through the stock market.

There have always been ups and downs to business, the economy, and the stock market, and there always will be. *This is normal.* You should ignore economic predictions and stock market predictions. They are wrong as often as they are right. You don't have to predict the future to invest safely and profitably in the stock market.

The best way to make money in the stock market is to invest on a regular basis, year after year. Make sure you own at least ten different stocks at any given time, which you will if you own a mutual fund because they always buy many different stocks. Don't worry about fluctuations in the economy or stock market. Just keep putting your money in on a regular basis, and plan to leave it there for at least several years. If you buy individual stocks, do not buy and sell them on a short-term basis. Hold each stock for at least several years on average.

The best way to make money in the stock market is boring to most people. The average stock market investor spends six months trying to make money in the stock market before he becomes discouraged and quits with less money than he started with. He uses a stockbroker who tells him to buy and sell stocks for a quick profit, earning commissions for the stockbroker, but losing money for the investor. Or he subscribes to some stock market guru's newsletter and loses money using the guru's "exciting secret techniques."

Don't let stock market gurus convince you to risk your money for short-term gains (less than a year). Use my "boring" but safe approach to the stock market and you will get the best investment returns for your money, instead of losing it. And you will be on a surefire path to building wealth. I know this from experience; I have made enough money in the stock market to take a year off from my other business pursuits and write this book!

Here is how to set up a stock market investment program using mutual funds. Mutual funds are the safest approach to the stock market, for most people, as long as you follow the plan outlined below. And mutual funds are the best way to get started in the stock market for those who lack the money to buy a broad selection of individual stocks.

Mutual funds are investment programs in which the money of many individuals is pooled together for investment in stocks, bonds, or other securities. Any profits earned from the investments are divided up equally among the fund shareholders, after paying a management fee to the organization responsible for the fund.

There are several ways that mutual funds are categorized according to the kinds of securities they invest in, such as stocks, bonds, options, futures, foreign stocks, etc. They are also categorized by the degree of risk involved in the investment approach. The assumption is that the higher the risk, the higher the potential rate of return (or loss) that may be achieved. Such risky approaches to investing may allow a fund to achieve very high rates of return during big price rises in the stock market, but also can result in large losses when the market drops. You are not looking for a high-risk or "aggressive growth" mutual fund.

In general these "growth" funds are not compatible with the long-term investment principles outlined in this chapter and I don't recommend them. They are prone to the gambling mode of short-term trading that I discourage. On the other hand there are a few funds falling into the "growth" category that are managed with long-term objectives in mind. Don't be concerned if the fund you choose is described as a "growth fund," as long as you use the approach I recommend.

There are other specialized types of funds that I would not recommend, including foreign stock or "global" funds, industry "sector" funds, or gold funds. There are too many disadvantages to mutual funds that specialize in only certain types of stocks.

The main benefit of a properly chosen mutual fund is that it will provide professional investment management on a small budget. You don't need a lot of money to get started investing in the stock market if you use mutual funds. Usually no more than $1,000, and sometimes less, is required, and you can add money in any amount as you go.

When shopping for a mutual fund you will discover that some are called "no-load" funds, as opposed to "load" funds. Load funds charge a commission for investing in the mutual fund, sometimes as much as 8%. This commission is a waste of money for the investor, since load funds don't perform any better than no-load funds, on average. Buy only no-load funds. Watch out for funds that charge on the "back end," that is, they charge you to sell shares. Buy funds that have no excessive sign-up fees (usually zero for no-loads), or extra fees for buying and selling shares at any time.

When shopping for a fund, choose only among highly rated, conservatively managed ones that have a long track record (at least five years) of consistent performance.

Here is how to find a good mutual fund.

Every August *Forbes* magazine publishes its "Annual Mutual Fund Survey." Buy this issue of *Forbes,* or look for it at the library. Look at what *Forbes* calls its "Honor Roll" of mutual funds. Check the columns showing the "Average annual total return" and "Maximum load." Pick the funds with the highest average annual total return listed, with the word "none" under maximum load. This will give you a top-performing no-load mutual fund.

Because the *Forbes* honor roll list contains load funds, and some funds with a minimum $5,000 initial investment, as well as international funds which you are not interested in, the list may narrow to just a couple of funds to choose from. These are acceptable investments, but if you want to broaden your choices, it also rates other top-performing mutual funds in its other lists as well, from which you can also safely choose.

I like the *Forbes* mutual fund ratings because they rate the performance of funds over long periods of time, and they rate their safety in down markets. Many mutual fund lists just rank funds according to which turned in the highest recent performance. This is a poor measure of long-term stock market success.

Consumer Reports magazine also rates mutual funds from time to time, and it applies similar measures of safety and long-term performance.

When you can afford it, I recommend that you own three different mutual funds. The success of a fund usually depends on the skills of just one or a few key individuals in charge of its management. If they leave, the fund's performance may be affected. By owning three different funds, you reduce the risk of a drop in future performance of one of your funds.

Because a mutual fund will not always perform as well in the future as it has in the past, you want a fund with a long-term track record. But even then, there are no guarantees. If one of your mutual funds turns in an especially poor performance over at least four or five years, you may need to switch it. Don't sell a fund just because it had one bad year. This is short-term thinking. Do not sell mutual fund shares when the overall stock market is down. Always hold on to your mutual funds during severe drops in the stock market, and wait until it returns to "normal" before deciding to switch from one fund to another.

Once you have purchased your mutual funds, you should give them at least several years to perform. An "average" market cycle, during which the market goes down and back up, or up and back down, is about three years. Sticking with your mutual fund somewhat longer than that will give it a chance to perform through a full cycle. The wrong thing to do is to buy at the top, watch it fall to the bottom, and then sell out.

It is not a good idea to put all of your savings into the stock market all at once, unless you only have $1,000 or so. Putting your money in a little at a time protects you from unexpected stock market price fluctuations. Dividing the savings you want to invest into ten monthly installments will accomplish this for you.

Do not buy your mutual fund through a stockbroker, or even a discount broker. No-load funds are available directly from the mutual fund management without commission costs. *Forbes* lists the address and phone number of the mutual funds they rate, so you can contact them directly.

So-called "switch" funds allow you to request that your mutual fund shares be sold and the cash placed in a money market account, or that your money market cash be used to buy into the stock mutual fund. In this way you can attempt to "time" the stock market, by getting out right before a major drop in stock prices, or by getting in right before a big rise. There are investment newsletters that recommend investing in mutual funds that allow you to switch back and forth like this, but I would avoid this kind of activity. It is nearly impossible to time the market in this fashion and you will probably do more harm than good attempting it.

That is about all you really need to know to invest successfully in the stock market. I wish someone had offered me these simple guidelines many years ago. I would be much richer today.

The rest of this chapter will focus on a more in-depth discussion of the stock market. It is of value to anyone who wishes to know more about the stock market.

Readers who prefer to use mutual funds and let professionals choose their stocks should feel free to skip ahead to the next chapter. The rest of you can explore one of my great passions—investing in the stock market.

I love the stock market, because nothing stands between me and making money. The more effort I am willing to put into studying and understanding the stock market, the more money I can make. As long as I have enough capital to invest in it, I can crank out wealth. It is like a candy store of American entrepreneurship. You get to shop among all the best businesses in America, and buy a little share of their success. The more you are willing to learn about excellence in business and investment strategies, the more you can participate in stock market wealth. It is such a clean and efficient way to apply the wealth-building tools I have described in this book, I get goose bumps just telling you about it.

If you put $1,000 in the stock market and let it compound at 20% a year for 25 years, you will end up with $95,396. But if you take away 5% for inflation over those years, you would have $32,918 in today's dollars. That is a nice chunk of change, but not exactly enough to retire in luxurious splendor. A 20% rate of return per year, over 25 years, is near the maximum you could hope to achieve; and without carefully applying the recommendations in this chapter, it is likely you will achieve somewhat less than that.

But if you combine stock market investing with the rest of your wealth-building activities, and continually add to the capital you have invested in the stock market, you could someday live on just the income from your stock market investments. That is a goal worthy of your best efforts—to achieve financial independence and personal freedom.

I have many friends who have tried their luck in the stock market and have come away broke and more deeply in despair of wealth. One of my friends listened to the advice of a stock market guru and invested in stock options. At first the money he put in exploded in value. He thought he had found the pot of gold at the end of the rainbow. His stockbroker told him to get out while the getting was good, but my friend continued to trust the advice of the newsletter he had read, and lost all of his money. But his problems did not end there. Greed had taken hold of his senses. He kept thinking about all that money he would have made if he had sold in time, so he *borrowed* several thousand dollars from a friend, and gave it another go. Following the advice of the same stock market guru, he bought more stock options but this time he lost all the money right away.

Stock options are a very high-stakes game. You can either make a lot of money or lose it all. Whatever you do, don't let anyone talk you into fooling around with them.

Instead, let's discuss how the stock market works and how to invest in it safely.

Stock exchanges in the United States trade a variety of financial instruments, but primarily trade stocks and bonds. **Stocks** are certificates of partial ownership in a business enterprise. When the business earns a profit, it may pay **dividends** to the stockholders of the company. The company declares a dividend and sends a check to its stockholders for the amount of dividends owed to them, according to how many shares of stock they own.

Bonds are agreements to pay back money borrowed by a business or the government, with interest.

The difference between stocks and bonds is that stocks represent ownership in a company, but bonds are debts of a company or government organization, created when it borrows money. Stocks are generally considered riskier than bonds, because if the company does not earn profits it may choose not to pay stockholders a dividend. Bonds pay interest, no matter what, unless the company or government agency goes bankrupt.

Although much more money changes hands every day in the bond market, most of the excitement and interest in the financial markets is centered on stocks.

For hundreds of years there have been periodic "crazes" during which people have become fascinated with the possibility of becoming rich in the stock market. Bernard Baruch, a legendary investor of the early twentieth century, said that he learned more about the stock market from a book published in 1841 entitled *Extraordinary Delusions and the Madness of Crowds* than from any other source. He found this book interesting because it chronicled several episodes early in the 18th century in which the passions of the public had been so inflamed with greed or panic over their investments that all common sense and rationality vanished.

Greed and fear are the two primary emotions controlling the fluctuations of stock prices. When stock prices spiral upward beyond all reason, the primary driving force is greed. When stock prices plunge well below the intrinsic value of the companies they represent, the driving force is fear. To succeed on your own as a stock market investor, you must learn to understand and control your greed and fear. I have read this in numerous stock market books, but it was not until I experienced this firsthand, that I understood its true meaning. It was greed that led me to put all my retirement savings into the stock market, just before the crash of 1987. And it was fear that caused me to panic after the crash.

Baruch realized that it is the loss of common sense, clear reasoning, and thoughtful study of the stock market that creates the greatest opportunities for the shrewd investor. When the crowd is rushing feverishly to buy, buy, buy, driving stock prices ever higher, the shrewd investor, resisting the impulses of the crowd, makes money selling stocks. When the crowd is fleeing the market in a panic, selling their stocks as fast as they can get rid of them, driving prices ever lower, the shrewd investor, once again mastering impulses to follow the crowd, will buy.

The steep rise in stock prices during the summer of 1987, followed by the dramatic October crash, demonstrated this phenomenon at work. The "crowd" that time consisted mainly of institutional investors, ever more excited by the unstoppable power of the great bull market of the 1980s. They were enticed into paying increasingly higher prices for stocks and taking a larger stake in the game. When the first winds of doubt began to blow, a hurricane panic ensued, producing a 36% drop in the Dow Jones Industrial Average in less than two months. On October 19, 1987, the Dow dropped 508 points for a *one-day decline of 22%*. It was the most dramatic crash in stock market history.

Those few investors who sold stocks prior to August 1987, and bought stocks again after October, made a killing.

Buying shares of stock when most people are selling them, and selling when most are buying, is called "contrarian" investing. When stocks become popular, as computer stocks did in the early 1980s, everyone wants to get in on the "latest thing" and this creates excessive demand in one area of the stock market, driving prices up. When an individual stock, or a category of stocks, lose their allure, investors move on to newly popular selections, selling off their previous favorites at reduced prices. By buying out-of-favor stocks, and selling those that have become overly popular, you can go against the crowd and make money in the stock market. This crowd mentality exists not just among amateur investors, as you might expect; these are mostly investment professionals riding each new wave of stock market excitement.

Mastering your own psychology is the first step toward successful investment in the stock market. Because the stock market continually fluctuates in value, and these fluctuations show up on the news every day, they can disturb your sense of equilibrium and color your investment judgment. You have to become familiar with your own reactions to news events, stock market price swings, and the opinions and pronouncements of the crowd.

When the news is bubbling with economic prosperity, business profits are up, and rising stock prices are lining the pockets of the wealthy with paper riches, it can stir twinges of envy and greed in you. And when the ship of economic prosperity founders, and the news turns pessimistic, chilling stock market enthusiasm, you can be filled with nagging doubts that stir fear and panic.

These are normal symptoms experienced by most stock market investors, amateur or professional. The battle for a cool head and a rational perspective is waged among all investors. The first lesson to learn is how these emotions affect your judgment, and how to deflect their influence and calmly stay your course, based on sound reasoning.

By studying the information contained in this chapter, you will achieve a clear understanding of the stock market that can be relied upon when placing orders to buy, when everyone else seems to be selling. That is how I knew to dive into the market in the fall of 1990, when everyone else was reacting to the invasion of Kuwait and the upcoming economic recession.

To understand how the stock market works you need to know why stocks exist at all. When a company is privately owned, all of the profits of the company are plowed back into it to help it grow, or they are paid out to the owners of the company. The value of that company to its owners is in the profits it pays out to them, or in the money they could get from selling the business. Its owners must either draw a salary from it, receive a share of the profits, or sell off shares of ownership in the company. The most efficient way to sell shares of ownership in the company is as stock.

If a privately owned company needs to raise more money than it is earning from its profits, it must either borrow the money, or sell shares of ownership to investors. Thus private companies will often decide to "go public," by selling shares of stock. (Private or public companies, and the government, may also issue bonds in order to borrow money.)

The stock market operates as a continuous auction for the buying and selling of either new stocks and bonds, or previously issued stocks and bonds that are changing ownership. Current owners of these securities may offer them for sale asking a set price, and buyers may place a bid offering to purchase at a set price. When the asking price of a seller matches the bid of a buyer, a sale is made.

It is also possible to buy or sell "at the market." This means that as a buyer you will purchase at the lowest price the stock is being offered at, or as a seller you will sell to the highest bidder.

If there are more buyers than sellers, prices tend to rise, as the excess demand applies upward pressure. With an excess of sellers, prices tend to fall. The stock market offers a good demonstration of how the forces of supply and demand cause prices to fluctuate. Sometimes the price of a stock will skyrocket as good news about the company excites a crowd of investors to buy. On another occasion the price may fall as some negative news or rumor casts doubt on the prospects of the company, causing a sell-off.

News about general business conditions or the economy may cause a large number of stocks to rise or fall in price at the same time. People react to news, no matter how sober and professional they are. Because there is always uncertainty in investments, people are on the lookout for any sign of how their investments will turn out. With investments, no news means no reaction, but news creates reactions.

The cycles of stock prices rising and falling can, in themselves, motivate buying and selling. There is an approach to stock market investing called "technical analysis" that relies heavily on the price movements of stocks to determine when to buy and sell them. Using charts and graphs, technical analysts trace price movements in hopes of predicting their future. Numerous books have been sold offering the promise of easy riches using technical analyses. Most sophisticated investors ignore these misleading ideas. Many stock brokerage firms maintain research departments promoting technical analysis, because it encourages people to buy and sell stocks on a short-term basis, which means more commissions for the brokerages.

A lot of people get hooked on technical analysis because they think it is a way to practice contrarian investing. By watching where prices are going, technical analysts think they are getting a fix on where the crowd is headed, and try to outguess them. Don't make the same mistake. Technical analysis is mostly stock market voodoo.

It is tempting to think that, based on the price history of a stock, we can somehow predict what its future price will be. And the price we pay for a stock has a strong influence over how we think the price of the stock should behave after we buy it. This is a serious mistake that many stock market investors make. You are better off forgetting what you paid for a stock, since it has no bearing on what the stock is worth thereafter.

The approach to stock market investment applied by the majority of serious-minded investors is fundamental analysis. Fundamental analysis assumes that the true value of a stock can be determined only by looking at the company that issued it. A stock represents shares of ownership in a company and in the assets and profits of that company. Assets are everything the company owns to help it do business and make money. Its profits are the money it makes doing business, after deducting its expenses. An increase in the value of the company's assets, and an increase in its profits, contribute to an increase in the value of that company's stock.

The fundamental factors of reality which have a positive or negative impact on the success of a company also have a direct effect on the value of its stock. These factors include how well its products and services are selling, how profitable it is, how good a job its management is doing, whether it has any exciting new products under development, or whether anything bad is happening to the company that might diminish its future profits.

To determine the appropriate price for the stock of a company you must analyze its business prospects and current financial health. Then, looking up the current price at which the stock is selling, decide whether the stock is overpriced, underpriced, or fairly priced, in comparison to the value of the company it represents. **When you look at the price of a stock, you have to see the value of the company that stands behind it, and the value that company is trying to create with its business.**

People forget that the price of a stock has something to do with owning a share of a company. The price of the stock starts to take on a life of its own, and loses touch with the real value of the company. If you lose touch with that, then you lose touch with what is protecting the price of your stock from falling.

One way to think of the stock market is that in the short-term it is like a voting machine. It counts the votes of investors, tallying up whether they think near term business or economic conditions are likely to be good or bad, and what their expectations for the stock market are. These votes will show up in the near term prices of stocks, as they rise or fall, indicating the optimism or pessimism of investors. In the long run the stock market is like a weighing machine. It weighs the effects of business and economic conditions, and investor attitudes, on the long-term action of stock prices. The voting machine measures investor opinion, the short-term outlook of investors. The weighing machine measures the sum of how all factors finally guide the price of stocks, in the long-term.

Popular opinion and theories about the economy and stock market are proven or disproven by long-term events. If popular opinion says that business conditions and the economy are on the decline, or that the stock market is overpriced and about to go down, then stock prices will fall in a self-fulfilling prophecy. But if, in reality, business conditions and the economy improve, people will change their minds about stock prices. Investors will then buy stocks, driving prices up to a level in accordance with what really happened. Here the scales of the weighing machine have swung back into balance. Long-term results cancel the effect of short-term opinions that vote stock prices up or down.

If a stock is worth $10 a share according to reasonable standards, and in five years the company doubles its profits and assets, it is reasonable to expect the price of the stock to double and sell for $20 a share. It does not matter if in the meantime the price of the stock fluctuates from $10 to $5, then up to $30, and back to $20. None of those price fluctuations has an effect on the *intrinsic value* of the company represented by those shares of stock. Eventually the stock market will recognize this inherent value, and the price should settle down to around $20 a share.

This is not to say that the interim price changes should be completely ignored. It might be nice to buy a lot more shares at $5 a share, or to sell some shares at $30 a share, but none of these price fluctuations have an effect on the inherent value of your investment.

If the price drops to $5 a share, no one can force you to sell them at that price. Just because some other fool is selling his shares and driving down the price does not mean you have to follow him down the road to ruin. Your company may still be healthy and growing, earning profits which it will eventually pay you in dividends. As long as the company is doing well, it does not matter if someone who is stupid or desperate sold at $5 a share. Eventually the price will return to a reasonable level.

Price fluctuation in the stock market is like having a manic-depressive business partner. Imagine you are in business with someone who is forever changing his mind, constantly moody, one day excited and optimistic, another day discouraged and depressed. Each day your partner shows up with a new offer to buy or sell his shares of the business. Some days the sun is shining, the flowers are in bloom, and your partner can see only the bright side of business opportunity. The future is golden and he is ready to buy. Any price will do. He sees unlimited potential. Though you like the business and are confident of its prospects, you cannot quite imagine the business growing fast enough or producing sufficient profits to justify the price your partner is willing to pay, so you sell all your shares in the business to him. The next day you drop in and discover that storm clouds have gathered. Your partner is in a dark mood. Some new business problems have arisen. Your poor partner is overcome with worry and doubt. He just did not expect such bad luck and cannot see beyond the immediate crisis. He wants to sell and wouldn't you please consider buying his shares back. You survey the damage and realize some unexpected reversals have occurred in the fortunes of the business, but nothing too dire. Your partner, in his despair, just wants out of the whole mess, and is offering to sell the business back to you at a price far lower than the current problems warrant, so you buy. But you don't give your partner back all his money from yesterday. You buy back the business for less. Your partner paid too much for the business yesterday and sold it too cheap today. This silly scenario repeats itself day after day, and you reap continuous profits from your hapless partner's foolish assumptions about the value of your business.

The metaphors of the voting machine, the weighing machine, and the manic-depressive business partner were originated by Benjamin Graham, perhaps the greatest stock market theorist ever. They clarify our understanding of short-term price fluctuations and keep them in perspective.

If you observe the wide range of price fluctuations which occur for many stocks, you realize the truth in these metaphors. How can the long-term prospects of a company gyrate so wildly day by day and month by month? The answer is they cannot. It is only the *opinions* of investors buying and selling the stock that are gyrating so dramatically.

In the short-term, stock prices depend on widely varying speculation as to their "correct" price, or whether their price is about to go up or down. Thus, comparing the stock market to a game of chance, a form of gambling, is not far from reality. However, in the long run the intrinsic value of a stock tends to be reflected in its price, providing a rational basis for stock selection. The almost whimsical nature of short-term price changes is overcome by the force of reason as events unfold. When people come to their senses, and realize how a company is doing in comparison to the price of its stock, they will react by buying or selling shares until the stock's price more closely matches the value of the company.

The apparent value of a company is in its current assets and profits. But when we invest in the company we are not so much concerned with today's assets and profits. We are far more interested in knowing how our investment will perform in the future. When we purchase a stock, we hope that it will pay us generous dividends, and/or continuously rise in price, offering the future opportunity to sell it at a good profit. The true value of a stock today depends on its profits, and its accumulation of assets, in the future.

Considering the present profits of a company, the assets it owns, and the expectation that the company will perform well in the future, we may decide to buy its stock at what seems to be a fair price. But since the future is uncertain, unexpected events may cause the fortunes of the company to decline. Profits may diminish or disappear altogether. Dividends may be canceled, and the assets of the company may become burdened with debt as it borrows money to survive. These problems degrade the value of our investment and drive down the price of our stock.

There are no guarantees in life or business. Great businesses of today may become the dinosaurs of tomorrow. The railroads of the nineteenth century were fabulous investments for a time. But the railroads were replaced by newer technologies and their fortunes declined, causing periodic shocks to the financial world as the value of their stocks and bonds collapsed with the news of another catastrophe in the railroad industry. Other industries whose good prospects have been ruined by unforeseen events include the American electronics and automobile industries, which have lost so much to the Japanese; the small plane industry, which could not bear the costs of liability insurance and litigation; the oil industry, which was caught off guard by the oil glut of the early 1980s; and the American tobacco industry, which is now besieged by health concerns regarding tobacco use and a continuing decline in the numbers of smokers.

Business managers are frequently caught unaware as events unfold, and they discover serious unforeseen problems that threaten the profits and future health of a company. If they are not able to assess the company's future, how would outside investors assess it, with a view toward buying its stock?

The answer is that no one can be sure of the future success of any company. All we can do is analyze its past performance as an indicator of future performance. We can use common sense about the business to consider whether it is likely to continue to do well.

Short-term stock prices are fickle and cannot be accurately and reliably predicted. Buying a stock because you expect that in a few days, weeks, or months, the price will go up, not down, and it can be sold at a profit, is a bad bet. You may as well be picking a number at the roulette wheel.

Short-term trading in the stock market also increases the cost of taxes to the government and commissions to your stockbroker.

Strangely, most of the stock market is made up of short-term investors. These are primarily institutional investors whose performance is usually evaluated on a quarterly basis, and who are therefore making investment decisions with near-term goals in mind. It is to your advantage that so many stock market professionals have customers breathing down their necks looking for quick profits. It forces them to make bad investment decisions which you can profit from. When they feel pressured into paying too high a price, or selling too cheap, you will find good investment opportunities.

The risks and disadvantages of short-term stock investing are well known. Various studies have demonstrated that by lengthening the holding period of stocks to several years, the risks of losing money are greatly reduced, the chances of making money from dividends and capital gains are greatly increased, and the rate of return is enhanced by fewer brokerage commissions and some tax advantages. Despite this evidence, people on

Wall Street continue to seek "higher performance" by following short-term strategies.

Ideally you want to select stocks of companies that will earn profits and grow during the several years following your investment. Because general economic conditions can have a large positive or negative effect on the circumstances under which businesses must operate, the future prospects of companies are not always certain. Therefore it would be useful to be able to predict future economic trends before you invest in any company.

But economists have proven themselves to be consistently unreliable in their predictions of economic cycles. Only a long time after economic events have occurred do the majority of economists agree on what has happened. The science of economics is not a "hard" science. It is a social science. It depends on the understanding of mass psychology—how large numbers of people are likely to behave toward their work, money, and investments, under a variety of uncertain circumstances. Weather forecasting may be more reliable than economic forecasting.

You can get a general picture of how past and present economic conditions affect business and the stock market. But I don't recommend paying heed to economic predictions as an important part of making investment decisions.

So far I have presented the following assumptions about how the stock market works:

• Mass psychology operates in the stock market, driven by fear and greed, driving stock prices up or down, often too far in either direction.

• The true value of a stock rests with the financial performance of the company represented by it.

• Stock prices gyrate up and down in the short term, often with little more rhyme or reason than a popularity contest, thus causing the market to act like a voting machine.

• In the long term the stock market acts like a weighing machine, weighing a company's performance, the effects of business and economic events on individual stock prices, and the stock market as a whole.

• Making short-term investments in the stock market is more like gambling than investing, offering few opportunities for safety, or adequate rates of return.

• Investing for the long term is safer and more reliable. It reduces risk and increases the chances of preserving capital and achieving a good rate of return.

These assumptions lead to the conclusion that it is safest and most profitable to invest in the stocks of well-run companies likely to grow substantially in assets and profits, and to hold on to those stocks for a number of years. To understand how to make money in the stock market, you have to place some faith in the future by relying on the past and on several logical assumptions.

Businesses exist to make money and earn a profit. You can assume when you buy most stocks that the businesses you choose are busy trying to make money.

The economy depends on the success of business. The government depends on the taxes of business and workers to operate. Therefore business has to keep doing well for our economy and government to succeed, and for people to have jobs. Unless you can justify the argument that the American economic system is falling into long-term decline, you have to assume that when all is said and done, the economy will do well, and the stock market will do well. Otherwise, you might choose to bet on a different horse than the American economy and business, perhaps by investing overseas.

Looking at the historical record of the stock market you can see that over the long-run it has performed well. Except during long periods of economic problems, such as the Great Depression of the 1930s, the stock market produced good results for long-term investors. Comparing stocks to bonds from 1939 to 1988, a period of 50 years, the Standard and Poor's list of stocks of the 500 largest companies returned 11.2% a year on average; small company stocks returned 15.8%; long-term corporate bonds 4.6%; long-term government bonds 4.2%; treasury bills 4.1%; and inflation averaged 4.4%.

The history of the stock market shows that in general, American businesses have succeeded in earning profits and rewarding investors. The long-term trend of stock prices has been, and continues to be, up. Despite the existence of business cycles and related economic cycles, the outlook for the future continues to look good. The stock market of the twentieth century has survived two world wars, the Great Depression, and spiraling inflation while maintaining an excellent track record overall. If the American government, the economy, and business fail, it will not matter what you invest in anyway.

With this background, and a drop of faith in the future, you can see that the stock market offers good investment opportunities. You may need to remember this from time to time when the newspapers are full of stories about the decline and fall of the American way of life, especially when politicians are spouting their ignorance of economics and crying out against the catastrophes in store for us all.

Looking back on the history of the stock market, notice that during three of its worst periods—in 1932, the most dismal time of the Great Depression, and in the severe recessions of 1974 and 1982 when stock prices were very low—the best stock-buying opportunities existed. These were good times to leap headlong in the opposite direction of the crowd, and invest heavily in the stock market.

Before we can get down to picking specific stocks for investment, we still need to review a few more general concepts about the stock market.

By selecting the stock of the one company that will produce the highest rate of growth in earnings (profits) over several years, you would theoretically have picked the best possible investment. For example you could have bought stock in Microsoft Corporation, the world's largest manufacturer of computer software, back in 1986 for as low as $2.30 a share when it was earning 17 cents a share for its stockholders. By 1991, Microsoft was earning $1.65 a share, representing a 57.5% compounded rate of growth in earnings over five years. By then you could have sold your Microsoft stock for as much as $88.80 a share. That is more than 38 times what you originally paid for it! An original $10,000 investment at $2.30 a share would have been worth $386,086 in 1992 at $88.80 a share, representing an 83.8% compounded annual rate of return over six years.

But now that is history. What does past experience say about the future of investing in Microsoft? It says that Microsoft was such a fabulous investment that many people rushed to buy it, and the stock is now very expensive. It also says that Microsoft must have done some things right, and will probably do fairly well in the future. But finally, going strictly by the numbers, it says very little about the future prospects of Microsoft stock as an investment. As I write this I note the headline on my most recent issue of *Forbes* magazine announces "New Threat to Microsoft," and the article warns of serious threats to Microsoft's future growth.

If I had put all of my investment capital in Microsoft stock back in 1986, I would have been delighted by the outcome, and it would have been hard to do much better. But what if I had put all of my money into the stock of Bolt Beranek & Newman, a leading high-tech electronics firm? Its stock price had gone from a low of $1.40 a share in 1981 to a high of $29.90 in 1987 for a 66% compounded annual rate of appreciation. By mid-1992, after the company lost money in 1989 and 1990, its stock price hit a low of $4.90. Ouch! I am glad I did not buy at $29.90 a share in 1987.

The example of Bolt Beranek & Newman demonstrates that past performance is not always equaled by future performance. It is best to invest in companies with a track record of success. But even that track record offers no guarantees.

So how do we achieve better-than-average investment returns, select stocks which offer above-average performance, and avoid the risk of concentrating our money in an overpriced Bolt Beranek & Newman? The answer lies in diversification and value.

There are two forms of diversification, which I will call "portfolio diversification" and "time diversification." A group of several investments is called an investment portfolio. When you own a portfolio of stocks, the risk that any one stock will lose money is offset by the potential of the other stocks to earn money. If you own only one stock and it drops in price by 50%, your stock portfolio has dropped 50% in price. But if you own 10 stocks of equal value pricewise, and one stock in this diversified portfolio drops by 50%, the value of your total portfolio has dropped by only 5%. By owning 10 stocks you have removed 90% of the risk of owning just one stock. This principle of risk diversification is similar to what insurance companies accomplish by dividing risk among large numbers of policyholders.

The principle of time diversification is similar to portfolio diversification, but relates to the risk of price fluctuations over time. Stock prices on average move up, providing the long-term returns I have already talked about. But stock prices don't move up in a straight line. They cycle up and down, day by day, week by week, year by year, gradually reaching higher and higher price levels. The shorter your time frame for holding stocks, the more likely you are to catch the top of a cycle and ride it to the bottom. The longer your time frame, the more the cycles average out and the long-term upward movement works to your advantage.

By holding on to your stocks over a long period of time you achieve time diversification. You avoid the risks caused by the short-term cycles. Time diversification can be achieved in two ways: first, you can lengthen the average time you hold stocks—five years being a good rule of thumb—and second, you can use dollar cost averaging.

Dollar cost averaging is the technique of buying and selling stocks gradually over a period of time. This reduces the risk of buying a stock just before it begins a long decline in price, or of selling a stock just before it begins a long rise in price. Dollar cost averaging works best when investing in mutual funds, because commission costs on buying individual stocks are higher when buying in small increments.

Value investing follows the theory that behind the price of every stock stands the value of the company it represents. By comparing the relationship of the stock price to the value of the company you should be able to select stocks that offer better values for your investment dollar.

This is where the secret of making money comes in.

The secret of making money is finding or creating value, and earning a good return on your time, effort, and money, year after year.

Hunt for companies in the stock market which offer good value for your money. It does not matter how good the company is if you pay too high a price for its stock. Sometimes average companies offer the best investments. Because the price of their stock is so low, they offer good value. But the best combination is buying top-performing companies at a bargain price.

To get a good return on your time, effort and money, year after year in the stock market, look for value. Put your time and effort into finding stocks at bargain prices. Then sit back and hold on to them for the long haul. This approach saves you time and effort compared to picking stocks for short-term gains, then selling them and having to search for new ones. Also, it is more reliable because it makes sense to put your money where the value is, instead of chasing prices and hoping for a quick killing.

A good return on your time, effort, and money also implies making money as quickly as possible; getting a good return on your money in the shortest amount of time. But in the stock market, overanxious greed results only in *losing* money. In the stock market, patience is crucial. But now and then you will strike it lucky and make a few quick killings. If you buy a stock at a bargain price, and it shoots up in price and becomes overvalued, sell it. No problem.

Be careful though. Once again, greed can overcome your patience and you can sell when there is still plenty of value left in the stock to drive its price even higher. Greed can also cause you to hold on to a stock too long. The price will peak out way too high, and suddenly plummet. It is always OK to buy a stock before it hits its lowest price, and to sell a stock before it hits its highest price. Nobody knows how to hit the peaks and valleys perfectly. If anyone did, successful short-term trading would be possible.

Because the future is uncertain and picking the best individual stocks is difficult to do, you want to reduce the risk of investment losses as much as possible, while maximizing the opportunities for gain. This provides a margin of safety between what we hope will happen and the possibility of failure. Diversification and value investing achieve this goal.

To maintain a margin of safety, the principle of value investing assumes that any given stock, at a specified price, may be considered undervalued, fairly valued, or overvalued. You want to buy undervalued stocks, and sell them if they become overvalued.

A stock that is undervalued is more likely to rise in price than one that is fairly valued or overvalued, and is the safest investment. In theory, a fairly valued stock will not have a strong tendency to rise or drop in price, unless the company's performance improves or gets worse. An overvalued stock is more likely to drop in price, so it is riskier and has a smaller margin of safety.

I find it useful to imagine a rubber band that is stretched when a stock, or the stock market, is undervalued or overvalued. One end of the rubber band is attached to the "fair price" of the stock, and the other end is attached to the actual price of the stock. The more undervalued a stock is (i.e. the lower the price), the more tension there is on the rubber band to pull the price of the stock up. The more overvalued a stock, the more tension pulling the price down. At fair value the rubber band is relaxed and the price is not tending in one direction or the other. I like a lot of upward tension in my investments.

In the past I often probed my friend, the investment adviser, on the subtleties of investing in the stock market, looking for the best "techniques." One evening while pestering him at a party he seemed to grow impatient with my questions and suddenly blurted, "The best way to make money in the stock market is to wait until it falls on its ass, which it does every few years, and then buy." Although I had already been making successful stock market investments by then, following the value approach I had learned to trust, I knew my friend's comment was especially relevant because I had read about highly successful stock market investors who plunge into the market when the time is ripe.

When the stock market fell dramatically during the summer of 1990 I recognized just such an opportunity, and invested heavily, making a killing in the market at that time.

By applying the contrarian strategy of seeing value where others did not, I was able to select stocks at prices representing excellent values. Ignoring the crowd that was stampeding past me to get out of the stock market, apparently panicked by the generally correct assessment that we were heading into a recession as well as concern over the Iraqi invasion of Kuwait, I selected sound businesses that were selling for peanuts. I had read various economic predictions anticipating a recession and knew that we were long overdue. But I also knew that all recessions and downward stock market cycles are followed by economic and stock market recoveries. I knew that war scares are common causes of market panics. And with stock prices so low (although they could have gone much lower), I could feel that rubber band of value stretching in my favor. To me there was much more likelihood that I would make money than lose money, under the circumstances.

Reviewing my investment performance of that period of time I calculated that from June 1990 to January 1992 I earned an average annual rate of return of 26% on my stock market portfolio. This is a high rate of return which would be nice to maintain, but my overall performance as a stock market investor has been lower than this. It was mainly due to the great opportunity during this sell-off of stocks in the fall of 1990 that I was able to turn in such a high performance.

Here are some stocks I bought and how they worked out. I bought Family Dollar Stores at $10.37 a share and later sold it for $23 a share, for a 122% increase. I bought Ford Motors at $27.62 a share, later sold for $40 a share, for a 45% increase. I bought Chrysler at $10, later sold for $14, for a 40% increase. I bought Interface at $9.37, later sold at $15, for a 60% increase. I bought Goodyear Tire at $15.87, later sold at $22.12 for a 39% increase. And so on. Of all the stocks I have bought during the last several years, I have sold only one at a loss, Western Digital, which I discuss later in the chapter.

Of course, the percentage increases I list for all these stocks are not annual rates of return. They are the percentage increase on the price of the stock, during the short period I owned them.

Looking back, my actions seem like a very safe bet, compared to the situation in mid-1992, when the Dow Jones Industrial Average surpassed the 3400 level for the first time ever. Then I found my rubber band of value stretched the *wrong way* and sold some of my stocks. Under those circumstances I found myself groping for signs to guide me, even though we were most likely on the verge of economic prosperity and a continuous upswing in corporate earnings.

Most of the value was priced out of the market as far as I could see, at least for the next year or so. But this is normal, as stock prices typically anticipate economic cycles. The record highs of 1992 were anticipating a likely economic recovery, which was partly under way.

Even when the stock market is reaching all-time highs, there are always some stocks available which offer good value. They are just harder to find. Once stocks have been popular and overpriced, they become especially unpopular after their price falls, and then can become good buys. Undervalued stocks can exist under any market conditions.

To understand the comparison between the price of a stock and the value underlying it, there are two important measures of value: the price-earnings ratio and the price-to-book ratio.

The price-to-earnings ratio is calculated by dividing the price per share of a stock by its earnings per share. Most tables of stock prices in the financial press provide a column titled "P/E" which lists this ratio. If a company earns a net profit of $1 per share and its stock is selling for $15 a share, then the stock can be had for a P/E of 15. The long-term average P/E of the Dow Industrials is 13.4, so 15 is a little high by comparison. If the price of the stock dropped to $8 per share, then the P/E would also drop to 8, which would be a below-average P/E, offering good value by comparison. For $8 you could buy $1 worth of earnings, plus the value of the company's other assets.

The value of a company is in its profits and assets. The P/E ratio measures the price you pay for profits, and the price-to-book ratio measures what you pay for assets.

The book value per share of a stock is determined by totaling the value of all the assets of a company, subtracting all the debts owed, and dividing what is left by the number of shares of stock owned by shareholders. For example, ABC Inc. owns land, equipment, and cash worth $10 million, and owes $3 million in debts, which leaves $7 million worth of assets to divide among, let us say, one million shareholders, resulting in $7 a share of book value. If the stock of ABC Inc. is selling for $14 a share, then the price-to-book ratio is 2.

A general rule of thumb for the price-to-book ratio is that 1.5 is fair value. Anything greater gets expensive, and anything less is a better value. ABC Inc., at 2, is pretty steep because for every dollar of assets you are paying $2 to buy the stock. Why would someone pay $2 for $1 worth of assets? Well in 1991 if you had bought Apple Computer at $40.30 a share, its lowest price that year, you would have paid a price-to-book of 2.7, but a P/E of 10.77. The book ratio was pretty high at 2.7, but the P/E was relatively low at 10.77, and there is the rub. Different measures of value don't always agree, so it becomes necessary to analyze other factors as well.

I bought Apple Computer at $25 a share in 1990, and as it rapidly rose in price, I decided if it reached a P/E of 20, or $74 a share, it would be somewhat overvalued and I would sell it. At $73.30 a share the price plummeted, bottoming out at $40. In 1992, Apple headed back up to $70 and later in the year dropped back to $45. This type of behavior is typical of many stocks, which is why keeping a cool head is so necessary to stock market investing. I will continue to hold on to Apple stock because I like what the company is doing in the computer industry. I think it has good future prospects. But if the stock price does get too high again, I will sell.

You can easily look up the price-earnings ratio (P/E) or the price-to-book ratio for stocks in stock guides available at most libraries, such as the *Standard and Poor's Stock Guide.* These guides contain many useful financial statistics for analyzing stocks. I use the *Value Line Survey,* which lists the "Book Value Per Share." I take that number and divide it by the current stock price to get the price-to-book ratio.

Remember that a stock is worth what the current earnings and assets of the company are, but more importantly, it is worth what the *future* earnings and assets of the company will be.

The preoccupation of securities analysts, those folks in the back room at stock brokerage firms, is to predict the future earnings of companies, and secondarily, to predict their growth in assets. Assets are considered secondary to earnings because dividends are usually paid from earnings, not assets, and because growth in earnings is the clearest indicator of ongoing profitability.

Benjamin Graham essentially put the profession of securities analysis on the map with his textbook, *Securities Analysis.* Paradoxically, Graham stated in his book, *The Intelligent Investor,* that future earnings and assets are extremely difficult to predict.

Studies by various academic researchers show that securities analysts seldom produce reliable future earnings estimates. On almost any given day you will find reports in the *Wall Street Journal* of stocks that shot up in price as "earnings exceeded analysts' expectations," or stocks that dropped in price as "reported earnings fell short of most analysts' predictions."

You have to consider the position the securities analyst is in. This person is paid by his or her employer, a stock brokerage or other type of investment organization, to predict the future. A securities analyst cannot go to his boss and say "You know, boss, studies have shown I cannot predict the future, so just tell our customers I don't know what to invest in." Analysts are in the business of making educated guesses, which often miss the mark by a wide margin.

It all boils down to finding the best values you can, diversifying among at least 10 stocks to minimize the damage from poor selections, and allowing the long-term upward bias of the market to work in your favor.

I should point out that three of the greatest minds ever to dedicate themselves to the problem of maximizing stock market returns have agreed to disagree on the best approach. Benjamin Graham is more or less on one side, Phil Fisher on the other, and Warren Buffet, the most successful of the three, somewhere in the middle. These are men who have made hundreds of millions of dollars in the stock market, far more than anyone playing games with short-term investment strategies using "technical analysis," charts, computers, economic predictive models, hedged options strategies, relative price strength indicators, or any of a hundred theories that have come and gone. When they discuss fundamental questions which challenge their investment philosophies, it is best to sit quietly and listen.

There is absolute agreement among these three investors that finding the right stock, at the right price, and holding on to it for relatively long periods of time is the key to investment success. But Fisher is more concerned with finding the right stock of a top-performing company than he is with the price he must pay. Graham was not so much concerned with which stock to buy (although he applied certain strict criteria to guarantee quality) as he was concerned with buying at the right price. Buffet seeks the right stock at a good price.

It is possible to comprehensively study the operations of a company, as Buffet and Fisher have done, to find the best quality companies. But Graham has proven that this is not essential to getting good results—as long as you buy bargains, apply strict financial standards for quality and safety, and diversify among at least 10 stocks.

The fundamental approach to valuing most companies is to analyze their earnings and assets, then attempt to predict their future prospects. Public companies publish their financial statements in their annual reports, and usually report quarterly changes as well. The income statement shows earnings and the balance sheet shows assets. There is just one problem. The figures for earnings and assets are open to broad interpretation. Accounting standards allow for a great deal of leeway in the determination of how much money was "earned" by a business, and in how assets are valued.

To truly understand the value of a company you cannot simply look up its earnings or the value of its assets in the annual report. You have to dig into the financial statements—not just for one year but for several years—and analyze the figures, to find out how they are derived. Often the most important information is contained in the "accounting footnotes" which are listed in the back of the annual report. These footnotes contain descriptions of what choices were made by the accountants in deriving certain key numbers.

Equally important as understanding the financial health of a company is studying its business and gathering information about how the company is being managed. A well-managed company with good market opportunities for its products and services will certainly do better than a company in similar financial condition, but with poor management.

But don't worry. If you don't want to learn accounting in order to carefully analyze the annual reports of companies, you don't have to. You also don't have to be a business management expert and try to figure out the business, either. Using common sense to think about how a business works will help you pick better-performing businesses. By employing the simplest measures of value, and leaving yourself lots of room for error, you will find many good stocks. Simply selecting from the stocks that have the lowest price-earnings ratio in the stock market, you are likely to achieve above-average investment performance. By checking that a company does not have too much debt, has been profitable for many years, and whose stock is selling for a low P/E ratio and low price-to-book ratio, you have a good set of criteria for selecting better-performing stocks. Later on I will describe how to apply these criteria, and a few others to help make your choices.

Throughout this book I repeat the theme that the economy and business pass through cycles of prosperity and decline. It is important that you keep these cycles in perspective as they occur, so you don't react to them in the wrong way. Predicting these cycles is very difficult, particularly since mass psychology plays such an important part in their occurrence. No one knows what events will trigger pessimism among businesses or the buying public to cause a major turning point in a cycle. I personally don't make an effort to predict economic or stock market events. I try as best I can to anticipate them, but I don't base my investment strategies on predicting the direction of events.

Instead, I maintain the perspective that I am in one part of the cycle or the other and that eventually the cycle will turn in the opposite direction. For me, the best position to be in is buying during bad times and selling during good times, or "Buy on bad news. Sell on good news." The reasoning here stems from the recognition that human emotions cause us to overreact to events. When bad news comes investors sell at prices lower than the bad news justifies, and when good news comes investors buy at prices higher than justified.

The importance of cycles is that they always change direction eventually. I hope I never have to wait out a Great Depression, but there are many extremely wealthy investors alive today who did. When a cycle is occurring and things are looking very bad, that may be the time to buy. Stocks may still go lower, but they cannot all go down to zero. At some point, so much upward tension on stock prices builds that the cycle turns around.

Think of my metaphor of the rubber band. The worse economic and business conditions get, the more people buckle down and say, "We just can't let this go on. We have got to turn this thing around." The tension to correct the situation increases as the situation worsens. Despair of wealth also plays its part in the scenario, pushing people toward hopelessness for part of the cycle.

The opposite situation occurs during economic prosperity. High employment and consumer spending reach a point of tension that limits further economic expansion and prosperity. Eventually the economic momentum stretches the rubber band too far, and the cyclic direction reverses.

During the 1980s as the public and business felt more prosperous and became more enthusiastic about spending and growing businesses, they took on more debts. As the debts piled up, they tugged harder and harder against prosperity until the cycle changed direction. When it did, the income that was needed to pay off debt disappeared and rapid economic decline ensued.

The character of every economic cycle will be different from the last. So it is easy to become caught up in the events of the day and focus on the short-term outlook. But the short-term outlook is always replaced by the averaging effects of long-term trends. These are the trends you should be counting on—the long-term upward bias of the stock market, and the overall economic expansion that has been occurring in America for over 200 years. Always remember to step back and take the long view.

You have to be careful not to confuse what is happening with individual businesses with the larger economic picture. Individual businesses will follow economic cycles, their fortunes declining and recovering along with the rest of the economy. But it is important to distinguish between temporary setbacks and permanent decline.

It requires experience and good judgment to recognize when companies are suffering temporary setbacks which are bound to be corrected, or find themselves mired in unsolvable problems. Even the best companies endure temporary setbacks, but many companies are mediocre and fall into decline. If you buy a stock and the company runs into serious financial trouble and the stock price goes down, down, down, look at the situation carefully. Unless there are definite signs the problems are only temporary, take your lumps and bail out.

This is hard to take emotionally. Psychologically, we always hate to see a stock hit a price and fall back, never to recover. We assume that once a stock has seen a price, it is bound to get back up there again someday. Not true! Also if your stock drops from $20 a share to $5 a share, the tendency is to think "It can't possibly go any lower." Again, not true!

When I loaded up on stocks during the fall of 1990, I bought a lot of Western Digital stock at $5 a share, down from a high of $14.90 that year. This company looked very attractive at the time, with a P/E on trailing earnings of 4.5, a price-to-sales ratio of only .15 (very low), a price-to-book ratio of .45, and acceptable levels of debt. A real bargain. Later on, problems which had already begun to surface in the company worsened, and it took on a lot more short-term debt. The stock price fell to a low of $2 a share in 1991, representing a 60% loss to me if I had sold. By early 1992 the price had recovered somewhat and I sold my shares at $4 per share for a 20% loss. I may have been premature in my decision to sell, as the disk drive market in which Western Digital specializes is improving, and the company has done a lot to put itself on a firm footing. But its debt situation is still precarious and I found it too risky for my taste.

Sometimes when the crowd is stampeding, you should stop and ask somebody what all the commotion is about. If they yell back, "There's a bear in there," maybe you better turn tail and run with them. The crowd is not always wrong.

When the stock market is generally trending upward in price, this is called a "bull market," but when prices are trending downward it is called a "bear market." You will find continuous debate and differing opinions in the financial press as to whether at present we are in a bull or bear market. Some people think they occur several times a year, some think they occur only every few years, and some think the stock market is just one long bull market, gradually rising higher and higher, despite short-term fluctuations.

Just like bull and bear markets, people talk about good markets and bad markets, tricky markets and stable markets, volatile markets and stagnant markets. What are all of these markets anyway? There are so many different ideas used to interpret whether you are going to get clobbered or not in the stock market, it is ridiculous to take them too seriously.

These debates are on par with making short-term predictions of any kind, including which way the economy is headed. You need not concern yourself with what sort of animal the stock market currently is. As long as you stick to good companies whose stock is selling at reasonable valuations, and you are willing to hold out for long-term results, you will do fine. In order to hold out through all market conditions, only invest money in the stock market that you will not have to withdraw on short notice—less than a year or two.

There are always some stocks worthy of investment. When the stock market is overvalued it is difficult to find stocks that represent good value, but they are there to be had if you could predict the future. When the stock market is exceptionally undervalued, finding good buys is like shooting fish in a barrel. When the stock market is fairly valued, stock prices may be headed up or down, but if you are conservative in your purchases, sticking to good values and holding for the long-term, you will do nicely regardless of which way the market heads.

Often when you consult with a financial adviser to establish an investment plan, she will want to know if you desire "income" or "capital appreciation," and whether your tolerance for risk classifies you as an "aggressive" or "conservative" investor. By classifying your investment goals in this way, they are trying to determine the type of companies you should buy stock in.

If you are seeking income, an adviser would suggest buying a "blue-chip" stock of a large, well-established company that has steadily paid dividends for years. Usually blue-chip stocks are selected from the list of 500 that make up the *Standard & Poor's 500 Index*. The idea is to find companies on which you can depend to pay you an income from dividends. IBM has long been considered a blue-chip stock, being one of the largest and most consistently successful companies in the world, with a long record of paying steadily rising dividends.

Companies with a consistent record of growth in earnings, or generally considered to have reliable prospects for future growth, are called "growth stocks." These are companies whose earnings and assets are expected to grow rapidly for at least several years. Often growth companies are smaller in size, and are members of a growth industry. Growth companies usually need to reinvest their earnings to maintain their growth rate, and often pay little or no dividends, but continually enhance their stock price by increasing earnings and assets.

Growth stocks are usually recommended for investors who prefer capital appreciation to current income. The preference for capital appreciation derives from the desire to see your investment capital compound without having to pay taxes on current income. Often, younger investors who are working, earning, and saving prefer capital appreciation. Older investors who live off their investments, need to invest for current income, on which they must pay taxes, but often at a lower tax bracket than during their active earning years.

Growth stocks may provide higher rates of return than blue-chip stocks, but they are accompanied by greater risk. Part of the risk stems from the higher price-earnings ratios paid for growth stocks, based on expectations for growth in earnings. If the earnings growth does not occur, the stock price is bound to suffer a rapid decline.

Younger investors may tolerate more risk, because their current income is not threatened by lower investment returns, although their savings and investment program will suffer. Older investors may prefer the lower risk and dependable income normally associated with a larger, slow-growth company. Their tolerance for risk is less than the younger investor, because they depend in large part on their investments for current income. Their standard of living would be directly impacted by reduced investment performance. Thus they are willing to forgo the potential for higher rates of return, in order to avoid the risks involved.

Typically, stock brokerage firms will have a list of "income" and "growth" stocks available for their brokers to recommend. They will divide up their mutual funds into income, growth, or income plus growth funds (providing both current income and some potential for future growth).

This sums up the conventional wisdom an investment adviser would probably use to evaluate your stock market investment goals and recommend a course of investment.

I disagree with this approach.

My objection to this standard pat formula is its overly simplistic interpretation of the investment problem. Although it is useful to consider risk factors in investment, and your needs for income as well as desire for capital appreciation, that should not be your approach to individual stock selection.

A better idea is to earn the maximum rate of return on your total investment portfolio, at a minimum of risk. You reduce risk and increase your returns by investing in the best quality companies. You reduce risk by using portfolio diversification, so that individual stocks that don't work out as planned will not hurt you too much. You increase your rate of return and reduce risk by buying stocks at bargain prices. And you reduce risk using time diversification to average out price fluctuations.

The need for income can be met by managing the balance in your portfolio between stocks and bonds or cash, as well as through selling your stocks, as they gradually increase in value over time. For most investors, it is not wise to have only non-dividend-paying "growth" stocks in their portfolio. Therefore a conservative investor will always seek both dividend income and capital appreciation.

If you depend on your investment portfolio for income, you may want to invest a sufficient proportion of your portfolio in high-grade bonds to provide adequate interest income, and invest the rest in stocks that never have to be liquidated in an untimely fashion (such as the bottom of a market cycle).

So ignore recommendations to buy "riskier growth stocks while you are young" and switching to "safer income stocks now that you are older." Focus instead on an overall investment program that minimizes risk while providing maximum investment returns, as well as income when needed, throughout your lifetime.

In addition to my objection to categorizing stocks according to income, growth, and degree of risk (which I don't believe is the best approach to designing a stock portfolio), I also object to the assumption that blue-chip stocks are "safe" and growth stocks are "risky."

Big stodgy companies who have long since lost their entrepreneurial vigor may suddenly run into serious business difficulties, causing their good old reliable dividends to be threatened, and the investment value of their stock to plummet. A collection of "risky" little growth companies may, on average, produce much higher and more reliable rates of return on investment than "safe," dividend-paying blue-chip companies, if purchased at the right price.

International Business Machines has been a wonderful blue-chip company over the years, with a consistent record of magnificent growth and generous dividend payments. But apart from recent problems with IBM's performance, there have also been times, such as in the 1970s, when IBM's stock price was bid up so high that the company's performance could not justify it. At such high prices, the stock was too risky and offered too low a rate of return.

There was a time during the early 1970s when the "Nifty Fifty" concept held sway among a large number of institutional investors. This approach to investment called for buying a favored group of about 50 blue-chip growth stocks, which institutional investors falsely believed to be good investments at any price, because of their future growth prospects. As a result, the number of institutions who bought Nifty Fifty stocks was so large that they drove the prices up beyond reason. During the recession of 1974 the Nifty Fifty fell from grace and their stock prices plummeted, even though as a group these companies continued to prosper and grow. For example, in 1972 Coca-Cola had a P/E of 40 and 1% dividend yield. By 1974, Coca-Cola had fallen 70% in price, with a new P/E of 15 and a dividend yield of 4%. This general drop in stock prices was caused by the realization that the Arab oil embargo, accelerating inflation, and a recession made future prospects less appealing.

The moral of this story is that blue-chip stocks are not always blue-chip investments.

The term "growth stock" has acquired several interpretations, including a stock whose price is likely to appreciate at an above-average rate; the stock of a company likely to experience above-average growth in earnings and assets; and the stock of a company in a growth industry or emerging market. Because the meaning of the term has been blurred by so many different casual interpretations, it is important to be clear on how it is being used.

The most useful meaning applies to stocks whose earnings and assets are likely to grow due to factors unique to the particular company.

Stocks whose prices rises at an above-average rate are not properly considered growth stocks, because the price rise is not necessarily explained by any growth factors inherent in the company.

Stocks of companies in growth industries or emerging markets are not growth stocks unless their company possesses unique characteristics that give it a competitive advantage within the industry or market. This is a confusing subject which deserves further explanation.

The stock market often pays particular attention to "hot" sectors of the stock market or "glamour" industries. When sales and profits in a particular industry rise rapidly, the stock market may exaggerate the value of those stocks by bidding up their prices beyond reasonable expectations for investment returns. Because people get excited and greedy about companies or industries that are earning a lot of money, they will pay too high a price for their stocks. And once an industry sector becomes popularized, investors may lose discrimination as to which companies offer the best potential for growth in earnings. A company may become classified as a growth stock merely by virtue of membership in a growth industry, especially if its stock price has already been bid up. The point is that following the crowd into a hot sector, or so-called growth sector, is a deadly investment error producing extreme risk and poor investment choices.

Numerous companies are attracted to the sales and profit potential found in every emerging market or growth industry. Only a few companies with the right qualities for success will survive the competition and grow. Most of the weaker competitors will vanish, taking the investments of their stockholders down with them. Within any growth industry or emerging market there are few true growth stocks, and their stock prices may already be too high to deserve serious investment consideration.

To me, the best definition of a growth stock applies to companies with the highest caliber of management expertise, many opportunities for innovation, and unique competitive advantages. Those companies don't have to be in a growth industry or a new market. Sometimes innovative companies invent new ways of earning a profit which surprise their competitors.

Sam Walton, the founder of Wal-Mart stores, created a revolution in the retail industry with "every day low prices," efficient new methods of inventory distribution, and friendly customer service. Wal-Mart stock was one of the best investments of the 1980s, and made Sam Walton the richest man in America. Currently Wal-Mart trades at a P/E of 32.7, a little rich for my blood. But in 1979 its P/E averaged only 10.7 on earnings of 4¢ a share, and as recently as 1989 its P/E averaged 20.7 on earnings of 95¢, a high P/E but not too high for a company of this caliber (although only in retrospect can I state this with confidence). The growth in earnings from 4¢ to 95¢ represents a 37% annually compounded rate of growth over 10 years!

There are at least two forms of risk associated with growth stock investments. One is that growth stocks are typically priced at a higher

P/E ratio, adding to the risk of stock price declines if the company fails to produce the growth expected. The idea that a top-quality growth stock is a good investment at any price is silly, despite the number of foolish people who have been taken in by this notion. A growth stock may justify a relatively higher price, as we saw with Wal-Mart above. However, the higher the price in relation to earnings and assets, the higher the risk that the stock will not perform well enough.

The other risk with investment in growth stocks is that companies often get ahead of themselves as they race to grow. For this reason Peter Lynch, in his book, *One Up on Wall Street,* says that he is leery of stocks with earnings growth rates higher than 25% a year.

Whereas growth stocks tend to be high priced, value stocks, by definition, are low priced. These are often stocks of ordinary companies who have been plugging along for years producing modest but steady growth, perhaps just enough to keep up with inflation. They are marked by conservative borrowing practices, have plenty of current assets to cover debts, and pay dividends steadily for years.

Value stocks are associated with boring companies, without much apparent growth potential, that nobody pays any attention to. But because no one has bid their stock price up, there is little downside risk and a large margin of safety. Using the margin-of-safety principle, you would invest only in companies with a long record of modest but consistent success, conservative management, and a long history of earnings and dividends. If the stock market takes a dive, dragging the price of your value stock down, don't worry about it. It's a steady little company which will weather the storm. Eventually its stock price will recover.

When the stock market does drop, value stocks become even more worthwhile, because their price will recover with the rest of the stock market. When the stock market gets expensive, sometimes value stocks really shine as investors hunt around for bargains, and that may be the time to unload yours. Also, there are cycles to value stocks, periods when they come into favor or fall out of favor again. If you are willing to buy value stocks when they are out of favor, and to wait until they come back into favor, your patience will pay off.

Keep in mind that "value stock" is a confusing term, because it relates directly to the price of the stock, as well as to certain general characteristics of a company. A value stock that goes way up in price is no longer a value stock, regardless of the characteristics of the company.

One measure of the value of a stock is its dividend yield, which indicates how much you are paying for the company's dividends. A stock that costs $100 a share, and pays a dividend of $5 a share, has a dividend yield of five percent, which is the dividend amount divided by the price of the stock.

Under normal circumstances, mature companies with little growth potential don't represent an inviting opportunity for investment, with average dividend yields ranging around 4.7% or so. But during periods when the stock market is very depressed overall, the dividend yield of such companies often rises well above 4.7%, sometimes reaching 7% or higher. At times like that, these companies can be very good investments, anticipating the time when institutional investors pour their money back into the stock market and need their blue-chip stocks again.

To buy stocks, all you have to do is establish an account with a stock brokerage firm and deposit enough assets to cover your purchases. There are no special credit requirements. If you have the cash, you can buy the stocks. You can also buy stock "on margin," borrowing against the value of stocks or bonds you have on deposit with your broker. But this involves the use of leverage, which increases your risk.

There are two kinds of brokers that you can open an account with: a "full-service" broker and a "discount" broker.

A full-service firm provides individual customers with stockbrokers who will recommend specific stocks to buy or sell, and reports from securities analysts detailing their opinions on the investment merits of a stock.

A discount broker does not provide stockbrokers who give investment advice although they will answer questions regarding the mechanics of buying and selling. The cost of commissions at discount brokers may be less than half of what a full-service broker would charge.

I would recommend against using a full-service broker, because they don't offer the informed investor enough value to justify their higher commission rates. And there are very few stockbrokers whom I would trust for investment advice. Most don't have the time to become savvy investors themselves; instead they are preoccupied with making trades, and are more concerned with the commissions they can earn buying and selling your stocks in the short term than with long-term investment results. A similar problem exists with the analyst reports they provide. While much of the information may be useful and pertinent, the opinions rendered seldom have much value because they are usually directed at short-term stock price and company earnings expectations that are not reliable. If you don't feel that you have adequate experience or judgment to make individual stock purchases without professional advice I would recommend investing in a mutual fund, a better idea than allowing a stockbroker to manage your investments.

You might also consider the services of a fee-based investment adviser, who will build your stock portfolio in accordance with your personal investment goals, and who is paid a percentage of the value of your portfolio (usually about one percent a year). The advantage of this fee structure is that your adviser is provided an incentive to increase the value of your portfolio and does not earn a commission for trading stocks (assuming he is not a crook who earns kickbacks from a stockbroker). Unfortunately most of the better fee-based advisers will not take on a client with less than $250,000 in assets to invest.

If you decide to make your own stock selections, here are some of the basics of placing orders.

Every stock has a stock market symbol, and trades on a specific stock exchange, or in the over-the-counter market. The stocks of the 5,000 largest publicly owned companies trade on the New York Stock Exchange, the American Stock Exchange, or in the NASDAQ National Market System, which is the main part of the over-the-counter markets. To monitor the price of your stock, you will need to know which stock exchange listing to look at in the financial section of your newspaper, and it is sometimes helpful to know its stock symbol.

For example, the symbol for Campbell Soup is "CPB" which trades on the New York Stock Exchange. The symbol for Adolph Coors brewing company is "ACCOB" which trades in the NASDAQ National Market System. The symbol for Coca-Cola is "KO." Coca-Cola Enterprises, on the other hand, is a separate company with a bottling franchise from Coca-Cola; its stock symbol is "CCE."

Your broker will usually know a company by name, but if there is confusion it helps to know the stock symbol and the exchange.

Next, you need to know how many shares you wish to buy. You should usually buy in "round lots" of 100 share increments, because "odd lots" often carry higher commission charges. You could buy 79 shares of a stock, but this requires that brokers break a round lot of 100 shares into odd lots of 79 and 21 shares, for which they will charge you extra. You don't have to specify that you are buying round lots. Just say "I would like to buy 200 shares of IBM," or 500, or 900, or 1,300, or 20,000—any quantity evenly divisible by 100.

You must decide at what price you wish to buy the stock. If you buy "at the market," your broker will purchase the stock at the lowest price currently available. Otherwise you can set a "limit price," in which case your broker will buy the stock only at or below the price you specify. For example, if the most recent price a stock sold at is $50 a share, and you don't want to pay more than $45 a share, then you could place a limit order to buy at $45, in which case you will not get the stock unless its price drops that low.

There are two types of limit orders: "good till canceled" and those specified to last only to a certain date. A "good till canceled" order will stay active until the stock becomes available at the specified price, or may expire after a standard time limit (usually 60 days), if not renewed.

A limit order may be specified to expire after a day, a week, a month, or at a specified date. Sometimes you will notice that the price of a stock hit your limit order price, but your broker didn't buy any. This results from a "stock ahead" situation, meaning someone else's order (not necessarily a customer of your broker) was ahead of yours at the exchange.

Now you are ready to place your order. Call your broker and say: "Hello, this is shrewd individual investor Shane Roberts. My account number is 101, and I would like to buy 100 shares of International Business Machines, stock symbol IBM, at the market." Your broker will then look up the stock, tell you what the current asking price is, and repeat your order back to you. I can always hear a beeping noise in the background when I place my orders, because my broker records all of its phone calls, to prove it gave me what I asked for.

Actually, I now place most of my orders without talking to a broker, because I get a 10% discount on the cost of the brokerage commission by using their automated telephone ordering system. Stock brokerage commissions can range from less than 1% to 6% or more, depending on the dollar amount of the stock you are buying or selling, and whether you use a full-service broker or discount broker.

Unless you placed a limit order, you should now own 100 shares of IBM. Your broker can usually confirm the purchase of market orders while you are on the phone, because of modern computerized trading systems. But in the case of some smaller company's stock it may take a little longer, while your broker waits for stock to become available.

Stock prices are quoted using a combination of whole numbers and fractions. For example a stock may be selling at 5 7/8. The fractions are usually some increment of an eighth but are sometimes quoted in sixteenths for low-priced stocks.

Once you have bought your stock, forget the price you paid for it. It is water over the dam. I keep a computer spreadsheet of all the stocks I own, and I list various financial statistics which apply to them. I also keep track of what price I paid, but only to remind myself of the valuation measures I used when I purchased the stock. You also have to record the date and amount you paid for a stock, for tax purposes.

There is an irresistible urge to value a stock according to the original price paid. Resist this urge at all costs. When the price of your stock falls below the purchase price, panic is the natural response, accompanied by guilt and shame. "How could I have wasted my money on that stupid stock? I could kick myself. Maybe I should sell it now before I lose even more money." At least that is how I always react. But the current price of the stock has little to do with the current *value* of the stock. Never confuse the price of the stock with its value. Today's stock price signifies only what you can buy or sell the stock for today, nothing more or less. It does not tell you what the stock is worth in the long-run, or what its price will be a year from now, two years from now, or five years from now.

If the price of your stock drops after you buy it, you may wish to review your reasons for buying it, how you determined its value, and consider buying *more.* This is the exact opposite behavior to what your panic reaction is telling you to do.

If, on the other hand, your stock rises in price after you buy it, you are likely to feel a wonderful sense of elation, evoking two possible reactions. One is "Gee, what a great stock; I should buy more of this," and the other is "Gee, what a great stock; maybe I should sell it while I'm ahead." Just because the stock goes up after you bought it does not mean it is any better than you originally thought it was. If it still seems to be a good buy at the higher price, and you have some new funds available to purchase it with, you may wish to buy more. Otherwise, a price rise is not a signal to buy except according to technical analysis, which often recommends buying on "price strength." But I strongly urge you to ignore such considerations.

The impulse to sell while you are ahead is also not advisable, since it is usually premature unless the stock has experienced a considerable run up in price, carrying it well into the overvalued range. Then there would be little harm in taking a quick profit and switching to a stock where there is substantially more value and less risk. A decision to switch stocks should account for the effects of trading commissions and taxes, though. This must include both a commission for selling the old stock and buying a new one.

There are a variety of old stock market adages or truisms that do more harm than good. One of them is "You can never go wrong by taking a profit." This tidbit of advice is terrible when it results in excess trading, selling your winners before you have given them their full run. An undervalued stock may require two or three years, even longer, to realize its full potential. And a quality company may provide good investment returns for many years due to consistent increases in earnings and dividends, without becoming overvalued. So hang on to your winners. Some of them can make you rich.

Let me stress once again that it is difficult to forget what you paid for a stock, but it has little bearing on the value of the stock once you have purchased it. Another tendency associated with stock pricing is the urge to look at the history of a stock's price, for signs of future price behavior. Somehow those charts of a stock's price history, with their mountains and valleys rising and falling before us, hold mystical power. When you look at the price history you cannot help but think, "That stock has seen 100, but is now at 10. Surely it has to climb back up again." Don't bet on it.

Remember, stocks rise and fall according to their popularity. Some stocks are popular for a while and then are ignored ever after. Graphic Industries stock rose from a low of $2.80 in 1984 to a high of $16.80 in 1987, and then fell continuously. By mid-1992 it was $5 a share. WMS Industries saw $8.50 a share in 1983; $1 in 1984; $6.10 in 1986; $1.20 in 1987; $7.50 in 1989; $1.80 in 1990, and hit $23.40 in 1992. What do all of these dramatic price changes mean? Nothing, in and of themselves. The stock market is reacting to news, both good and bad, as we have discussed. More important than these price fluctuations is the internal condition of the company.

When buying stock it is best to think of yourself as owning a share of a business. You should be more concerned with the success or failure of the business than with what its stock price does. If the operations of a business degenerate, and its financial condition reflects this, then you will want to sell its stock regardless of whether the price is up or down. Eventually, you can bet the stock price will match the poor results of the company. On the other hand, if a company is well managed for profits you will want to buy its stock at any reasonable price and hold on to it as long as the company does well, or until the stock becomes excessively overpriced.

Selling stock is as simple as buying it. You call your broker and place an order to sell either at the market or at a limit price. If you sell at the market price, your broker will sell at the highest price currently offered. If you sell at a limit price, your stock will sell at the specified price, when all other orders ahead of you for that price have sold and there are more buyers left willing to purchase at your price.

Sometimes investment books recommend that you place a "stop-loss order" to sell, which is a limit order set at some price below the current price. It limits the loss you would experience if the stock falls much in price. I don't recommend this practice because it guarantees that you will sell at a loss from the current price if the stop-loss order is executed.

For example, let's say your stock is currently quoted at $90 a share, and you could not live with yourself if the price dropped to $70 a share and never recovered. So you place a stop-loss order to sell at $85 a share, and one week later the price drops and your stock is gone. Are you happy? Probably not, especially if two weeks later the stock is back up to $95.

At $85 a share the price is 5.5% below $90, not really much of a drop. At $70 a share there is a potential loss of 22%. A substantial loss, but is that the price you want to sell your stock at when it may be worth much more? The problem with stop-loss orders is that if you set it just below the current price, you are almost guaranteeing you will sell the stock, in which case you might as well sell it at the higher price. If you set it well below the current price and the stock dives down, you are selling at the wrong time. You don't want to sell just because everyone else is depressed about your stock and is selling it. You should only sell based on a conscious decision that your stock is worth less than what the market is offering for it.

The one time a stop loss order may be useful is when your stock experiences a rapid run up in price. In this case, if you are prepared to sell at the current price but would be willing to risk a slightly lower price in return for the potential of a slightly higher price, you might place a stop-loss order just below the current price. Sometimes when a large investor is accumulating a huge chunk of shares in a stock, the price will go up and up, in which case by ratcheting your stop-loss order higher and higher, you may achieve substantial gains.

The question of when to sell stock is much more difficult to answer than when to buy. It is hard for me to explain why this is true, except to say I have found it to be so in my own experience, and other stock market authorities agree with me on this, including some who go so far as to say the best time to sell a stock is never.

Ken Fisher, a regular columnist for *Forbes* magazine, says he finds it annoying when the price of one of his stocks goes so high he feels compelled to sell it, because then he must go to the trouble of finding an equally good company to replace it with. Since Ken looks for "Super Stocks" which are hard to find, you can appreciate his dilemma.

My criteria for selling a stock are as follows:

- When the quality of the company deteriorates substantially, including risks brought on by the addition of too much debt.
- When other stocks present a large advantage over existing ones, offering equivalent value at, let us say, half the price (a highly subjective determination which should be made as an exceptional case only).
- When the overall market reaches extremely high valuation levels and you wish to reduce portfolio risk by liquidating stocks for cash or bonds.

Liquidating stocks to reduce risk should be done in such a way as to maintain portfolio diversification, perhaps by selling shares in proportionate amounts for each stock, or by reducing a long list of stocks to a shorter list. By selling small amounts of individual stocks, you will incur higher commission costs than by selling large amounts of just one stock. Also, when I say to reduce your portfolio at high levels of valuation, I am not advocating market timing techniques. I am only acknowledging the extraordinary risk that is associated with the stock market on unusual occasions, such as August 1987.

Finally, you may have to sell a stock just because you need the money. But you might consider borrowing the money against the value of your stocks, if your financial need is a temporary one. Your can arrange for such a loan with the brokerage firm holding your stocks.

As your stocks rise to high levels of valuation during a hot market cycle, you may find yourself selling them off one by one as they become overvalued, and not replacing them due to a lack of good buys. This may be the most natural way to achieve the theoretical benefits of market timing, without making a conscious effort to predict market tops, which is nearly impossible. Becoming fully invested near market bottoms may be a natural occurrence as well, as you find more and more bargains to choose from.

When you first start selecting individual stocks to invest in, you may be at a loss to decide which are best. One approach to getting comfortable with your new role as a stock market investor is to practice without actually spending any money. Some people will put together a list of stocks and monitor them for a couple of years.

Finding good stocks to buy is probably not as hard as you think. I always thought it would be very difficult before I began to do it. The secret is to apply strict criteria of value, searching for the real bargains, and not just buy any old stock some expert recommends. You can read about a lot of good companies in business magazines and investment newspapers. I read the *Wall Street Journal*, and I especially like *Forbes* magazine for the quality of its reporting on business and investments.

Leafing through stock guides at the library, you can easily compare a wide variety of stocks for their financial statistics and the summary of their business operations offered by securities analysts.

Line up some stocks side by side and measure them against various standards of value and safety. Buy the ones offering the most value. The reason for applying different standards is that no single measure of value works for every stock. As in the example of Apple computer above, it was cheap according to its price-earnings ratio, but not its price-to-book ratio. It is usually some combination of factors about a company that indicates that it is a good buy.

Here are some useful financial statistics for finding cheap stocks.

A low price-to-earnings ratio (P/E) is one of the simplest and most effective measures of value. The price-to-earnings ratio is calculated by dividing the current price per share of a stock by the annual earnings per share. To get a more long-term view of a company's earnings, take the last three years' earnings combined, and divide them by three to get the average earnings per share over the three years. Then calculate the P/E from that. This helps to smooth out short-term blips.

To find a list of low P/E stocks, look at *The Value Line Investment Survey* (at your local library) in its "Summary & Index" section that supplements the stock guide every week.

Another measure of value is high-dividend-yield stocks. The dividend yield is calculated by dividing the annual dividend of a stock by its current price. The blue-chip stocks of the Dow Jones Industrials have averaged a dividend yield of 4.7% for over 60 years. So when their dividend yield gets above 6% it may be a good time to buy, and when it falls below 3% it might be time to sell.

Any stock that is selling at a large discount to its fair value is a good buy, as long as there is adequate safety in the financial structure and operation of the business. You determine safety by relying on the financial track record of the company and by looking at how much debt the company has. You also add safety to individual stocks by making them only a small portion of your total stock portfolio. This guards against excessive losses on the few companies whose future performance ends up much worse than their past performance. To maintain a diversified portfolio you should own at least ten and no more than thirty stocks. Ten stocks are a minimum to maintain diversification, and thirty are a maximum, because it is too difficult to keep track of more, and reduces your investment risk by only a little.

A good measure of value is to look at net current assets. Few companies are worth less than their net current assets. To figure the net current assets subtract current liabilities (bills the company must pay within the current year) from current assets (money due from customers in current year, cash in bank, stocks, bonds, inventory, and anything else convertible to cash in the short term). Stock guides, or the annual report of a company, will list current liabilities and current assets. Net current assets ignores all the other assets of the company, like land, buildings, equipment, etc. You get all those assets for *free,* if you buy the stock for less than the value of the net current assets per share.

A good way of measuring the long-term financial performance of a company is to notice how long it has been earning a profit. Many companies go on for decades without ever losing money. It is also a good sign if its earnings keep growing year after year, and it has been consistent about paying dividends and increasing them from time to time.

Other general guidelines for safety are that total debt does not exceed stockholders' equity (book value), it has a strong current financial position (check *Standard and Poor's* or *Value Line* financial ratings), and a low stock-price-to-book-value per share (something less than 1.0—the lower the better).

Two other ways to look at debt for a margin of protection is to be sure that current assets are at least twice current liabilities, or that net current assets are twice the total debt.

To give you some historical perspective, here are some long-term financial statistics on the stock market. From 1920 to 1989 the Dow Jones Industrial Average for each year showed an average price-earnings ratio of 13.4, average dividend yield of 4.7%, average earnings growth rate of 4.2%, average dividend growth rate of 5.8%, and an average book value growth rate of 4.9%. Presumably, better valuations than these measures for the Dow Jones Industrial Average would indicate better investment values. In other words, lower price-earnings ratios, higher dividend yields, and higher growth rates for earnings, dividends, and book value, represent better-than-average values.

The relationship between the financial ratios of a specific stock to the average financial ratios of the stock market can be used under all market conditions to evaluate a specific stock. For example, if the average price-to-earnings ratio of all stocks is 15, and a particular stock is selling for a price-to-earnings of 10, then it is worth looking at, because it is relatively undervalued for the market. In a highflying market, the average P/E may be 20, in which case 15 might be comparatively cheap. In a depressed market, the average might be 10, in which case a lower P/E would be the better value.

When the market is really depressed, you don't need to focus so much on finding the cheapest stocks. This is a good time to pick up the best quality companies at bargain basement prices.

Buying the most undervalued stocks in the market does not guarantee that the stocks' prices will not go down. If the market takes a dive, then most stocks will drop in price, including those that are relatively undervalued. But there is less risk that undervalued stocks will fall, and they are less likely to fall as far. This is the margin-of-safety principle at work again.

For example, on Black Monday, October 19, 1987, when the Dow Jones Industrial Average dropped 22%, the undervalued stocks of Geraldine Weiss, author of *Dividends Don't Lie,* dropped only 2%.

If you really want to delve into statistics on stocks there are computer software packages you can get that will sift through a large number of stocks and tally up all kinds of different numbers for you. You can tell the computer what financial measures to apply, and it will search for stocks that match them. This is called "screening" for stocks, a convenient and timesaving tool.

When you sell your stocks you need to decide where to put your cash to earn interest, until you are ready to buy more stocks with it. The easiest thing to do is put it in a "money market fund." Money market funds are mutual funds that invest in "commercial paper," certificates of deposit, extremely short-term bonds, and other low-risk short-term debt instruments. A money market fund is useful for storing cash because it pays a higher interest rate than a bank savings account and is very liquid. You can withdraw your money at any time, although some have minimum withdrawal amounts, such as $500. My discount stock brokerage firm provides me with a money market fund and check-writing privileges.

When I sell a stock, the cash automatically goes into my money market fund.

Be sure not to let your bank confuse you into using its "money market account." This is a name it uses for a normal type of savings account to get your money away from a true money market fund, which pays higher interest.

Other places to earn higher interest on your money are bank certificates of deposit, government bonds, and corporate bonds. You might want to put some cash in bank certificates of deposit, or short-term government bonds, to earn a higher return than a money market pays. But if you do this, you will have to tie up your cash anywhere from three months to several years.

I would not recommend that you put a lot of your money in long-term bonds, those that mature in more than five years. The problem with investing in bonds is they have not performed as well as stocks over the long run, and sometimes they can be just as risky. As you read more about investing in the stock market, you will hear a lot about bonds, so I am including a short description of what they are and how they work.

Bonds are an agreement by a business or government to borrow money and pay it back with interest. When a corporation issues a bond, it may write special terms into the bond agreement which make it riskier, or less valuable, as an investment. Because of these special provisions written into different bond agreements, it can be just as complex to select a good bond investment as it is to select stocks.

Because most bonds guarantee interest payments, they are considered a safer form of income than stocks, which pay dividends. A company does not have to pay a dividend, but it is required to pay the interest on its bonds. Bonds are also considered safer investments because they have first claim on the assets of a business. If a business goes bankrupt, its bonds are paid off before the stockholders can collect any money.

The safety provided by bonds compared to stocks means that people are willing to accept a lower rate of return on a bond. But stocks have the advantage that their price can go up, and so can their dividend payments. The decision to choose either stocks or bonds is not a direct trade-off between risk and the rate of return.

The interest rate, or yield, on all types of bonds currently for sale, changes according to the supply and demand of money in the credit markets. The government, in particular the Federal Reserve Board, has the most control over the money supply, and therefore the biggest effect on interest rates. When interest rates go up, the price of existing bonds goes down. When interest rates go down, the price of existing bonds goes up. You will hear this described as "the inverse relationship between bond prices and interest rates."

Bonds can be a conservative investment, a safe way to earn income. They can also be a risky investment, causing you to lose money.

Let us say that inflation is 3% and you are earning 6% interest on your bond. You are only earning a "real" return of 3%, because the other 3% is getting eaten up by inflation. Now suppose inflation goes up to 5%, and interest rates go up to 8% to compensate. When interest rates go up, bond prices go down, so your bond just dropped in value. That might not matter if you don't have to sell your bond. You can wait until it matures and collect what you originally paid for it. The problem is that with inflation at 5%, the real return on your 6% bond is now only 1%. The real return dropped from 3% to 1%, which means that the value of your bond income has dropped by two thirds! Inflation is a killer for fixed-income investments such as bonds.

The price of bonds is determined not only by interest rates, but also by how "risky" the bond is. U.S. Treasury bonds are considered the safest investment in the world, as far as paying interest and getting back the original money. Corporate bonds for the most part are riskier than government bonds, and so pay a higher interest rate.

The safest corporate bonds have an AAA or Aaa rating. Bonds with lower ratings sell for lower prices, thus providing a higher rate of interest. The more risk you are willing to take, the higher the rate of interest you can earn on a bond. The highest rate of interest is offered on so-called "junk bonds," because they have a low rating, such as BB or below.

Because corporate bonds can have so many different gimmicks in their bond agreements, it is not that simple to pick a high-grade corporate bond. Often bonds have special features to make them more attractive to investors. Convertible bonds are similar to other bonds, but they give you the right to convert the bond into a certain number of shares of stock in the company.

Corporate bonds are generally purchased by wealthy individuals or institutions, because they usually cost $1,000 each, and you often have to buy $5,000 worth to avoid paying a high commission. It is possible to gain some of the benefits of corporate bond interest by investing in a bond mutual fund. However I don't recommend using bond mutual funds. Most bond mutual funds speculate on price fluctuations in the bond market, trying to earn higher rates of return. This is risky and you don't want any part of it.

If you have a lot of money, you may want to invest in bonds to get a higher rate of return than you can get from money market accounts or bank certificates of deposits. Bonds can provide you with safe income when the stock market is in the doldrums and you don't want to sell any of your stocks.

Here is a summary of how to invest in the stock market:

• The way to make money in the stock market is to buy stocks that go up in price *over the long term.*

• Reduce your risk of losing money on any one stock by owning at least ten different stocks.

• Never buy stocks that are popular or expensive; instead look for stocks that are "cheap"—reasonably priced in relation to earnings, sales, dividends, and assets.

• Do not invest in stocks. Invest in companies. Look for good quality companies with a long history (at least five years) of consistent earnings and growth. Or look for good companies that are temporarily available at bargain prices due to conditions from which they are likely to recover.

• Never attempt to trade short-term. Always plan for long-term investing. You could buy stock in a good company and hold it for a lifetime if the company continues to do well, taking income from your investment by collecting dividends, or selling off 100 shares as needed.

• Pay little attention to stock market or economic predictions; they are seldom accurate and only liable to stir your emotions and color your judgment.

• The stock market and the economy always cycle, so buy on bad news and despair, and sell on good news and excitement.

• Remember 1% over 25 years is a 25% increase on your return.

It is a good idea to read other books about the stock market to broaden your understanding and refresh your thinking on the topic. Be sure to check out the list of books I recommend in "Resources."

The stock market can be an exciting and rewarding adventure in wealth-building as long as you play it safe and invest for the long haul. You can count on the information in this chapter to guide you in the stock market for a lifetime. The principles I have shared with you here are time tested and classic. If you use the wealth-building equation to refine your attitudes, knowledge, skill, effort, and resources, and apply them to the stock market, you will be richly rewarded.

CHAPTER NINE

Real Estate

In ancient times, the primary form of wealth was real estate. Land was the principal asset of kings, and the purpose of most wars was to expand or defend territory—real estate.

Rulers of commerce and government were the landowners. The churches also acquired land. Land and the dominion over its peoples were the source of most intrigues between government and religion. The common people were usually enslaved to the land or its owners, in one fashion or another. To own your own land was the highest standard of affluence and social rank, and in many ways it still is. Home ownership is a key measure of success.

The instincts to own land, and the desire for home ownership, are deeply imbedded in the history of Western civilization. Our need to own a home is a powerful emotion based on long tradition. In *Love and Death,* Woody Allen's father is a Russian immigrant who prizes land over all other possessions. "Land, my own piece of land," he cries, removing a piece of sod from his pocket and kissing it reverently.

With the world in chaos, nothing provides quite the same sense of protection and safety as gathering with your loved ones in your own home. For many people a home of their own means security and independence, the ultimate in quality of life, and the fulfillment of the American Dream.

Renting a home, whether it is a house, apartment, or other dwelling, can never provide the same sense of belonging as a home of your own. As a renter, there is always a measure of impermanence and illegitimacy to the arrangement. Every time you want to hang a picture, or paint a wall, you have to worry what the landlord will think. Your home is not yours to do with as you wish; it belongs to someone else.

Renting does have personal and financial advantages though. As a renter you don't bear the responsibility of making costly repairs if the roof needs replacement, the water heater breaks, or termites are found gnawing away at the framework. It is much easier as a renter to pick up and move, since you don't have to sell your house or condominium first (which can be difficult when the real estate market slows down). And financially, renting is sometimes more advantageous than buying.

If security, stability, and the responsibilities of home ownership are not your thing, you may prefer to rent your home. A friend of mine once said; "The second greatest day of my life, was the day I bought my own home. The greatest day, was when I sold it." He now rents in a mobile home park and is quite content.

Since the founding of the nation Americans have used real estate to build their wealth. Other than starting your own business, real estate investment is the most common way people become wealthy. A large proportion of the richest Americans have amassed their wealth through real estate.

My parents struggled against poverty most of their lives, but one of my mother's proudest accomplishments was her success in real estate. She did so well in fact that she eventually got her real estate sales license and later qualified for a broker's license.

When I was a boy my mother managed to buy a little house on two lots in a shabby neighborhood of Sacramento. She bought the house with a small down payment, and we lived there for a couple of years. Using this house as collateral, she bought some land in the country, and then sold it to buy a 10-acre farm. We moved to the farm and my mother rented out our house in Sacramento, arranging to build a duplex on its adjoining lot. Eventually she sold the house and duplex in Sacramento, divided up the farmland, built another house on it, and sold that house and several parcels of the farmland. Finally we ended up with a large house with a swimming pool in a nice neighborhood of Sacramento.

Within a few years, my mother had built the family fortune up to a net worth exceeding $100,000. This was a lot of money in the early 1960s. And she accomplished all of this dealing in real estate, starting with very little money. If it were not for the financial and emotional devastation resulting from my parents' divorce, there is no telling where my mother would have gone from there. Although she continued to dabble in real estate throughout her life, her despair of wealth discouraged her from repeating her early successes.

Those years of my childhood are among the happiest of my life. We lived in homes that belonged to us, and we were together as a family, with a place we could call our own. After that, living in various rented apartments and houses, I felt like a vagabond—someone without a legitimate place in the world.

Now that I have my own home with some land, a place to raise my family in security, I feel rooted. I have a retreat I can claim as my own, and make a stand against the cold realities of an uncaring world. I am one of those people who needs the sense of belonging that home ownership can provide.

Part of what made it possible to own the wonderful home I now live in is the successful investment we made in our previous home. By finding and investing in good value in our home in Los Angeles, we were able to trade up into a country estate that has substantially raised the quality of our life and increased our wealth.

Early in my marriage I could not imagine where we would come by the financial resources to own a home. I had to apply every part of the wealth-building equation to make this dream a reality.

First I had to adjust my attitude and see myself as a wealth-builder and a homeowner, instead of a perpetual failure destined to poverty. I also had to view the world as an open-ended sea of possibilities and trust the old saying, "Where there's a will, there's a way."

I remember trying to convince my wife that there are houses that have been in families for years, and they don't realize how much the property has gone up in value. She scoffed at the idea, saying that even if such houses exist, they are too difficult to find. When we finally bought our house it was a moment of supreme marital triumph for me, since we picked it up four hours after it went on the market at a bargain price, from a couple who had inherited it forty years after the husband's parents built it. It was immature of me to gloat, but I couldn't resist.

But we never would have found and purchased this home if we had not put in two years of effort, increasing our knowledge and skill about home values and buying real estate. It took a great deal of effort to shop for homes until we found this unique bargain, a gorgeous home at a price we could afford. We constantly had to struggle with our attitudes and not give in to discouragement and despair of wealth. And we had to cultivate many different resources to make our dream a reality, including time, money, knowledge, contacts and information.

Many Americans have built their fortunes in real estate in a similar fashion. It is one of the few means of becoming wealthy in which an average individual can leverage their way up fairly quickly. We made a lot of money in three years from our home. We were able to exercise our knowledge, skill, and effort to find and acquire good value. And real estate can be a good investment whether you buy a home to live in, or an income property to rent out.

Real estate provides tremendous wealth-building opportunities because, unlike buying a business or other financial assets, real estate does not necessarily require in-depth business or investment knowledge. At the same time, real estate is worth a lot of money, so there is plenty of room for profiting on shrewd buying and selling, as well as adding value by fixing up properties.

Most people who would have difficulty sizing up the value of a business would not have nearly so much trouble sizing up the value of a house. The value of real estate is much more tangible than the value of a business. We all know what it is like to live in a home, what works and what doesn't. If you look at a lot of properties and compare their selling prices against what the houses have to offer in terms of beauty, convenience, comfort, and location, you can easily get a gut feel for value. Then the trick becomes putting in the effort to fine-tune your sense of real estate values and compete against others to uncover the buying opportunities that can make you the most money.

Successfully investing in real estate is also somewhat akin to investing in the stock market. You have to know when to go against accepted beliefs about market and economic conditions that affect the timing of buying and selling.

A friend of mine recently called to ask if I knew that it is a bad time to buy real estate. I asked him why he thought this was so. He said that he had just heard an expert on a nationally televised investment program explain that real estate is very illiquid (meaning hard to sell), and real estate prices keep going down, so it is a bad time to buy. I told him that the experts are always describing what has *just* happened as if that is what will *continue* to happen. And I explained that this might be the *best* time to buy real estate, because so many past problems with the economy, savings and loan companies, and exaggerated real estate prices have now produced lower prices. Contrary to what his expert had said, you don't want to wait until real estate is selling well, and prices are going up, before you *buy*. That is when you want to *sell.*

The way to get the best deals on real estate is to wait until the real estate market goes sour and properties are selling at bargain prices, then *buy*. Rent out the properties for several years until the market recovers again, and then *sell.*

But you can invest in real estate at any time, if you are careful to apply high standards of value in making your purchase. Buying your own home is one of the surest ways to succeed at investing in real estate.

The financial benefits of home ownership are that you can save on taxes, build up equity (ownership) in your home by paying down the mortgage, and allow inflation to increase the value of the house over the long term. This works as an automatic savings plan as well.

Setting personal and emotional considerations aside, whether it is better financially to rent or buy depends on several factors in your situation. In most cases you must be willing to stay put for several years to justify the costs of buying and selling a home. There are various fees associated with any real estate transaction, including up-front fees for taking out a mortgage when you buy, and commission costs to the real estate broker when you sell. Unless the property goes up in value during the time you own it, or you live in the house long enough to get plenty of use out of it, you are better off renting. There is not much point in going to the trouble of finding and buying a home, and paying all the associated fees of buying and selling, just to move out in a year or so.

When you rent a home, the money is down the drain. You get one month's shelter for one month's rent, and then start over again. When you buy a home, your mortgage payments build ownership value or equity in the property. But your equity buildup on most loans is slow, since most of your payment goes toward the interest costs of the loan in the early years. And paying interest on a loan is not much different from money out the window for rent.

One advantage that paying interest has over paying rent is that mortgage interest is deductible from your taxes. Part of your interest costs can be offset by savings on your taxes.

In many parts of the country real estate prices have gotten so far ahead of rents that by the time you make your mortgage payment, pay property taxes, insurance costs, and the costs of fixing up the house when it needs repairs, you would be better off renting. If you compare the costs of buying a home to what you might save by renting, you may find that putting the money you save into other investments is a better bet.

In other parts of the country where renting more closely matches the costs of buying (and such places do exist, believe it or not), the advantages of buying outweigh those of renting.

The decision to rent or buy does not follow hard-and-fast rules, especially when the emotional considerations of home ownership come into play. In general, I agree with the recommendations of most financial planners that owning your own home is one of the best investments you can make. I would qualify that recommendation by emphasizing that home ownership makes sense only when you are sure that you can safely cope with your mortgage payments, and that you buy a house only at "fair market value" or less.

Another consideration for investing in your own home is whether to buy a condominium or townhouse. Here there are some advantages, and many disadvantages. Condominiums usually cost a lot less than a house, so they can be an affordable way to achieve home ownership. There is less maintenance responsibility in owning a condominium because the outside areas and many shared features of the building, like plumbing and heating, are taken care of by the homeowners association. The drawbacks of condominium or townhouse ownership relate mainly to the cooperative nature of the arrangement. You may not like all the rules you are subject to as a member of the homeowners association. There can be problems if other owners don't pay their fees and don't follow the rules. And the value of your unit may decline if the whole place is not properly maintained or the operation is otherwise mismanaged.

Condominiums or townhouses may be good or bad investments, depending on market conditions. In many areas of the country, condominiums have become overbuilt, and prices have plummeted in recent years.

If you don't care about real estate as an investment and you just want to own a nice home, it pays to shop for a good deal. A home purchase is the single largest investment most people make, and you can save thousands of dollars with a little extra effort. Also bear in mind, that to "buy low, sell high," or buying bargains and selling at or above prevailing market prices, is the most effective way to protect your investment in a home or other real estate.

The financial opportunities in real estate are tremendous. Many among the *Forbes 400* richest Americans made their money in real estate. Contrast this with the fact that only one member of the *Forbes 400,* Warren Buffet, acquired his wealth solely through investment in the stock market. So despite the opinions of naysayers, and the usual band of pessimistic "experts," real estate holds tremendous opportunities for those willing to invest the time and effort required to succeed.

But real estate investment carries many risks along with it. There are high carrying costs to cover insurance, property taxes, repairs, vacancies, and other expenses. If properties don't appreciate according to expectations, substantial losses may be incurred. Declining neighborhoods may erode property values for decades. Local government could impose rent controls or raise taxes. And real estate is an illiquid investment that you cannot sell off quickly if you hit a cash crunch.

Real estate investing is a nuts-and-bolts kind of business. And it *is* a business. It is not like the stock market, where you can study the financial news and put in a call to your broker to buy or sell. In real estate, you have to do a lot of legwork to keep after all of the details. You have to get to know neighborhoods, study the market, look at lots of properties, handle paperwork, deal with a variety of people. It can be full of hassles.

But some people love real estate investing. It can be fun getting out and looking at all the different houses there are, how they are designed and decorated, and amusing to see the grotesque things some people do to houses. If you like working with your hands fixing things or doing renovations, real estate can keep you very busy. And there is an empire-building sensation to real estate investment. You accumulate properties, fix them up, buy and sell them, move money around refinancing and renegotiating.

One thing is for sure: Real estate investment is not a free ride, an easy way to get rich. It takes a lot of work to do it right and make money at it.

Three primary benefits of real estate as an investment are 1) the potential increase in the value of the property; 2) the possibility of rental income; 3) the tax advantages. The two main tax advantages derived from real estate are deductions for interest expenses and depreciation. The taxes on any rental income from the property are directly offset by these deductions.

The tax deduction you get from depreciation results from the assumption that a property deteriorates in value as the building and any appliances it contains wear out. You don't get to claim depreciation on your personal residence, because depreciation is considered a business expense, which applies only when you are investing in properties and collecting rent.

Depending on which area of the country you live in, you may have to place more emphasis on either rents or price appreciation as a primary characteristic of your investment strategy. Where property prices have not gotten too far ahead of rents, a property may pay for itself just from the rental income. But there may not be much potential for price appreciation in that local real estate market. Where prices have gotten ahead of rents, you cannot collect enough rent to make a large mortgage payment. In this case you must hope that by the time you are ready to sell the property, its value will have gone up sufficiently to compensate for your extra out-of-pocket expenses, or that rising rents will someday cover negative cash flow.

Be wary of depending on price appreciation to bail you out of negative cash flow situations. There have been real estate booms in the past that were conducive to this approach, and in certain areas that are still growing rapidly today, or will grow rapidly in the future, this approach can be successful. Still, never assume because prices have gone up in the past, they will continue to go up in the future.

The average rate of price appreciation for single-family dwellings from 1970 to 1990 has been 7.5%, compared to an average inflation rate of around 6.3%, a high-grade corporate bond average yield of 9.8%, and an 11.2% return on the Dow Jones Industrial Average list of stocks, with dividends reinvested.

Don't you love statistics? I have been reading statistics like these for years in books on investment, and I could never understand how they relate to each other. Well the truth is they don't, but don't tell anyone I told you so.

Statistics like these often appear in the financial press with little elaboration. You are supposed to take these boiled-down numbers and pick the best investment for yourself. I don't know how you can interrelate these numbers in such a simplistic fashion.

But here is what I do know. The average price of single-family homes has been rising slightly faster than the price of everything else. If you had put $100 into top-rated corporate bonds every year for the last 20 years, you would have earned an average of 9.8% interest on your money every year. If you had stuck a dollar under your mattress in 1970 and pulled it out today, it would be worth only 29¢. If you had bought a single-family home at the median price of $23,400 in 1970, you would have gotten about $100,000 for it in 1990.

So why don't the above statistics relate to each other? Because each of the statistics applies to a completely different area of economics and investment. If you say that stocks returned 11.2% with dividends reinvested, and that is better than bonds which provided only 9.8% a year in interest, you are comparing apples and oranges.

To get the maximum yield on stocks you have to buy a share of each of the Dow Jones Industrial Average at the beginning, put all of your dividends back into stocks every year at the average stock price for that year, and then sell all of your stocks at the average price during the 20th year. The 11.2% statistic assumes all of these factors. In the real world this would never happen. Only a robot can invest this efficiently, and even it could not buy the incremental shares it would need.

Once you understand what goes into statistics like these, you realize they are just ballpark figures, vague comparisons of long-term relationships. The value of such statistics is just to give you a "feeling" for how various investments stack up. They don't provide an exact basis for comparison.

Whether you are better off investing in stocks, bonds, real estate, or some other investment depends on your own interests, skills, financial circumstances, and how these investments relate to current economic conditions. It is not so much a matter that stocks are always better than real estate, or vice versa.

With a 7.5% average rate of appreciation on the median price of single-family homes since 1970, you might think you would be better off with stocks or bonds. Actually this statistic is pretty bare-bones. It is just the increase in prices, not the financial benefits that accrue from saving on taxes, or the extent to which your renters have been adding to your equity by paying down the mortgage.

Many people have gotten rich in real estate accumulating various properties at the beginning of a big upsurge in prices. And many people have gone broke in real estate accumulating various properties at the beginning of a plateau or big drop in prices. The primary force at work here is leverage.

Leverage is the added buying power you get from borrowing. In real estate it is typical to borrow 80% of the price of a property. You put up a $20,000 down payment and borrow $80,000 to purchase a $100,000 property. If the price of the property goes up $20,000 and you sell it for $120,000, you pay off the $80,000 dollar mortgage and pocket $40,000. You have doubled your original $20,000 down payment. Double your money. You can get rich fast doing that.

If, on the other hand, the price of the property drops $20,000 and you sell it for $80,000, you can just barely pay off the mortgage and are left with nothing. You just went broke.

That is the power and the danger of leverage. It increases the risks and the rewards of investment. It is common for people to use leverage for investing in real estate, and although some are more conservative than others, few real estate investors buy properties outright for cash. Almost everyone borrows part of the cost of purchasing real estate, and it makes sense to do so, as long as you can collect enough rent to pay your expenses, including mortgage payments. The problems with leverage arise when people borrow too much money to buy a property that is overpriced to begin with. Or they take on large mortgage payments, with unrealistic ideas about costs associated with the property, including the cost of vacancies.

The mathematics of real estate investment (including investment for home ownership) are complicated by the fact that so many uncertainties go into the equation. To figure tax savings, you have to predict your income and tax rates. If you have a variable-rate mortgage you have to predict interest rates. To value the property for sale in five years you have to understand and predict economic forces that affect the rate of increase or decrease in real estate prices. There are unpredictable costs of upkeep such as replacing the furnace or water heater, or repairing a leaky roof. And there are other costs such as insurance and property taxes. And finally, on income properties, you have to figure how much time houses or apartments may remain vacant, or what percentage of tenants may stiff you for the rent.

All of the numbers and guesstimates associated with real estate investing can seem daunting at first, and you may feel confronted by an impossible task. But once you get accustomed to the various items involved, it becomes no more difficult to do these calculations than working up a personal budget, or paying your bills and balancing your checkbook.

If you have difficulties in this area, a good accountant familiar with real estate investing should be able to review the financial ramifications of a real estate investment for you. But don't get lazy and let your accountant convince you of the value of the property you are buying, or how much it is likely to appreciate in the future. This is where you need to do your own research and thinking.

If you want to synthesize an exact index to measure the quality of a particular real estate investment, you will have to run the numbers through an internal rate-of-return calculation. In essence, "internal rate of return" is a "magic" interest rate you are earning on your investment, which you can decipher only by plugging in the proper cash flows. This is normally done using a computer spreadsheet program, or a financial calculator. Your accountant should be able to help you do internal rate-of-return calculations, if you want to compare a real estate investment with other investment opportunities.

The internal rate of return distills all of the financial complexities of an investment down to one simple number: the compounded rate of return on your investment. For example, you would be doing terrifically well in the stock market if you combined all of your earnings from dividends and price appreciation on your stocks over the last five years and discovered you were earning a 20% internal rate of return.

The one important and crucial question not measured in the internal rate-of-return formula is relative risk. Relative risk is a measure of the likelihood of success of one investment over another in earning the income projected for it.

One complication to applying a strictly rational approach to real estate investment is the difficulty in estimating income, expenses, and price appreciation on properties. Getting these numbers right, in order to predict your investment profits, requires judgment that comes only from experience. This is where the help of someone with knowledge and experience in real estate investment can be very important. Seek out a friend, accountant, real estate professional, or other qualified adviser who can give you objective advice on these matters.

Among the important questions to settle in your mind regarding any real estate investment is whether property values will be maintained or rise in the future. Real estate has been through many boom-and-bust cycles in the last century, and, like the stock market, few people have consistently predicted these cycles. There is a large degree of uncertainty in any long-term economic projections. Then what, you may ask, is the point of even brewing up these concoctions? The main value is in what they force you to think about. If you can see current conditions within the larger picture, even if you cannot predict where we are going, you at least have a framework for understanding what is happening now. Contemplating various trends, population changes, long-term interest rate changes, and other factors that may affect your investments improves your decision-making.

In the 1970s and 1980s there were tremendous surges in real estate prices, but now, in the early 1990s, real estate prices have generally declined. Sometimes surges in prices occur in one part of the country while prices are falling elsewhere.

Real estate cycles tend to follow long-term changes in interest rates and population cycles, and also respond to the effects of inflation.

As interest rates go up, it becomes more expensive to borrow money. Your interest payments are higher, so it is more difficult to afford mortgage payments. When interest rates go, up fewer people can afford to buy real estate, and prices tend to fall.

As population increases there is a greater demand for housing, and prices tend to rise until that demand is met. During the 1950s and the 1960s there were both a "baby boom" and growing economic prosperity, that drove real estate prices higher over the last 30 years. By the 1990s much of that demand has been met.

For every boom cycle in real estate, there have always been experts warning of danger. And sure enough, in every bust cycle, a lot of overleveraged players get swept out of the game. But the cycles have repeated themselves over and over again, continually confounding the "experts."

Now in the 1990s, with real estate in the doldrums again, many experts are predicting that the golden days of real estate are over, just as they did in the early 1980s and 1970s. But the truth is that there are always opportunities for investment in real estate, just as there are always opportunities in the stock market, or in business. You just have to know how to interpret current conditions. That does not mean you have to understand the large issues and complexities of the national economy, interest rates, current banking policies, and national demographic trends. It means that you have to look at specific deals and decide whether they add up.

Real estate markets are very localized in their characteristics. From one neighborhood to the next, conditions vary; some areas are growing while others are on the decline. In order to succeed at any time in real estate, you have to select properties based on the three most important features: location, location, and location. This old joke is still a truism in real estate. Probably no other single factor contributes more to the success of a purchase. Buying the right kind of property, in the right place, at the right price, will succeed no matter what the current economic conditions are. And there are people who have made money in real estate decade after decade, despite all the cycles and trends that have occurred.

The big bust in real estate in the late 1980s provided tremendous opportunities in distressed properties for those who had the cash or financing available to buy them. Now in the early 1990s, when mortgage interest rates have fallen to their lowest level in years, many attractive deals are possible.

Real estate has always been a good business, and always will be, as long as you approach it as a business and do your homework properly. Many of the warnings and complaints about failed real estate investments are reflections of the naiveté of the investors involved. Failure to understand the principles and forces at work in real estate investment is bound to have the same effect that ignorance always has. Ignorance subjects you to random outcome and blind luck. If you don't know what you are doing, then you are stumbling in the dark and bound to fall.

Often in real estate, as in other investments, people will say that what has happened before will continue to happen. Thus, if prices have gone up in the past, they will continue to go up in the future.

Throughout the 1970s and 1980s a lot of home buyers and real estate "investors" relied on the fact that most of the time, in certain areas of the country, real estate appreciated rapidly in price. The popular wisdom was that real estate always goes up, so buy it at any price and sit tight; eventually you will make a profit. In financial markets, this type of wisdom tends to feed on itself, producing price speculation and forcing prices up "unnaturally." This happens all the time in the stock market, which cycles up and down in violent swings, much more rapidly than real estate.

The more people believe that real estate prices will go up, the more they are willing to pay for properties, in the hopes that prices will go up even more. And this cycle continues as a self-fulfilling prophecy. Eventually some form of economic reality steps into the picture and bursts the bubble, awakening the crowd from their dreams of ever-rising prices. When this happens, and everybody realizes that prices might stabilize or fall, and that their "investment strategy" relies on rising prices, look out. Stampede! Everybody wants to sell and prices go through the floor, until they find their economic equilibrium again.

In the real estate market of 1992, numerous factors contributed to dampening this speculative fever. The savings-and-loan debacle dumped a lot of properties on the market, since so many savings and loans lent money on overvalued properties to begin with. The baby boom generation does not have many first-time home buyers left to contribute to demand. Some overbuilding occurred as a result of excess speculation. The price of rents did not keep up with the cost of mortgage payments on investment properties. All of these real-world economic factors eventually had an effect on real estate prices and forced a rebalancing of values.

The key to successful real estate investment is in finding or adding value. In the popular real estate books the classic examples of this are the distressed property and the fixer-upper.

The distressed property is one that wants to be sold so badly that the seller will let it go for substantially less than its market value. This may happen when properties are being sold in tax lien sales, or due to divorce or death in the family, or if the sellers are in over their heads on their mortgage payments.

The fixer-upper is the property that is run down, and that you can add value to by fixing it up. This is sometimes called "sweat" equity. It is very important with a fixer-upper to analyze what can and cannot be done to effectively add value. This is an art that requires determining where you can get the most bang for your buck, putting time, effort, and money into the property to improve its price potential. New paint, floor coverings, and landscaping are usually the most cost-effective items for adding value.

Most people know about looking for fixer-uppers to make money in real estate. There is a lot of competition in this approach. To beat the competition, a very effective technique is simple *hard work*. If you can put in the time and effort to look at many properties, study and understand the market, and try out many different angles on financing and buying properties cheap, you will learn to automatically recognize where the values are and how to acquire them. The key is diligent adherence to high standards of value to make sure you get "good buys."

A good buy should include several important characteristics:

1) Never pay more than a fair or preferably a "bargain" price. Pricing is a slippery subject, because the cheapest of 100 overpriced properties is still overpriced. You have to study general market conditions and historical standards of value in real estate pricing. Usually, local real estate agents can quote you a price per square foot as a rule of thumb for making price comparisons.

2) Never finance a property in a manner that would not allow you to hold it indefinitely. That means the net income from the property, after deducting expenses from rents, and the combination of your own income from other sources for the foreseeable future, would be adequate to cover all costs of holding on to the property. Conservative financing (not too large a mortgage) on the property safeguards against a forced sale during a down real estate market.

3) A realistic look at the costs of purchasing and holding the property, measured against the income and price appreciation likely to be earned from the property, must suggest a favorable rate of return on your investment. Here it is especially important to think clearly and honestly about potential income and costs. What if a water heater breaks, the tenants don't pay the rent, or the property remains vacant? All of these cash flow variables have to be analyzed realistically. Only in this way can your calculations offer a true picture of the investment potential that exists.

Finding an especially low-priced deal might justify buying a property with negative cash flow. Quick action might net a profit if you are confident that you could resell the property at a fair market price in a short period of time. In that case, it might be reasonable to take on costs that you would not be able to sustain in the long run.

To explain where investment opportunities lie in real estate, I have developed a theory which I call the "Inefficient Market Theory of Real Estate," which states that since real estate is not a liquid asset, easily bought and sold, the value of a property is not continuously determined by buyers and sellers.

Many homes are unique and not easily compared with other homes. The decision to buy a home involves very subjective and personal criteria that affect the buying decision, providing a large margin for error in the pricing of homes by both buyers and sellers. When you are talking about a 10% margin for error on a $100,000 asset, that is a lot of money.

This inefficiency in home pricing offers one advantage for real estate investment over the stock market or other investments that are priced more efficiently. An experienced investor can take advantage of this inefficiency by profiting from the difference between a seller's lower opinion of the value of his property, and the higher opinion of the property's value formed by some future buyer.

To get top dollar for a property, it is important that it be marketed effectively. A property that has not been presented to a large number of prospects and shown in its best light may not command the price it deserves.

If the price of a property has been held low by poor marketing techniques, you might make a successful bid at below full market value. Then you put the property back on the market, possibly adding to its value by doing certain repairs or improvements, and sell it at a substantial profit. To succeed in this approach, you need an adequate spread between the buying and selling prices, to cover the costs involved and provide a reasonable reward for the money and effort invested.

Will Rogers' comment, "Buy land; they ain't making any more of it," is a classic bit of false logic for real estate investing. Following his wisdom, you could buy land and wait a whole lifetime for demand to drive up the price on your particular chunk of this irreplaceable commodity.

Another standard pearl of wisdom is to buy land on the edge of town and wait for the town to expand around it, driving up the value. This brings to mind my boyhood home in a poor neighborhood of Sacramento, currently one of the fastest-growing communities in the United States. The house my parents bought is still standing, including the duplex they built on the lot next door. But the neighbors' homes I used to play in have been torn down and turned into vacant lots. This poor neighborhood has actually deteriorated since my childhood, despite the fantastic growth in other surrounding areas. Other one-horse towns on the edge of Sacramento, which I remember from childhood, have exploded with strip malls and tract homes, but not my old neighborhood.

So be wary of pat formulas in real estate. Countless investors have simplemindedly poured their savings into real estate investments, only to see them tied up in empty towering office buildings that "expert advisers" and "sophisticated investors" had planned and developed.

Speaking of sophisticated investors, let's talk about real estate investment trusts. Congress created legislation in the early 1960s to provide small investors with a vehicle for investing in large real estate projects and enjoying some of the tax benefits available. This legislation authorized the formation of real estate investment trusts, or REITs.

Shares of REITs trade on the stock exchange just like shares of stock mutual funds. REITs are required by law to earn 75% of their income from rents, dividends, interest, and capital gains from the sale of real estate property. They are also required to pay out 95% of this income to shareholders. REITs that meet these restrictions are exempt from taxation at the corporate level, thus avoiding the double taxation of earnings that stockholders of normal corporations suffer.

REITs have a troubled history. In the 1970s many of them ran into severe financial hardships that depressed the industry. Later REITs achieved greater successes and regained popularity, but by the early 1990s they were bombing out again.

There are several types of REITs. Equity REITs invest directly in real estate developments, either those created by the REIT, which becomes the developer, or those created by other developers.

Mortgage REITs don't invest directly in real estate, but instead provide mortgage money to the real estate industry. They may also have some equity participation in deals they finance.

Then there are REITs that operate as a mix between the mortgage type and the equity type.

Finally there are the FREITs, or Finite-Life Real Estate Investment Trusts, which are more like traditional real estate limited partnerships and are intended to have a fixed life. They are supposed to dissolve themselves as they sell off their properties and pay out profits to investors. This is a new type and since few have a long track record, it is difficult to judge them.

REITs are a large and complex subject deserving specialized treatment. I think most financial planning authors treat the subject too casually, devoting only a couple of pages to it, and leaving their readers vulnerable to the wiles of the REIT salespersons. I am a firm believer in educating yourself thoroughly before trying something new. Therefore, I recommend you give this subject in-depth study if this is an investment that holds appeal for you. Bear in mind that REITs have been hyped and sold by untrustworthy individuals and organizations, so proceed with caution. There are many well-run and excellent REIT investments, but there are also some REINs (Real Estate Investment Nightmares).

Real estate partnerships, another category of real estate investment, are legal business entities formed to invest in real estate. Anybody can form a real estate partnership. You get a group of people to pool money for investing in real estate, and hire an attorney to draw up an agreement that specifies how the partnership will be controlled. Limited partnerships, which are similar to standard partnerships, limit the legal liability of investors who will not participate in active management of the partnership.

Partnerships have significant disadvantages compared to doing your own thing. You cannot cash out your shares at will. Also, if you disagree with how the partnership is being run, an arrangement like this can be aggravating and troublesome.

The advantage of partnerships is that they allow investors to pool their resources and buy properties they could not otherwise afford. If you are lucky, the partnership will have honest and competent management, and you will get a good return on your money.

Investment in raw land can be approached in one of two ways, as a speculation or for development.

Speculating in raw land is based on buying at a bargain price and reselling it quickly (assuming there is a big market for raw land in the area, which in most areas is not likely), or buying land that you expect to become more valuable in the not-too-distant future.

The other approach is buying raw land with the intent to develop it. This can take many forms:

• Buying a lot on which to build a "spec house," a house built for sale at a profit. Do not attempt this unless you are an experienced home-builder, or form a partnership with a trustworthy builder.

• Buying a large tract of land to develop a subdivision. You need to have a lot of experience as a real estate investor before you attempt your own subdivisions.

• Buying a lot in a business district to build a commercial property on. Be careful here. Commercial real estate is overbuilt as of the early 1990s, and it may be many years before the excess space is put into use.

Raw land is an especially risky investment because you have to carry the costs of any financing or taxes on it until it is sold, without the benefit of income from rents (unless it is farmland, grazing land, rich in minerals, or contains some other inherent income-producing potential).

All in all, you are better off staying away from raw land until you have substantial experience in real estate. But by way of contradicting myself, I have a story:

An attorney I know who had no prior experience as a real estate investor decided to invest in some land. A real estate agent took him to view a lakefront parcel. It was clear from studying the parcel map that the majority of the parcel was actually underwater in the lake. The agent pointed this out and suggested my friend would not want any "underwater land." He said, "Just make an offer for the dry land. Let them keep their underwater land."

But my friend instructed the agent, "Tell them I will buy the whole thing if they will reduce the price per acre for the dry land." The agent thought he was nuts.

The attorney made the purchase and brought in dredging equipment to dredge canals in the lake. He used the dredged-up mud to create strips of land. He built an extensive development that stretched out into the lake as "keys" and he made millions selling these lakefront lots.

This is an excellent example of seeing value where no one else does.

A number of people have popularized strategies for acquiring real estate with little or no down payment, offering the promise of making a killing in real estate to people with small incomes. The basic idea is to find bargain-priced properties that can be bought with little or no down payment, on "good terms." A bargain-priced property is one that is selling for less than the average price of a comparable property of the same quality. If real estate prices are rapidly appreciating (be careful with this assumption!), a property selling at the average price could be considered a bargain.

Buying the property on "good terms" means that you don't have to make a normal down payment, and you don't have to get a bank loan to pay the balance of the price. To buy a $100,000 property you would normally pay a $20,000 down payment and have to get a bank loan for the other $80,000. Since most people would have a hard time coming up with $20,000 and would not be able to qualify for an $80,000 loan to invest in real estate, they would not be able to do the deal. The alternative is to try and get good terms from the seller. If the seller will accept a smaller down payment, perhaps $5,000 or $10,000, and will keep his existing mortgage and let you make the payments, it becomes easier to buy the property.

Some of these "no-money-down" strategies do work. The catch is that you have to strive to find bargain properties and convince their sellers to give you good terms. It can be very discouraging to have real estate agents and friends scoff at these approaches, and for sellers to reject dozens of offers before one is finally accepted. But with sufficient motivation and stamina, these strategies can make you money.

You find a seller who has a "don't wanter." The seller is highly motivated to get rid of it because the tenants are always complaining, or the seller needs cash, or he wants to move out of the area, etc. The property is worth $100,000 in present condition. You offer $90,000 with a $5,000 down payment, and you offer to take over the existing mortgage payments and all other expenses. The seller agrees.

It is springtime and you mow the lawns, plant a couple of flower beds, clean up the back yard, kick out the bad tenant, put a fresh coat of paint on the walls, and hang up a for sale sign: "For sale—cute little house, $110,000, great buy!"

Along come a young couple. They drive a hard bargain and you let the thing go for $105,000. How did you do?

Sales price	$ 105,000
Down payment	-5,000
Expenses	-1,000
Mortgage payoff	-85,000
Real estate commission	-6,300
Net profit after deal	$ 7,700

You just made $7,700 on the $6,000 you put into the deal ($5,000 down payment plus $1,000 in expenses). But you also put in a lot of hard work finding the deal, closing the deal, fixing the place up, and selling it.

If the arithmetic did not scare you off, and all the hard work did not scare you off, and the rejection by numerous sellers who turned down your offers did not bother you, and you have a little cash or the courage to try and negotiate strictly no-money-down deals, and you can live with all the hassles and risks, you may be the perfect candidate to become a real estate magnate.

The first real estate investment I made was a no-money-down deal from a friend of mine, a real estate agent and expert in no-money-down deals. He had gotten his mother to invest in a property that he was now living in. He offered to go partners with me, buying it from her with no money down, if I would sign a note and take on the negative cash flow on the property. It was a classic greenhorn venture. I was eager to make my big move into amassing a real estate fortune and bought at too high a price, with too much leverage, in a bad market. After a year of pouring money into this pit I realized that we had overpaid and it would be several years before the market would catch up enough to break even on the deal. So we bailed out and let my friend's mother have her property back for "no money down." Actually there was some money down, ours, which was down the tubes.

While gathering material for this book I contacted a friend of mine who has been in real estate for fifteen years and has put together numerous deals for investors, as well as himself. John Klus has developed raw land and built and sold custom houses, so I felt he was eminently qualified to share his firsthand views. In particular I was interested in John's reactions to all of the "get-rich-quick" real estate books. His responses were interesting.

When someone comes to John with a no-money-down book in hand, he has two immediate problems: 1) The financing strategies may not be in the best interests of the seller, and as a real estate agent he has a fiduciary responsibility under the law to serve the interests of the seller in that regard. If he helps to structure financing that puts the seller in a tough situation, he is opening himself up to lawsuits, and possibly the loss of his license. 2) The no-money-down approach involves a lot of legwork hunting up potential properties. To find a "don't wanter" you have to make a lot of offers, most of which will get turned down. A real estate agent cannot justify putting that much time and effort into deals to get his commission. He will do a lot more deals and make much more in commissions just sticking to average buyers and sellers.

So someone trying to do no-money-down deals is not going to get much encouragement from real estate agents. If you want to attempt real estate investment on a shoestring budget, you will have to get used to seeking out rare opportunities. Rather than working through real estate agents, you may have to deal with sellers directly, to find cooperation for your unusual offers.

The first step on the road to success as a real estate investor is getting the proper education. Read books about real estate and familiarize yourself with the ideas and techniques they contain. Then get out and take a firsthand look. Drive around to familiarize yourself with different neighborhoods you might want to invest in. Find the real estate agents in that area and make an appointment to see properties with them. Give them a clear picture of the kind of properties you might be interested in, such as apartment buildings, duplexes, fourplexes, single-family homes, upscale or moderately priced.

Remember when dealing with agents that they don't necessarily know any more than you do about investing in real estate. Many agents take up real estate sales as a part-time vocation and don't last very long. You are trying to get an education when starting out, so find someone who can educate you. That means a knowledgeable real estate agent, preferably someone who understands real estate as an investment. Qualify the agents you use. Feel them out for what they know about real estate investment.

You don't need to act like an expert with real estate agents. Let them know that you are learning and need their advice. Tell them you are interested in putting some money into real estate, and would like to see some properties and evaluate them for investment purposes. Be sure that they provide a work sheet to show you how any properties they suggest would size up as an investment. Go over their numbers with them to see what assumptions they made.

Keep track of the properties you look at, make general notes about their appearance and other characteristics, and any first impressions that hit you. Write down anything that will help jog your memory about the property. After seeing three or four, it gets hard to keep them straight in your mind.

This part of real estate investing can be a lot of fun. My wife and I have always enjoyed wandering through homes, seeing how other people live, and the intriguing variations of design that exist among homes.

Go home with your notes and compare the properties you have seen with the ideas in your real estate books, or other knowledge you have picked up by now. You will immediately realize that you have many more questions about the properties. What is the existing financing? How long has the property been on the market? Did they start out asking a higher price and lower it? Are there schools in the neighborhood? Where is the closest shopping? Is the house on a noisy street? How are other houses in the neighborhood selling? Are there any "comps" (comparable sales prices) for similar houses that have sold in the neighborhood recently?

List all of your questions and call the real estate agent back and get answers. Do not let him put you off with kindly reassurances; you need all the facts.

The agent may not have all of the information you need, but can direct many of your questions to the homeowner for answers. You will also have to do some of your own research, perhaps by driving around the neighborhood and asking the people you see out and about. You can also visit the county clerk, assessor's office, or zoning department and gather information there.

Local government offices maintain a wealth of information that is useful to you as a real estate investor. You should learn how to get it. This can be very confusing at first, but after a couple of hours of marching from one department to another, asking questions and getting the lay of the land, you will sort out who keeps track of what, and where.

Normally, it works something like this. The county clerk records deeds of ownership and maintains these records on file. You can go there to look at copies of deeds and discover interesting facts about a property, shown on its deed. The assessor's office determines how much property tax the county will charge on a property, and can often give you clues about how much the previous owner paid for the property. The building department issues building permits and can explain regulations that control how a building must be constructed and maintained. The planning department manages the local zoning laws, which control what types of businesses or residences can be located in various areas of the county.

You need to know how to do title searches; that is, to look up the deeds to properties and see who owns them, for how long, whether there are restrictions on the title, and what was the original purchase price. Sometimes different departments keep separate track of these records.

Another resource available to you is your local title company. It offers many free services answering questions and providing information, hoping to get your business when you need to buy or sell a property.

It is important to learn and understand the zoning laws applying to areas in which you intend to buy a home or real estate investment. You may purchase a house with pleasant surroundings only to discover later that a gas station, store, or apartment house is being built next door.

My wife and I once offered to purchase a home in a quiet residential area. The back yard overlooked a serene setting of trees and bushes in a neighbor's back yard. A very private and pleasant scene. A couple of weeks before we were to close the deal, we stopped by for another glance at our dream home, only to find the neighbor's house gone and the whole back yard bulldozed. After several urgent phone calls we were able to establish that an apartment building was going to be built overlooking our back yard. We quickly extricated ourselves from the deal at the last minute, barely avoiding a disaster. If we had checked the zoning laws ahead of time, we would have discovered that the neighborhood was zoned for multiple family dwellings.

As I pointed out in Chapter 7, "Investment Strategies," most investments are mediocre, so it pays to shop hard to find the best opportunities. There are more places to find properties than the local real estate agent. Some properties are offered "for sale by owner" and may be advertised only in the local paper, or by a for sale sign in the front yard.

There are also people who would like to sell their property but have not gotten around to listing it with a real estate agent or otherwise advertising it. You may want to mail leaflets to all the residents in a neighborhood, offering to inspect their property with a view toward buying it.

You can get on a mailing list with the county treasurer, who periodically sends out notices of properties being auctioned off for unpaid taxes. And these tax lien auctions are advertised in the local paper from time to time, as well as bank foreclosures.

You can also check the obituaries and inquire about possible estate sales.

These are all different avenues to investigate, and each of these situations puts a twist on the type of deals you can make, sometimes with special advantages.

Among the safest real estate investments are small single-family dwellings and older apartment buildings. They are also where the best fixer-upper opportunities lie.

Typical two- or three-bedroom homes in blue-collar neighborhoods are in greater demand than other types of houses, and are easier to buy and sell. One problem with these types of properties is that they have become such popular investments, they may be overpriced and the rents won't cover the mortgage payments.

Avoid expensive neighborhoods or prestige homes. The market for selling these is much smaller. Also remember a cardinal rule of real estate is to buy the smallest or least expensive home in a neighborhood, not the best. It is much easier to fix up a home to bring it up to the standards of the neighborhood than to raise the standard of the neighborhood to match your fine home.

Apartment buildings offer several advantages for investment. They provide economies of scale in the costs of purchasing, maintaining, and selling the property. The bigger the apartment complex, the better. A bigger complex reduces management and maintenance costs per unit.

If you have enough money to buy several houses or one apartment complex, you will do better with the apartment complex, because you end up paying fees on only one transaction. You also get economies of scale because you can standardize the paint colors, floor coverings, plumbing fixtures, and many other items needed to maintain the property. When you own many different properties on the other hand, each one has unique problems that you most cope with on an individual basis, adding to your expenses.

The fixer-upper strategy applies double to investing in apartment buildings, but with a different twist. You want to buy an apartment complex in an attractive residential area (not ritzy, just avoid slummy neighborhoods), but the building should have obvious flaws—ugly exterior, ugly landscaping, poorly maintained pool area, whatever would turn prospective tenants off—which could easily be fixed. The idea is that if the neighborhood is nice enough, but the apartment building is unattractive, you may be able to buy the apartment building for a cheap price because it has a high vacancy rate. After you paint, landscape, and clean up the place, you will be able to attract tenants and improve the value of the building for sale.

Troublesome tenants and poor management are factors that reduce the profitability of apartment buildings for their owners. If you can find these types of apartments and solve their problems by kicking out the bad tenants and managers, upgrading the overall appearance, cleanliness and amenities, and possibly raising rents, you will increase profitability and add to the resale value of the property.

Apartment buildings are usually offered as investments based on their "cap rate" (capitalization rate). Normally this is around 10 but can vary widely in different parts of the country and under varying economic conditions. The cap rate is calculated by dividing the sales price of a property by the net annual income on the property after expenses. If an apartment building is selling for $300,000 and earns $30,000 a year after expenses, it is being offered for sale with a cap rate of 10 (300,000 divided by 30,000).

The cap rate relates to our discussion because a property may not be making much profit due to problems that you could fix. If the property is netting $30,000 in income, and you increase this to $40,000, then based on a cap rate of 10, the property is worth $400,000 instead of $300,000. A 33% increase in value.

Now look what happens with leverage. You buy the property for $300,000 with a $60,000 down payment, you spend another $30,000 fixing the place up, and you sell it for $400,000. Let us assume you also have other costs of buying and selling (sales commissions, loan fees, etc.) of around $30,000. So your net cash out after the sale is $400,000 - $240,000 (loan) - $30,000 (other fees) equals $130,000. You put $90,000 into the deal and came out with $130,000, so you made over 44% on your money.

Even though you are only increasing the sales price of the property by 33% (from $300,000 to $400,000), you are getting a 44% return on your money using leverage. If you reduce your down payment to $50,000, your net cash out equals $120,000, which is a 50% return on your money. The less money you put in (the more you borrow), the greater your leverage and the return on your investment.

The most crucial factor in apartment building investments is verifying the income and costs. The previous owner may fudge the figures, so be sure to use a good accountant to audit the bookkeeping before you buy.

Because real estate investing, like other investments, involves competing with other investors to find good deals, you may have to pursue some alternative approaches for striking gold.

Real estate options are contracts that guarantee the buyer the right to purchase a property at a set price within a given time period, if she chooses to exercise her option. Options are the ultimate form of leverage, not only in real estate, but also in the stock and commodities markets. But real estate options are much safer than stock options or commodities futures contracts, because real estate is a less volatile market, and real estate options contracts are written for longer time periods.

For as little as let us say $1,000 (there is no minimum), you could control as much as say $200,000 (there is no maximum) of real estate for several years.

Here is how it works. You approach a property owner with the proposal of purchasing his or her property at some fixed price, within a set period of time. "I'd like to purchase your house sometime in the next two years at your full asking price of $200,000. I don't have all the money for the down payment yet, and I don't know if I can get financing. But if you will sell me an option to buy it at that price at any time within two years, I will pay you the nonrefundable amount of $5,000 now."

If the seller agrees to that proposal, you have secured his legal obligation to sell you the property. Now you, for all intents and purposes, own the property for two years, without having to pay the mortgage, taxes, upkeep, or any other costs. You also don't have to worry about keeping it rented or dealing with tenant complaints. Your only concern is to purchase the property at the specified price, within the time allotted, and turn a profit on your investment. The option angle is a slick idea, but like no-money-down deals, it requires finding willing sellers and negotiating the unusual terms involved.

You must be careful when entering into options contracts because of legal pitfalls. It is important to record a "memorandum" of the option with the county recorder. This is a legal document that must be drawn up by an attorney familiar with the legalities involved. Under some options arrangements you may have trouble enforcing your rights, if the seller balks when you attempt to exercise your option and buy the property at the option price. Therefore, it is important to maintain legal protections.

You can also purchase your personal residence using a lease option. You lease a property with an option to buy. This is a good strategy if you don't have the money to buy a property right away, or if you want to try the house on for size before agreeing to buy it.

One investment idea is to look for properties with expiring options. When people lease a home with an option to buy, they often decide not to follow through, letting their option expire, worthless. If you locate them before this happens, you may be able to get a good deal and put some money in their pocket as well. To find such deals, advertise in the local newspaper: "We buy real estate options."

Let's say someone paid for the option to buy a house within five years for $100,000. Now four years later, it is worth $120,000, but they cannot afford to exercise their right to buy it at $100,000. You come along and offer them $5,000 for their option contract, and pick up the property for $15,000 less than it is worth.

A similar approach is to locate tenancies in common. When two or more people own a property as tenants in common, they may disagree on how to manage or dispose of the property. You may get a bargain buying out one of the partners, although you will then face the possibility of becoming an unwelcome partner in the deal. But if you have the force of personality and legal fortitude to pull it off, this may be an effective investment strategy. You can find such properties searching through deeds at the county recorder's office, where the title records will show joint ownership. Once you buy into a property, you can use legal means to force a sale.

A "deed" or "title" is a legal document that describes the passing of ownership of a property from one or more persons to another person or group. It is always necessary to consult with a title company or other legal expert to verify ownership on a property. The title to a property can get "clouded" by conflicting claims to a share in its ownership. If you become expert in this area you might make money buying properties by settling disputes over its ownership and buying out the claims of others.

Yet another alternative investment approach is tax sale redemptions. After a property has been sold in a property tax auction, the original owner still has a few months in which he can redeem the property. If the property sold for a low price in the auction, you may want to buy it via the previous owner. Get him to exercise his right to buy it back, in exchange for selling it to you, with a small profit for him.

If you are interested in becoming a full-time real estate investor, you might consider getting your real estate license. The most successful real estate investors I have known started out as real estate agents. The disadvantage of this approach is that in some states you are limited by certain legal restrictions in the way you participate in real estate investments. But as a real estate professional you would be among the first people to know when bargain properties come on the market.

There is really no replacement for experience in negotiating business deals. You can get a lot of ideas from books, but in the end you just have to go for it. There is an old joke that says that in every deal there is a sucker, and if you don't know who the sucker is, then you are it. That is a pretty cynical approach to business negotiations, but it does remind you to carefully guard your own interests.

In every deal everyone wants to come out ahead. The seller wants to get top dollar, the buyer wants to get a steal, and the agent wants to push the deal through and get her commission. Along the way there are always some compromises to be made on all sides. Just be sure to keep track of your own chips, and don't worry too much about the other person's.

Probably the hardest thing to learn about deal-making is when to pick up your chips and go home. It is easy to get to the point where you feel, "I have just got to have this deal!" especially when you are starting out. Even experienced deal makers can succumb to this temptation.

The best way to approach your first several deals is as a learning experience. Unless you are confident of getting the best possible terms, just let them go. You should approach these deals with great caution, in the hopes of gaining as much knowledge as possible without getting burned. You can always find new properties, new neighborhoods, new real estate agents, and new sellers. But you cannot easily escape legal and financial entanglements if you get in over your head. By taking the most cautious approach, you have the freedom to experiment and learn, without the fear of failure.

One key feature of any purchase offer you make is "the back door." This is a contingency clause that lets you out of the deal if unfavorable facts come to light later on. You can make your purchase "subject to inspection by a contractor," "subject to review by legal counsel," "subject to approval by spouse." Any of a number of contingencies can be written into your offer, including some that might apply right up to the last minute.

When you are looking for properties to buy carry a flashlight with you and peek in all the nooks and crannies. Look for cracks in the foundation, leaky plumbing, old-fashioned wiring, broken appliances, evidence of termites or rot, any sign of significant wear and tear.

One problem to be particularly careful of is hazardous materials or environmental hazards. Watch out for asbestos ceilings, ducting, and siding. Notice any conditions such as stored chemicals or old fuel tanks that may have leaked and contaminated the soil. Such problems, when discovered by authorities, always land on the shoulders of the *current* owner. The law does not care who originated the problem, since they may be long gone. Make sure that when buying a property the seller provides a written warranty against such problems, or at least gives full disclosure on them.

While investigating a property take a walk around the neighborhood and get a feel for things. Look over the neighbors' fences for nuisance factors in adjoining yards.

Once you have satisfied yourself about the condition of the property, go ahead and make your offer. Be sure you make your offer "contingent on inspection by qualified expert." It is well worth the couple of hundred dollars to get a good home inspector to go over the property. She will come in with an expert eye for problems, and can save you a lot of heartache or help you get a lower purchase price.

Remember that the rules of real estate deal making are flexible. There is a lot of room for creativity in writing agreements that protect your interests and create favorable terms.

Before making your offer or negotiating terms, try and find out as much about the sellers as possible. You want to know what they hope to accomplish. Do they just want to get rid of some headaches? Are they looking for a certain amount of cash, or would they rather take payments and not have to pay taxes on all the income at once? Are they looking for someone to really take care of their home? You want to offer reassurances that they are getting what they want out of the deal. This will make negotiations go much more smoothly.

You will also gain some leverage in the deal if you offer to move quickly. This indicates your seriousness as a buyer and will encourage the seller to be more flexible on other negotiation points.

Carefully determine the maximum price you would pay for a property, then offer a price 10 to 25 percent lower. You never know when someone might accept a low bid. As you negotiate, there are several factors you may adjust to increase the appeal of your offer to the seller: 1) the total purchase price; 2) the down payment; 3) the interest rate on the loan (if the seller is lending you money); 4) the length of time over which the loan will be repaid (if the seller is lending you money); 5) the length of escrow. This can be very important to some sellers. The faster you can close escrow and get the seller some cash, the more eager he may be to sell.

An "escrow" is an arrangement whereby a disinterested third party handles the disbursement of money in a complicated transaction, according to prearranged instructions agreed upon by all parties to the transaction. Real estate transactions are almost always conducted with the aid of an escrow company. There can be a long list of conditions that must be met before an escrow company will transfer funds between parties in a transaction. What goes into the escrow instructions can be an important part of negotiating a real estate transaction.

Sellers may loan money to help you finance a deal for two reasons: 1) they are anxious to complete the sale at the price you are offering; 2) they want to take their money in payments because under certain circumstances they can pay less in taxes (ask your accountant about "installment sales").

Wherever you can see tax advantages for the seller, point them out. If you have properties you would like to use in trade to purchase another property, be sure to discuss the tax advantages with the seller.

When you start shopping for a real estate loan, you will discover a large number of institutions that participate in mortgage lending, each of which has its own rules and guidelines. There are mortgage banks, credit unions, savings and loan associations, commercial banks, and loan brokers. Avoid loan brokers like the plague. They are seldom reputable, and there are endless horror stories associated with them.

At the various lenders you may qualify for special loans backed by government agencies including the Federal Housing Administration (for FHA loans), and the Department of Veterans Affairs (for VA loans).

Even though your mortgage financing costs are the most important aspect of your real estate financing, it can be complicated and confusing to nail down exactly what those costs will be. But the Truth-in-Lending Act requires that lenders cooperate in explaining exactly what those costs are.

You can start shopping for mortgages by looking up "Real Estate Loans" in the phone book. Call around to different banks and get the lay of the land. But first you should have the following facts in hand:

1) The price of the property.

2) The amount of your down payment.

3) The source of your down payment (the bank does not want you to borrow the down payment, thereby increasing your monthly debt payments).

4) The amount you wish to borrow (this is not always the difference between the price and the down payment, if the seller is financing part of the cost).

5) The term of the loan (5, 10, 15, 20, or 30 years). The interest rate on shorter-term loans is sometimes lower than for longer-term loans.

6) Whether you want a fixed-rate or variable-rate mortgage (FRM or ARM). More about this later.

Armed with this information, find out how much the banks charge for application fees, processing fees, points, and the interest rate on the loan. They will charge you something just for applying for a loan, and this is paid when you apply. In order to avoid wasting your money on this fee, try to prequalify yourself as much as possible. Talk about your income and debts, to discover how these will affect your eligibility. Most banks will not want your mortgage payment to be more than one third of your net monthly income after taxes.

The processing fee gets paid out of escrow—by you or the bank, if you finance it as part of the loan—after the loan goes through.

The points also get paid out of escrow, and may be paid by you directly or financed as part of the loan. The points are a percentage of the amount borrowed that the bank charges up front, on top of all the interest they will earn. It is like the money you pay on a cash advance with a credit card. "Two points" on the loan, means you pay 2% of the amount borrowed.

Most banks will let you put down 20% and will loan 80% of the cost of a house you will be living in (an owner-occupied property). But they will not always tell you that. They may give you the impression you would have to put down 30% or more, when in fact some lenders will allow you to put down as little as 10%.

How much a bank will lend on a property depends on the appraised value. The bank uses an appraisal to decide how valuable the property is, and therefore how well protected their money is, if you default on the loan. They hire an appraiser to go out and look over the property, comparing it with similar properties that have sold in the neighborhood, in order to figure out what it is worth.

If you head for a bank looking for a loan without adequate preparation, you may find yourself eyeball to eyeball with a "loan representative" trying to figure out what to specify as a down payment. If you offer too little, it may appear as if you cannot afford the house and should not be trying for a loan in the first place. If you offer too much, you get stuck with a bigger down payment, and you might not have enough left over for fixing up the house and buying furniture.

The best way to cope with this encounter is to come prepared. Spend a lot of time phoning around in advance and educating yourself on the qualifications necessary to get a loan. Ask questions until you are confident you know what you are doing.

If you can comfortably afford the payments on a 15-year mortgage, you may get a lower rate of interest. You will also save a lot of money on the interest that would have accrued during the second 15 years of a 30-year loan. A $100,000 loan for 30 years at 10% interest would cost a total of $315,925 in principal and interest. A $100,000 loan for 15 years at 10% interest would cost "only" a total of $193,428 in principal and interest. The payments on the 30-year loan would be $877 a month, and on the 15-year loan $1,074 a month.

Your monthly payment is quite a bit lower on the 30-year loan, but the interest rate may be higher and the overall cost of the loan is higher. However, you can make extra payments on it each year, to help pay it off early. Be sure to ask your bank about this when you take out your loan. You don't want a loan with prepayment penalties.

You are charged interest on the outstanding balance of your loan every month. Anything you pay over the interest portion of your payment reduces the principal amount on the loan. If you pay off the loan in 20 years instead of 30 you can save a lot of money in interest.

After the inflation of the 1970s, banks became more nervous about offering fixed interest rates on their loans. So they came up with adjustable-rate mortgages or "ARMs." With an ARM, a bank will occasionally "adjust" the interest rate it charges according to changes in the general interest rate market. Some banks use the prime rate of the Federal Reserve as the basis for their ARM rates; others use a different index. Regardless of the index used, if it goes up or down it can cause the bank to adjust the rate on its ARMs.

There are advantages and disadvantages to ARMs. The main advantage is that when you take out an adjustable-rate mortgage the interest rate is lower than on a comparable fixed-rate mortgage. If interest rates go down, your payments and interest costs on an ARM go down. On the other hand, if interest rates go up, then your payments and interest costs go up as well.

If you get an ARM, be sure it contains an interest rate "cap" that limits how high the interest rate on the loan can go. Your loan should specify the maximum interest rate increase that can occur within any one year, and a maximum increase over the life of the loan. But even with an interest rate cap, you might end up paying 13 or 14% interest on your loan. Ouch!

With a fixed-rate loan, you start out with a higher interest rate, and higher payments, but you have the security of knowing that your payments and your interest rate costs will not change. This is good if interest rates are generally higher in the future. This is bad if future interest rates are significantly lower.

If you think interest rates are low now, you may want to lock in a fixed-rate loan. In 1992, mortgage rates hit their lowest level in over 20 years. If you get an ARM, interest rates may go even lower and stay there. If you get a fixed-rate mortgage, interest rates may go up and stay there. It is a coin toss, and no one can give you the right answer. Don't believe experts who presume to predict interest rates, not even the President's panel of economic advisers or the chairman of the Federal Reserve can predict interest rates. You have to choose whatever you feel most comfortable with.

Some adjustable-rate mortgages have fixed monthly payments, no matter which way interest rates go. If you are not careful you may be *increasing* your loan balance, not reducing it. This is called negative amortization. In the early years of a mortgage, most of the monthly payment goes toward paying the interest, not paying down the principal. If interest rates go up, and your monthly mortgage payment is not sufficient to pay the monthly interest on your loan, the excess interest due on the loan will be added to your loan balance, resulting in negative amortization. Then you will be another day older and deeper in debt.

A "graduated payment mortgage" is based on the concept that as people progress in their careers, their earning power gradually increases. With a GPM you start out with low payments, even lower than an adjustable-rate mortgage. Your payments don't cover all of your interest costs in the beginning, thus you have negative amortization and a growing loan balance. Over the years your payments are gradually increased and eventually begin to cover interest costs and reduce your loan principle. A GPM can make it easier to afford a mortgage, but in the long run costs more, and adds the burden of negative amortization. Be sure to study the financial ramifications carefully before going this route. If you do choose a GPM, get a fixed interest rate. If you get an adjustable-rate GPM, the negative amortization could burden you with debt.

A "renegotiable mortgage" is similar to an adjustable-rate mortgage. With this beast you get lower interest rates and payments. The term of the loan is 20 or 30 years, but it comes up for renegotiation every few years. At that time the bank will change the interest rate on the loan, according to prevailing rates, and has the option of canceling the loan if it feels you are no longer creditworthy. These loans are probably not such a great deal, and you may be better off with an adjustable-rate mortgage. At least then you know the bank cannot suddenly cancel the loan (assuming you are keeping up with your payments).

A very popular mortgage these days is the "two step." Two-step mortgages are a new type that is fixed interest for the first five or seven years, then for remaining 23 or 25 years the interest rate is reset to a new fixed amount. The interest on the first step is usually a little lower than on conventional fixed mortgages.

A "balloon mortgage" is usually a short-term arrangement, often no more than several years. You make small payments on the loan, with one gigantic payment (the balloon payment) when the loan comes due. People have been known to get them without understanding how they work, only to lose their home when the balloon payment comes due. A balloon mortgage can be a useful tool when looking for flexible terms from a seller on an investment property. If you need time to collect a down payment, or you are planning to resell the property in a few years, you might arrange for the seller to finance a balloon mortgage.

To qualify for a loan on investment properties, you have to meet more stringent requirements than if you are borrowing for your own home. One rule of thumb is that banks will credit only from 50 to 75 percent of the rental income from a property toward making the mortgage payments. Any shortfall must come from your personal income.

Banks are reticent about lending money to individuals for real estate investment, especially after the savings and loan debacle of the 1980s. They will want to see a larger down payment, and clear evidence that you can meet the mortgage payments. The no-money-down books seldom talk about mortgage financing from banks, because they know no bank in its right mind would lend on a property where the owner has not made a down payment (although some of the books discuss ways of tricking the banks into making such a loan). The no-money-down books discuss endless ways of getting sellers to finance deals—loaning them your second home, offering outrageous rates of interest, inviting them to orgies, anything to get sellers to accept deeds of trust as part of the financing.

Your ability to finance real estate investment will depend on how much investment capital you already have available, or can raise from nonconventional sources (i.e., anywhere but banks). The greater your knowledge of alternative financing arrangements, the less cash you may need to finance purchases.

You will discover there are many useful methods for financing your purchases—as well as some that are pure garbage, possibly illegal, and which may have adverse tax or legal consequences for you or a seller (especially if he sues you for talking him into something that goes sour). Run any ideas you want to try past your qualified accountant or tax attorney. Remember, they get paid for being conservative. Do not let them rain on your parade completely.

To compare mortgage rates, here are some services that publish comparisons: HSH Associates, 1200 Rte. 23, Butler, NJ 07405, (800) 873-2837 or (201) 838-3330, or Gary S. Myers & Associates, 308 W. Erie St., Suite 300, Chicago, IL 60610, (312) 642-9000.

When you decide to sell your property, you have to switch hats. Most of the things that apply to buying a property, apply to selling a property. **Remember: buy low, *sell high.*** Selling high does not mean selling too high. You are just shooting yourself in the foot if you hold your property on the market too long because it is overpriced. There are many ways to enhance the selling price of your property.

The secret of making money is "finding or creating value." Presumably you went about finding value when you bought your property at a bargain price. Now that you are selling your property you need to apply the principle of creating value.

First of all, there are a lot of low-cost decorative ways of dressing up your property. Plant flower beds, trim the lawn and bushes, put on a coat of fresh paint, install new floor coverings, and generally clean and spruce up the place. This adds value and gives your property "curb appeal."

Next make sure you do an effective job of marketing your property. We don't often think of marketing as adding any value for the consumer, but this is not true. You are providing a service to consumers when you make them aware of your products and services. You can be helpful and friendly and avoid intimidating them when they have questions or are confused about the product you are offering.

You may help your buyers locate financing, or offer some financing yourself. You can take back a second or third deed of trust from buyers to help them finance your property; this may encourage them to pay a higher price. Lending money carries with it many of the same risks as borrowing money. When borrowing, you risk using too much leverage and not being able to keep up the payments. When lending, you risk not getting your payments, and having to foreclose on your borrower (which is no fun for you or him).

You should do a credit check on borrowers before lending to them. Have them fill out a standard credit application, available from a stationery store or your local real estate board. Call on all of their references and verify them. To some extent, you have to treat your buyers in the opposite fashion as you would want to be treated as a buyer. Make sure they put up a substantial down payment, have plenty of income, and a strong credit background.

Normally, when a property is sold through a broker, the seller pays the real estate agents' commission. Because you, as the seller, are paying their commission, even though you did not formally hire the buyer's agent, by law both your agent and the buyer's agent are working for you. Both agents have a fiduciary responsibility to keep your best interests at heart.

As a buyer, your agent is in some sense on the seller's side of the table. Even though you are confiding in him, he is also busy representing the interests of the seller (and his own interest in earning a commission). For this reason it may not be wise to fully reveal your intentions when making an offer.

When agreeing to list your property with a real estate agent, she will probably quote you her standard selling fee of 6% or so. You don't have to agree to that rate. There is no commission rate established by law, and it is open to negotiation. Your agent will probably have to talk to the manager of her office, but you should be able to get a lower commission rate if you push for it. The drawback of negotiating for a lower commission rate is that your property will not be as lucrative to sell as another property, and your agent may not work as hard for you. On the other hand a property that is worth more does not necessarily take any more effort to sell, and therefore does not have to offer a higher commission.

At $1 million a property would pay a $60,000 commission at 6%. At $800,000 a property would pay a $48,000 commission at 6%. Why not pay the $48,000 commission on the $1 million property, which is a 4.8% commission? You could save yourself $12,000 (that is, if you happen to be selling a $1 million property).

You could advertise and sell a house yourself, and avoid paying the cost of a commission. This seems straightforward, but to do it effectively you have to make a bigger effort to market your property. And you lose the professional legal advice that comes as part of the service of a real estate agent.

Once you become familiar with real estate transactions, you will discover they are not such a mystery.

A real estate transaction follows these steps, more or less:

1) A seller contracts with a real estate broker to list her house for sale.

2) A buyer makes an offer to the seller, usually contingent on his ability to secure financing.

3) The seller's real estate agent opens an escrow account, at an escrow company, on behalf of the seller. A small deposit of perhaps $1,000, that was submitted by the buyer with his offer, is deposited into escrow.

4) The buyer applies for a bank loan, orders the property to be inspected by a professional building inspector, and generally frets and worries over buying a home.

5) The seller orders a termite inspection (usually provided by the seller, but not necessarily), fulfills any other obligations agreed to in the purchase offer, and generally frets and worries over selling her home.

6) Somebody orders a title search from a title company (which may also be the escrow company, since both services are often available from the same source). The title company verifies that the seller actually owns the property, indicates whether there are any other claims against it, and provides title insurance guaranteeing that the new owner will hold legal title to the property.

7) The bank orders an appraisal of the property's value (everybody prays this is high enough).

8) The bank agrees to loan the money (God willing, since this is what the buyer, the seller, and the real estate agents are all counting on, to make the deal go through).

9) Closing day arrives. The escrow company collects a check from the bank, pays off the old loan, pays its own fees, pays for title insurance and title search fees, pays the real estate agents their commissions, pays inspectors and termite people and anybody else their money, and finally pays the seller anything that is left. The buyer probably does not get paid anything (unless he is one of those no-money-down hustlers, who knows how to take cash out of a deal), but he does receive the deed to his new property.

10) It's a done deal!

Real estate is an important wealth-building tool whether investing in your own home or buying income properties. Throughout this chapter I have stressed the importance of increasing your knowledge and understanding. But don't give up if you feel confused and the subject seems overwhelming. You don't have to have all the answers, or feel completely comfortable with what you are doing, to succeed at investing in your own home or other real estate. All you need are an understanding of the basics and the help of competent professionals to walk you through the legal formalities. You can easily apply these fundamentals to protect your interests:

- Take the time to look at a lot of properties in different areas and price ranges, to reassure yourself about the value of your investment.
- Make sure you understand the size of the down payment you will need.
- Finally, be careful not to take on mortgage payments you would not be able to meet in an emergency.

Most other aspects of a real estate transaction involve technicalities that should be readily handled by your real estate agent, the title or escrow company, and your bank.

CHAPTER TEN

Art, Gold, Collectibles, and Other Speculations

My life has been a laboratory experiment for the contents of this book. I have seen or done almost everything I have written about here. I wish someone else had been the guinea pig for more of these experiments. I am tired of egg on my face.

When inflation was raging out of control in the late 1970s, many investment advisers were recommending "hard-money" investments that should go up in price with inflation. Their logic made sense to me in my neophyte state of investment knowledge, and I bought gold, silver, diamonds, and real estate with the expectation that their value would have to rise with inflation. Somebody forgot to explain to me that high inflation is not guaranteed to continue. And my investments were overpriced, regardless of inflation.

This is how I learned that there are various items that are promoted as "investments," when they are really "speculations."

These include: gold, silver, and other precious metals; art, stamps, rare coins, antiques, baseball cards, and other collectibles; raw land, stock options, commodities futures contracts, foreign currencies, interest-rate-sensitive securities, famous documents, record masters, and more.

"Investment advisers," promoters, and scamsters would have you believe that these are solid forms of investment, guaranteed to make you a lot of money. In fact, most people lose money on these so-called investments. Never mind if they don't go up in price according to promise, the high commissions charged for buying and selling them can take a big bite out of your capital.

I distinguish between a speculation and an investment as follows: **investments produce income, speculations don't**. To make money from a speculation, either its market price must change, or you have to buy it at wholesale and sell it at retail.

Take real estate for example. If you buy a house and rent it out you earn income from the rent. That is an investment. The price of the house does not have to change for you to make money. You can buy the house for $100,000, charge $6,000 a year in rent, then sell the house in a few years for $100,000, earning income on your investment. Not exactly a great investment, but it qualifies.

Buying raw land, on the other hand, is usually a speculation, unless you can rent the land out for farming or some other use. There is no point in buying raw land that does not provide income unless you expect the price to go up. You are speculating that for some reason the price will rise. But why should it?

If you bought the raw land at fair market value, the price should go up due to the effects of inflation. That's not really an investment. That's just a way to beat inflation. In terms of the real value of money, you have not gained anything. If you pay $100,000 for a piece of land, inflation is 5%, and after a year you sell the land for $105,000, you have not increased the spending power of the money you originally put in. You have maintained its value against inflation, but you have not earned any real investment income.

Similar comparisons can be made in the stock market. When you buy a stock on a hot tip, because someone tells you the price is going to go up, you are speculating on a quick rise in price. Suppose one of your friends calls you and says that Goliath Industries is about to buy a little company called Pipsqueak Technologies. She says Goliath has already driven up the price of Pipsqueak stock, in order to acquire 5% of the company. She tells you to buy some shares now, and sell them when the price peaks as Goliath buys the rest of the stock of the company. This sounds like a sure thing and you buy $5,000 worth of Pipsqueak Technologies stock. Soon thereafter the management of Goliath and Pipsqueak announce an agreement to merge the two companies, issuing shares of Goliath stock to replace all existing shares of Pipsqueak stock. The price of Pipsqueak stock immediately drops through the floor as people rush to sell their shares. Nobody wants to trade his Pipsqueak stock for shares of big mediocre Goliath Industries, even if it includes ownership of exciting little Pipsqueak Technologies. Speculating on a quick profit in Pipsqueak Technologies stock thus proved to be a bad bet.

You were not investing in the stock to earn income from dividends, or from capital gains as the company grows. You were betting on short-term changes in the price of the stock, because of a speculative idea you got on a hot tip.

Indulge me in a quote from the dictionary, because it defines speculation so well.

Webster's Ninth New Collegiate Dictionary:

Speculation: "to review something idly or casually and often inconclusively," "to buy or sell in expectation of profiting from market fluctuations," "to take to be true on the basis of insufficient evidence."

I am all too familiar with the pitfalls of speculation because I lost a lot of money speculating many years ago, when I first attempted to invest. I paid too much money to buy a house, in the hopes that the price would go even higher. Instead, the bottom fell out of the real estate market. I started buying gold when it was selling for $450 an ounce. More than a decade later it was selling for less than $400 an ounce, and has never seen the price I paid for it again. Ditto for silver. I bought a gold mining stock on a hot tip, which eventually became almost worthless.

Every speculation has a "story" that goes along with it, that salespeople use to convince you to get in on the action.

Here are some examples of the kinds of stories you will hear.

Story 1: *The price of diamonds has to go up because the DeBeers company of London has a monopoly on most of the market. It controls the price and will always limit the supply so that the price goes up. It is in its best interests to support the price of diamonds, since it is the largest supplier.*

This is a nice theory, but it has not worked out as described. DeBeers has not supported the price of diamonds sufficiently to make diamonds a good investment over the last decade. I own a high-quality diamond that I have had for a *long* time. Someday I will have it made into an elegant ring for my wife, because no one has ever been willing to offer me what I paid for it.

Story 2: *The price of gold and silver must go up because there is a limited supply of these commodities. With increasing demand for them due to industrial uses and governments that use them to back their money, the price has to go up.*

Wrong again. The price of gold and silver, along with many other commodities, has fallen in real terms over the last decade.

Story 3: *Commodities futures contracts, or stock options, are a great investment once you learn my secret system for making money on them. Look at the proof of how I made money trading options. Here is a list of people I taught my winning system. They all got rich.*

This story gets told over and over in a thousand different forms. There are dozens of books and newsletters on these subjects claiming to offer unique methods for getting rich. People have to be really gullible to think these hucksters, out of the goodness of their hearts, are spending time writing these books and newsletters to make *other* people rich. If the systems work so well, why do these promoters have to sell them to make money? Why don't they just apply their own systems?

Of course, they always claim that they do apply the system but that they just couldn't bear to keep it a secret. They had to share their wonderful discovery with all the other needy people in the world. These guys are especially evil, because what they recommend does not lose just *some* of your hard-earned savings; it loses *all* of it.

Story 4: *The price of raw land in such and such an area is going to skyrocket because the government is putting in a new military base and all kinds of businesses will open up around it that will need land.*

• *Or the city is expanding rapidly in this or that direction and when the growth gets out to this area real estate prices will surge upward.*

• *Or we are building a fabulous recreation resort with all sorts of facilities that will attract second-home buyers like flies. Buy into the first phase of the project, purchase some lots, and you will be able to sell them at great prices.*

These and many more real estate stories are used to convince you to speculate on raw land prices. Enticing people to buy raw land is one of the oldest schemes around. But raw land is among the riskiest forms of real estate investment and should be approached with extreme caution.

Story 5: *Because the national debt and the federal budget deficit are so large, the government cannot afford to stimulate the economy with fiscal policy. The president and Congress would like to spend money on federally sponsored projects to stimulate various parts of the economy, but the excessive debts of the government will not allow them to.*

Since inflation has not been a serious problem, but the threat of a depression is, it is up to the Federal Reserve to apply monetary policy to prevent total economic stagnation, by lowering interest rates. They are "bound to do this" over the next year.

Therefore, bond prices will rise, as they always do when interest rates fall.

This is a fairly logical story to promote speculation on interest rates and bond prices. The problem is that nobody can tell one of the most powerful people in the country, the chairman of the Federal Reserve Board, what to do. And he or she is the one with the power to decide whether to set interest rates higher or lower. Nobody *really* knows what the Federal Reserve may decide to do next. Financial markets are always reacting to new decisions of the Federal Reserve.

So even though a simple logical argument can be made for why interest rates should go up or down, thus affecting bond prices, nobody knows for sure whether they will or not.

Story 6: *Problems facing our economy, government, and society will lead to inevitable catastrophe. Because of the budget deficit and government, consumer and business debt, the economy faces collapse, and everyone who does not listen to the advice in my newsletter will be financially ruined. Worldwide economic imbalances, historical social and economic cycles, government mismanagement and irresponsible behavior among corporations leave no doubt that we are all headed for ruin.*

There is a whole category of investment newsletters called "gloom and doom" that play on people's fears to get them to subscribe. These people generally have no clue about how to make money except by selling fear in their newsletters. They are always recommending speculative investment ideas. It does not matter that their recommendations don't pay off, because by the time people get wise and cancel their subscriptions, the guru has signed up some new suckers.

As a young man trying to understand the complexities of the investment game, I was rather gullible in my acceptance of what I was reading. I knew nothing about economics or investing, so it was easy to put grand theories over on me. An intelligent author can string together a series of logical ideas to make a story sound true, or a financial prediction sound plausible. He is not going to include the facts or arguments against his favorite theory, especially when he is trying to sell you something. But there is hardly any argument for an economic or investment truth that cannot be countered by a logical explanation to the contrary.

Skepticism is always the best policy, especially when it comes to spending your money on speculations.

The reason I did not simply include speculation as a subject of discussion in Chapter 11, "Avoiding Fraud," is that there are legitimate ways of making money on some speculations.

Take baseball cards, for example.

A baseball fanatic may find it fascinating to collect baseball cards and study the fascinating statistics of his favorite players.

He may also want to go to baseball card trading shows where he can buy cards for some of his favorite players from the old days, cards that are no longer printed and have become "collector's editions," which command higher prices. If he really gets into this whole thing, he may wind up becoming a baseball card dealer and setting up his own booth at the trading shows.

As a dealer he will constantly observe the buying and selling of baseball cards and notice the various prices people are willing to pay for some of the vintage editions. Some rare cards containing popular players will, of course, go for higher prices. The dealer becomes an expert on the market, familiarizing himself with the quality of the cards he trades in, and what they are "worth" among baseball card traders and collectors. From his position as a dealer he can recognize the difference between a "wholesale" price and a "retail" price. He has to, because in order to make money he must buy at wholesale and sell at retail.

In this case he is not speculating on baseball card prices. He is trading on the difference between the wholesale price and the retail price. He is a professional in the business, constantly watching prices, and never paying more than wholesale, or selling for less than retail.

An individual collector, no matter how dedicated, can never spend as much time as a dealer, familiarizing himself with the market and the prices of particular cards. If he does know as much as a dealer, then he must *be* a dealer. Because dealers know prices by constantly dealing in the cards.

Sometimes the price for a Hall of Fame player, let's say Babe Ruth, will go through the roof. This particular card may get "hot." Everybody wants it. A smart dealer is never going to buy this card, even at "wholesale." He knows that interest in hot cards waxes and wanes. Sometimes they are hot, sometimes not. He could get caught holding the bag if people lose interest and he cannot even sell the card wholesale. So he deals in these cards in a special way.

If a collector comes to him with a Babe Ruth in mint condition and offers to sell it, the dealer will question him about price. The collector of course wants top dollar and the dealer is willing to pay only way below normal wholesale, to protect himself against any big price drop. So he tells the collector to hang on to the card and leave his name and phone number. The dealer passes the word around to other dealers that he can get his hands on a mint condition Babe Ruth, if any collectors come looking for one. Before long, someone shows up, wanting a Babe Ruth. The dealer gets the word from another dealer. He calls the owner of the Babe Ruth and says he can unload at full market price, for a 25% commission, and so goes the deal.

As a dealer or a *serious* collector, you can make good money in antiques, art, gold, diamonds, precious gems, stuffed dingbats, rare stamps, classic cars, or anything else you can think of that people buy and sell. But it requires constant time and attention to understand the quality and market price of the items you are trading in.

As an amateur, forget it.

The only reason to get involved in any of these areas is if you want to buy something simply to own it.

You have lots of money and want to own a Picasso. Fine. Buy one. But don't think you are "investing" in art. You would only be deluding yourself. What you are doing is buying expensive art. And if you hope to sell it someday at a profit, then you are speculating on a price rise that may, or may not, occur.

Various speculations experience periods of extreme popularity that, in the investment field, are called "bubbles" or "manias." They call them manias when people go nuts over them. Prices will start to rise, and somebody notices and decides to speculate on further price rises. Then somebody else notices and starts buying. Then many people notice, and everybody starts buying in a frenzy, because the price rises so fast and so high, people spot an opportunity for easy riches. Then everybody owns a piece of the action. There is no one left to get in. Prices flatten out. And "pop," the bubble bursts.

Somebody sells because he or she needs money to pay a doctor bill. Then somebody sells because he or she got in early, has noticed prices flatten, and now figures the show is over. Then, somebody sells because prices are not only flat, but have fallen a tad. Then panic. Everybody sells and prices drop through the floor.

Among the most famous speculative manias occurred in Holland during the 17th century when tulip bulbs were all the rage. Collecting various types of tulip bulbs became popular during that period. Wealthy individuals took up the hobby and spent more money on tulips. The price began to rise. Eventually somebody noticed. Finally everybody noticed and some common folk put their whole life savings into a few tulip bulbs, in hopes of greatly advancing their fortunes. It was a sad day among the picturesque canals, dikes, and glorious fields of tulips in Holland when the bubble burst. So much of its credit was tied up in tulip bulbs, it almost bankrupted the country.

One quaint story from this era tells of a merchant who had his tulip bulb collection out on the kitchen table. The cook had let a hungry sailor into the kitchen to offer him food, while the merchant was out of the room. Thinking the tulip bulbs were onions, the sailor partook of a few; when the merchant returned he almost fainted at the sight of so much of his wealth disappearing.

I used the example of baseball card collecting to discuss the difference between collecting, trading, and speculating, because in the latter half of the 1980s, baseball cards became a hot speculation (translate: a new mania).

Speculative manias can make you a lot of money—if you get in when the first price rises begin, and get out before the newspaper carrier and your local barber get in. Actually the barber may get in early, since he hears all the news first.

But how do you know that when the price first starts rising, it will keep rising, and how far it will go?

You don't.

The price on famous pieces of art by dead masters has gone through the roof and on toward Mars during the last decade. These works have become so expensive that museums can barely afford to collect them. I say barely, because somehow museums still manage to pay astronomical prices, with the help of their leading patrons.

Sotheby's of New York, a leading fine art auctioneer, made a great deal of money on art during this period. It sells art by auction and earns a commission on whatever price it gets. But even its earnings dropped off dramatically in 1991, following a big dive in the art market.

Never trust a "story" when it comes to speculating on short-term price fluctuations of financial instruments like stocks, bonds, commodities futures contracts, stock options, currency exchange rates, and others. And never trust the storyteller. Every broker, promoter, dealer, or salesperson who advocates speculating has a story to convince you to waste your money.

If you are going to speculate on short-term prices, you had better be an expert and devote your attention to it full time.

For example, speculating on commodities futures contracts is very risky—even for experts. You might wonder why commodities futures contracts even exist if they are so risky. Why would anyone bother to create them if everybody just loses money on them?

Commodities futures contracts serve a specific business purpose for farmers, other commodities producers, and commodities buyers. They are a form of risk insurance. A farmer planning to grow a crop of wheat wants to lock in the sales price of his wheat now, rather than when his harvest comes in. If the price of wheat goes down in the meantime, he still makes enough money to justify growing the crop. Likewise a wheat cereal manufacturer wants to lock in the price, now, that she will pay for wheat in the future, because her company's getting ready to advertise discount prices on its "Tasty Wheat Flakes." She doesn't want the price of wheat to rise during the time her company is discounting the price of the breakfast cereal, or it could lose money. So the wheat farmer and the cereal maker get together and write a futures contract to guarantee the future price of the wheat they buy and sell. This is a simplified explanation of how this market works. Actually the two of them don't have to get together; they write the contract with a commodities exchange brokerage company, which buys and sells these contracts. It would love for *you* to buy and sell them as well, so it can give some of your money to the cereal maker and farmer, while pocketing commissions in the process. But steer clear of this high-risk venture for making a fast buck *or losing all of your money.* Better leave it to the farmers and cereal makers for whom it serves a realistic purpose.

The same goes for stock options. There may be a good reason for them to exist, but there are not many good reasons for you to invest in them. I cannot think of one. Peter Lynch, who headed the top-ranked *Fidelity Magellan* stock mutual fund for many years, says he has never bought a stock option in his life.

So don't bother investing in speculative financial instruments unless you really, really, really, I mean REALLY, know what you are doing. Have I said it?

When it comes to other speculations such as collectibles, stamps, antiques, gold, and precious gems, there are only two good reasons to fool around with them.

One is that you like them for personal reasons, and you know how to shop for bargains. You enjoy collecting expensive antiques. That is your thing, and you have the money to do it. No problem. Do your thing. You like gold, and make it into jewelry. You like gold coins, and collect them. You enjoy collecting stamps. These are all valid reasons for putting your money into this stuff. As long as you realize you are not investing.

The other reason to buy and sell such items is that you want to deal in them as a professional. You may be an experienced collector whose enthusiasm has developed to the point of making a profession out of it. Then you are a professional dealer who buys wholesale, sells retail, and speculates only as an expert who understands the risk. Smart dealers don't normally speculate. If they are unsure of the market value of an item, they will take it on consignment and sell it for a commission. But they may speculate occasionally, when they feel the market is really hot, and they are confident of turning a fat profit on an especially fine item.

The best advice I can give you on speculations is to treat them like a hot stove. Don't touch, or you could get burned.

CHAPTER ELEVEN

Avoiding Fraud

Americans lose billions of dollars to investment fraud every year. Con artists and fast-buck schemers trick both the rich and the poor out of their hard-earned savings. Every imaginable ploy is used to fool people into placing their hope, faith, and money into the hands of these crooks and scam artists. Not only people foolish enough to believe in get-rich-quick fantasies are taken in. These scams often revolve around normal- and legitimate-sounding investments.

Swindlers rely on human nature, our greed and ignorance, to weaken common sense and better judgment. They know that most people can be misled by the information and promises provided by salespeople. Their advertisements and sales pitches are filled with half-truths and insinuations to lure people into believing in false promises of easy riches.

Very little money is ever recovered from these crooks, even if they are caught. The best way to protect your money from swindlers is to make sure they never get their hands on it to begin with. Verify the legitimacy of any organization or promotional offering before giving over any money, including any deposits or upfront fees.

Most of the schemes perpetrated on the unsuspecting have been around for years and would be easily recognized by the Better Business Bureau or a local law enforcement agency. A simple phone call to a consumer protection organization might be enough to avert financial disaster.

A convincing salesperson can make an investment opportunity sound very exciting. When your heart starts racing and you see dollar signs everywhere you look, that is when the warning bells should go off in your head. Train yourself to be wary of that signal. Emotional excitement is what con artists use to defeat your common sense and better judgment. The biggest mistake people make with investment opportunities is failing to take time out and investigate the facts.

Salespeople know that if you have time to let your emotions cool off and think about their offer, you will see through the hype, and the facts may not add up. This is why they use high-pressure tactics to make you think the opportunity will be lost if you don't make a quick decision. That is a trap you can easily avoid with a little forethought and common sense. No authentic business or investment opportunity is going to disappear in a week. Give yourself at least a week to make some phone calls and investigate.

Most business and investment opportunities are legitimate. You can usually tell the difference because you are not presented with wild claims and unrealistic promises of instant wealth. Any legitimate enterprise should be able to give you a long list of satisfied customers. Contact others who have participated in the venture—preferably someone with whom you might be able to meet.

Remember, con artists run into a lot of skepticism. They are very experienced at countering your questions and objections. You need a strategy for defending yourself against their persuasive message. Watch out for phrases like "ground-floor opportunity not to be missed," "limited-time offer," "you have been specially selected," or "don't worry; your money will be completely refunded."

Con artists will play on every emotion—greed, guilt, fear, pity—to weaken your good judgment. Sometimes the only defense is to resolve not to give any money or sign anything without sleeping on it first. This will give you time to let your emotions settle down so that you can think more clearly.

Here are some warnings flags to watch for when considering a business opportunity:

1. Failure to answer questions clearly and thoroughly. Anyone who passes off your concerns and dismisses your cautious attitude is being unprofessional. A serious business transaction should always be conducted with complete communication of all pertinent facts.

2. Claims of minimal or zero risk are pure hype. There are always risks in business. Starting any new business is full of risk. Any claim to the contrary is false.

3. Unreasonable sign-up fees for a direct sales business. The cost of enrollment, sales literature, and enough product to start selling, should not be very high.

4. Extravagant claims of enormous profits should put you on the alert. If there is so much money to be made, then why is the promoter giving the opportunity to you, instead of keeping it for himself?

Psychologists have identified certain personality traits that cause people to become vulnerable to rip-offs. Beware of these traits in yourself. They include the following:

Many sophisticated investors have a "need to believe" attitude. They need to feel that they have discovered a special angle on investing that gives them an edge and ensures a high rate of return on their investments. This attitude sometimes obscures their judgment. Despite their experience and qualifications as investors, they fall into the swindler's trap.

Some investors are driven by the nagging suspicion that the high rollers on Wall Street are making all the big money and leaving out the little guys. This resentment makes them susceptible to the con artist who promises a "big win" with high returns.

Another type is the lazy individual who relies solely on the advice of friends or acquaintances. Rather than doing his homework to find a safe investment offering a reasonable return, this person is on the lookout for hot tips and inside angles. He becomes an easy mark for the dishonest promoter.

Some people are "perceptual" types. Instead of analyzing investment proposals and exercising their skepticism, they accept situations at face value—going by their perception of appearances. Con artists who talk a good line and put on a convincing show can pull the wool over the eyes of the perceptual type. A "smooth operator" will likely arouse the suspicions of an analytical and skeptical person, but a perceptual type is persuaded by this style.

People who are susceptible to hypnotic suggestion can be commanded to act against their own best interests. A Texas disc jockey once commanded listeners to make out twenty-dollar checks to the radio station. Thousands of listeners responded. The radio station was flooded with money—with no offer of a prize or benefit of any kind. With the proper command phrases or suggestions, a swindler can control the suggestible type. Afterwards they may be unable to explain their own behavior beyond a vague: "It seemed like the right thing to do at the time."

Impulsive people lack discrimination, act without thinking, and leap without looking. They are often jolted when they realize that they have been had.

Finally there is the chronic victim who refuses to accept responsibility for his actions, and places the blame for his misfortune on "bad luck" or other circumstances beyond his control. *Forbes* magazine reports that "sucker" lists get passed around by swindlers who *repeatedly* victimize these same individuals. Incredible.

Of course, no one is limited to a single personality trait. Several may appear together. But the same defenses against fraud are effective for any personality type they include:

- Use discrimination to understand and investigate all business and investment offers.
- Maintain skepticism at all times toward investment offers, especially claims of easy money or high rates of return.
- Trust the old saw, "You can't get something for nothing."
- Never sign anything or pay money without taking time to think it over.

The first rule of detecting investment fraud: "When something looks too good to be true, it usually is."

Swindlers and their victims are not limited to those of modest means or on the fringes of society. The "Gentleman Scamster," George Bissell of Palm Beach, was a rich member of Palm Beach's jet set crowd. Having inherited a fortune, he lived in style with his million-dollar home and fancy cars. Nevertheless, for four years he bilked millions of dollars from his rich friends whom he convinced to invest in exotic orchids and palm trees. He sometimes took his investors to visit these impressive crops. There was only one problem. He kept selling the same orchids and palm trees over and over again.

Financial planners make it easier for the average person to get advice on managing his or her personal financial affairs and making sound investments. Once available only to the rich, financial planners are now accessible to everyone. Nationwide, over 200,000 people advertise themselves to be financial planners. While most financial planners provide an honest and useful service, many unscrupulous people also work this profession as a scam. A December 1988 article in *Business Week* estimated that $500 million a year in losses due to fraud are attributable to "financial planners" alone.

Because anyone approaching a financial planner, or approached by a financial planner, has potentially large amounts of savings to turn over for "investment," financial planning is a profession ripe for the picking as far as many con artists are concerned. For this reason, extra precautions need to be taken in verifying the reputation and credentials of financial planners before entrusting them with hard-earned money.

Financial planning is a relatively new and loosely regulated field. Many financial planners are not registered with the Securities and Exchange Commission. Before working with a financial planner or giving your money to one, be sure to verify her credentials either with the Institute of Certified Financial Planners, Two Denver Highlands, 10065 East Harvard Avenue, Suite 320, Denver, CO 80231, (303) 751-7600; or with the International Association for Financial Planning, 2 Concourse Parkway, Suite 800, Atlanta, GA 30328, (404) 395-1605.

The deregulation of the financial services industry during the 1980s resulted in many new types of investments and services. With so many to choose from, it is hard to understand them all and evaluate their merits. It is also difficult to distinguish between the services offered by traditional institutions. Stock brokerage firms now sell real estate. Banks sell insurance. Insurance companies own brokerage firms. And department stores sell financial services. All of these firms offer their services under the banner of "financial planning."

The purpose of financial planning is to evaluate all of your financial needs over a lifetime. These include educating your children, insuring against accidents, protecting your health, supporting your retirement, owning a home, saving to achieve special goals, managing debt, and building wealth. A qualified financial planner should understand how to meet your needs in all of these areas and construct a plan that matches your circumstances. Your financial planner should be objective in selecting from the range of financial services available, and select only those programs that best fit your needs.

Unfortunately many of these so-called "financial planners" are merely salespeople for specific products and will sell those exclusively. Insurance companies will offer financial planning to sell life insurance, disability insurance, and health insurance. Investment brokerage firms will offer financial planning to sign you up for a brokerage account and their line of stocks, bonds, mutual funds, money markets, and real estate investment trusts. Many small financial planning firms have real estate limited partnerships, oil and gas limited partnerships, life insurance, and other products in their back pocket. And they earn a commission from any product they can get you to buy.

The financial planning associations work hard to maintain the level of education and integrity of their membership and the reputation of their industry. But they cannot police their whole industry, and irregularities are all too common.

One new approach, intended to eliminate conflict of interest, is that taken by the National Association of Personal Financial Advisers. Its members charge set fees for their services and don't earn any commissions from the investments they recommend. To find a member in your area contact the International Association for Financial Planning, 2 Concourse Parkway, Suite 800, Atlanta, GA 30328, (404) 395-1605.

There are actually three types of financial planners: those that design a financial plan and give advice for a set fee; those that earn a fee for advice, and commissions for selling products; and those that earn commissions only by selling products. Obviously with this last type, the potential for a conflict of interest is the greatest.

The Investment Advisers Act of 1940 states that anyone who offers to furnish advice on the purchase and sale of securities for a fee is considered to be an "investment adviser" and is required to register with the Securities and Exchange Commission. Investment advisers are required to follow certain rules regarding advertising, recordkeeping and the information they disclose to clients.

Registering as a financial adviser with the SEC is no guarantee of the qualifications of a financial adviser. Although the SEC requires statements regarding any criminal background of the applicant, there are no educational requirements specified and no testing given. Various states have passed laws that require investment advisers to be licensed and to meet testing requirements. These are sometimes administered by the various financial planning associations or the National Association of Securities Dealers.

Naturally every possible precaution should be taken to protect your financial assets and to ensure that you get reliable financial counseling and investment advice. A popular book to help guide you in financial planning is *Money Dynamics for the 1990s*, by the widely respected and acknowledged expert, Venita VanCaspel. But to show how rampant the problems are in the financial planning industry, VanCaspel herself was the subject of controversy in the late 1980s. Questions arose about her ownership interests in real estate partnership deals that she was promoting.

There is an endless variety of money scams cleverly concocted by swindlers to trick you out of your nest egg. Here are some examples to alert you to common themes.

Deferred Delivery

Beware of this gold and silver scam. The dealer offers gold or silver at a discount from the spot market price they normally sell at, even offering to forgo the standard commission charged by dealers. The catch is that the customer agrees to wait as much as several months for delivery. When the delivery date nears the dealer calls with an irresistible offer of monthly bonus checks if the customer will wait longer for delivery. The dealer starts sending checks amounting to a small percentage of the original investment, and few customers demand delivery of the gold or silver. All of these tactics buy time for the scam artists, while they continue to advertise their scam and trap more customers. Finally the whole thing collapses and the perpetrators disappear.

Sometimes the dealer will even convince customers to send in gold or silver "to increase their special advantages." The dealer then ships the gold or silver out to customers who have demanded delivery.

New Mining Techniques

Fortune magazine has reported on the proliferation of gold mining promotions in California and Nevada. Hustlers operating from banks of telephones call people up out of the blue to interest them in gold mining investments. Tantalizing their prospects with visions of skyrocketing gold prices, supposedly stimulated by oil shortages and inflation, they paint a picture of fabulous profits in the near future. Relying on news reports of major gold mining acquisitions by various companies, the promoters predict a new boom in gold prices. Descriptions of "new methods" for extracting gold are intended to mislead their prospects into thinking they would be investing in a special new opportunity. *Fortune* reported that some programs require an up-front investment of $5,000 and monthly payments of $150, for which the investors receive a "certificate" and "regular progress reports." These types of scams inevitably result in the loss of most or all of the investors' money.

Junk Gems

An especially difficult problem exists with precious and semiprecious gemstones. It takes a lot of experience to distinguish between good-quality, poor-quality, or fake gemstones, and many dishonest people will use this fact to take advantage. Various firms advertise low-quality gemstones as solid investments and lure people into thinking they are making a savvy investment in a "can't miss" opportunity.

According to one source, Americans spend over $100 million each year on poor-quality or fake gems and jewelry at prices far above their true worth. The Gemline Recovery Service, a consumer counseling division of American Gemological Laboratories of New York, says that honest dealers are outnumbered by junk-gem dealers, and the problem continues to increase. This is an area where people are especially gullible and is a rich opportunity for crooks.

The law is very weak in the area of prosecuting dishonest gem dealers. There is very little regulation over the industry, and it is hard to prove outright fraud. Gem dealers will often buy poor-quality stones at a legitimate gem and mineral show and then sell them over the phone at exorbitant prices. Generally these activities are legal, while at times bordering on the illegal, and unfortunate victims have little recourse.

To protect yourself when purchasing gemstones or precious metals, work with reputable dealers only. You can get the names of dealers from the American Gem Society, 5901 West 3rd Street, Los Angeles, CA 90036-2898, (213) 936-4367, and from Professional Coin Grading Service, P.O. Box 9458, Newport Beach, CA 92658, (714) 833-0600.

Keep the following points in mind when investing in gems:

• The market for precious metals and gems is volatile and you may not be able to sell your investment for as much as you paid for it.

• Resist all pressure to make a quick decision and hand over money, without first investigating the validity of any claims that have been made.

• Make the sale subject to professional appraisal and get an independent appraiser to verify the authenticity and value of your purchase.

• Be suspicious of getting a good deal due to bankruptcy, excess inventory, unusual market conditions, or various other persuasive arguments.

• Do business at established storefront locations, instead of through the mail or over the phone.

Commodities and Futures

The commodities futures trading business is very complicated, with new types of contracts being created all the time. Commodities traders and brokers themselves have difficulty understanding all of the different types of contracts and how they work. There are so many different types of commodities that are volatile in their price behavior that it is difficult to trade in them safely. Even expert commodities traders who have been trading for years lose their shirts from time to time.

The lack of complete information for understanding how all of the various types of commodities instruments work causes many brokers to be evasive about giving details. Because the brokers themselves often don't understand what they are working with, they cannot easily answer a customer's questions and may pretend to know more than they do. The brokers may have to deal with some lawsuits along the way for not completely informing clients about the investments. But they seem to accept that as part of the cost of doing business.

Many commodities brokerage firms continue to conduct business the same way year after year, bringing in new recruits as their older brokers get burned out, and bringing in new customers as the older ones go broke. This is literally how some firms make most of their money. Their employees never last long enough to fully understand what they are selling, and clients lose their money so fast the brokers have to constantly resupply themselves with customers.

Even worse, some con artists may not be brokers at all. In one instance two brothers in business together noticed the rapid rise in exotic fruit prices in the produce departments of many of their grocery store customers. Mangoes, papayas, guava fruits, and others were shooting up in price. When a supposed commodities expert from a Hong Kong trading firm approached the brothers with a contract for a new exotic banana about to come on the market, they thought it had great potential. They were sure that when these new bananas started to sell in a few months their "contract" would be worth a lot of money. They wrote a check for $15,000 to open a margin account. The brothers were very excited about the great play they were going to pull off, until they discovered that they had been had. There was no such fruit. The trader was a sophisticated con artist. There was no commodities contract. The money vanished without a trace.

Most people would not fall for such an off-the-wall investment idea from some guy out of nowhere. However, even well-known firms have promoted bad or even crooked deals. A major crackdown on dishonest traders in the Chicago commodities exchange took place in 1990, resulting in criminal prosecutions. If you cannot trust the traders right there in the exchange, you had better know what you are doing if you are going to trade commodities.

During prosecution of firms engaged in illegal or questionable trading in commodities, the managers often plead ignorance. They claim that salespersons have been acting without authorization. In many cases, this is probably true. A salesperson, seeing an opportunity for a fast buck, will convince a client to invest based on false claims and promises of big returns. High-pressure telephone sales techniques are used to convince a client to jump into the market "because the timing is perfect, a once-in-a-lifetime setup."

Real Estate

Real estate fraud is one of the most notorious forms of fraud known. Everyone has heard of stories about buying desert land, underwater land, choice Hawaiian property covered with fresh lava rock, and land that does not even exist. The complex paperwork and financing that go along with most real estate deals contain a treasure trove of opportunities for fraud and misrepresentation by hustlers and crooks.

One scenario involves homeowners attempting to sell their homes themselves, without the assistance of a professional real estate broker. It goes like this: A group of conspirators cooperate to create the illusion of making a sincere effort to purchase the home. Initially, a friendly buyer approaches the homeowner with typical questions about the home for sale: price, terms of financing, condition of appliances, upkeep, etc. The prospective buyer may even be accompanied by his "wife" and "children." Next, the buyer returns with a well-dressed "friend" who offers to help purchase the home. Tough negotiations ensue in which the buyer tries to get various concessions from the homeowner, creating the appearance of an authentic homebuyer. Other participants in the ruse are the "loan broker" who offers reassurances about the financing, and the "escrow company" where the buyer has requested that the escrow be handled.

All of the events surrounding the transaction are orchestrated to appear as if a normal real estate sale is taking place. Eventually the home seller is presented with a deed of trust by the "escrow officer," which, once signed, legally deeds away the property. This is the crucial event in the scam. Once the perpetrators have secured a signed deed of trust from the homeowner and registered it with the county, the homeowner no longer owns his home. At this point, the crooks may have taken physical possession of the house, and the former homeowner, now perhaps homeless, may win back his home only after considerable time, expense, and legal wrangling.

Once again, the key to avoiding problems of this kind is to investigate the reputation and credentials of all parties to the transaction. In one instance, the "escrow company" turned out to be nothing more than a local mail drop and an 800 phone number that was being answered from out of state. Any attempt to visit the offices would have revealed the fraud.

Another scam that has become popular is to offer money to "investors" in return for their cooperation in securing real estate loans. The promoters will buy a cheap piece of land and do some initial construction work to substantiate the existence of a development project. Banks are duped into making loans to the borrowers hired by the promoters. The promoters then pay a few thousand dollars to the "investors" in return for their cooperation and some initial investment funds. The promoters walk away with millions of dollars in loans payed out to purchase units in the development. The banks end up with a lousy piece of property and bad loans. The investors end up with a few thousand dollars and the responsibility to pay back hundreds of thousands of dollars on loans for worthless property.

There are numerous accounts of land that is advertised to be a vacation or recreation haven, when it is in fact worthless. No facilities, no lakes, no water, no horses or riding trails, not even any roads in some cases. The same lots may have even been deeded to more than one buyer.

One subtle technique used to dupe land buyers is to sell on a "contract of sale." The buyer makes a down payment, and subsequent installment payments, without taking title to the property. Usually, the buyers are unaware of the irregularity involved in this type of transaction, in which their purchase agreement specifies that they don't take title to the property until they have made all of their payments. If the seller goes bankrupt or disappears, the buyer has little recourse for establishing his claim on the property, particularly if others have contracted for the same parcel.

Keep in mind the following points to avoid being taken in on such deals:

- Inspect the property personally before paying any money.
- Use an independent appraiser to assess the current market value of the property.
- Use an established and reputable title company who can guarantee you clear title to the property.
- Make sure all moneys are handled by an independent bank or escrow company, and not by a private individual.
- Use an attorney familiar with real estate transactions to review all contracts and agreements.

Penny Stocks

Penny stocks are stocks that are not listed on the standard stock market exchanges but instead appear on the "pink sheets" in the over-the-counter market. They are called penny stocks because their price per share is often less than a dollar when they are first offered.

Penny stocks originate in initial public offerings of small companies with uncertain prospects. Sometimes these stock offerings are based on "blind pool" start-up companies. The "blind pool" refers to the accumulation of investment funds for an unspecified purpose. The prospectus provided states only that the company intends to invest the proceeds of the stock sale in the hopes of some return. It doesn't even have an established line of business!

Why would anyone invest in penny stocks? Because when some company invents a promising new product or technology, there is the possibility of that company growing from almost nothing into a huge success. All of the initial investors in a company such as Xerox or Apple Computer became fabulously wealthy from their investments. Many people dream of riding a start-up company to riches by investing in its initial public offering of stock. Unscrupulous "stockbrokers" develop elaborate telephone sales techniques for tricking people into believing that a particular company is about to be very successful.

A typical scenario is for a salesperson to call up out of the blue, on the pretext of conducting a survey. After gaining the prospect's confidence, the salesperson promises to call back if any good investment opportunities develop. A few days or weeks later the salesperson will call again and alert the prospect that a very promising situation is developing and to be prepared to act quickly if the situation gels. In a final phone call, the prospect is told that a certain number of shares have been reserved in his name. The broker would like to have reserved more, but they are going fast. The investor is then encouraged to buy these shares, which have been so generously reserved "exclusively for him."

The resulting investment is uncertain at best. Perhaps the investor will get out ahead of the game, if manipulators succeed in pumping up the price of the stock. But as likely as not, the stock will soon become worthless and stop trading on any basis.

One way to avoid getting taken in by penny stock hucksters is never to invest in *any* penny stocks to begin with. Fraudulent or not, penny stocks are very risky investments. Never accept telephone solicitations for investments, since invariably these calls come from less-than-reputable individuals.

Ponzi Schemes

The Italian immigrant Charles Ponzi is attributed with the invention of the scam that bears his name. In 1919, he devised a scheme of offering very high rates of return on money invested with him. His modus operandi was to pay money to early investors at the promised rate of return, using the money of newer investors. The enthusiasm generated among early investors was the best advertising available for signing up new pigeons.

Eventually his scheme, along with all "Ponzi" schemes perpetrated thereafter, reached a mathematical destruction point and collapsed. Ponzi schemes invariably involve huge amounts of money because they are so successful in duping their participants. This scam works so well that it continues to flourish, and there are always new Ponzi schemes popping up under different guises.

The Ponzi scheme is not hard to recognize because it always follows the same pattern of operation. Investors are offered a very high return on their investment within just a few months. When investors get a big initial return on their investment, they are encouraged to reinvest in larger amounts to achieve even greater profits. Appealing to greed never seems to fail.

There is always some secret investment formula the Ponzi operator promotes as the key to his program of success. The specifics of the formula are never important and usually don't even matter to the investors involved. What gets their attention is all the money the early investors seem to be raking in, and their testimonials of instant riches.

I am familiar with one Ponzi scheme on a firsthand basis. A group of my friends made the acquaintance of an out-of-town individual who sold them on a concept of "medical factoring." Medical factoring is apparently a legitimate business whereby medical practices sell their accounts receivable at a slight discount, in order to speed up their cash flow. This was the "story" my friends were given to explain the opportunity. They were told that doctors were actually foolish enough to sell their accounts receivable for half of what they were worth, and that a "gold mine" existed in reselling them to certain organizations in the financial community. Over a period of several months there was a great flurry of excitement among this circle of friends, as they unwittingly drew other friends and relatives into the trap.

Suddenly a dark cloud crept over the scene. Some of the investors were not getting the lavish checks they had grown accustomed to. The initial concerns and inquiries were soothed with calming explanations. A brief slump in medical factoring was occurring; only a seasonal phenomenon, they were assured. Within weeks though, the house of cards crumbled. Panic and quick action resulted in a series of phone calls and meetings which resulted in nothing. They had been duped. All the money was lost without recourse. In the case of some families, retired parents had handed over large chunks of their life's savings to be lost in this horrid scam.

The North American Securities Administrators Association estimates that the Ponzi scheme "now appears to be the biggest single fraud threat confronting average American investors."

Pyramids versus Ponzi versus Multilevel Marketing

Pyramid schemes are similar to Ponzi schemes, and sometimes difficult to distinguish from legitimate multilevel marketing programs.

The pyramid scheme is a program in which everyone involved is encouraged to sign up new recruits. The "chain of gold" pyramid scheme has become illegal in many states and is the classic example. A new recruit enthusiastically contacts all of his or her friends and relatives to entice their participation in a fabulous new way to make money. They are told to put up a nominal amount of money, perhaps $100, in return for which they will receive "thousands of dollars." But it is emphasized that it will work only if they can get "just a few other people to keep the chain going." Under no circumstances should they "break the chain" or the formula will not work.

Sure enough, those who work the hardest to build the pyramid beneath them are rewarded with huge amounts of money. They in turn flash this money around, and put a lot of it back into the pyramid to keep it going. The question arises as to how those at the bottom will profit, once the pyramid encompasses the total world population, which it will do within

32 levels growing by twos. The absurd answer always comes that "the pyramid just keeps going around, nobody would get out, once they find out all the money they can make." Unbelievable.

In recent years, pyramid schemes have been dressing themselves up with "products" to sell along with the scheme, and unfortunately this has created a lot of problems for the multilevel marketing industry, which offers legitimate business opportunities.

Stockbrokers

While most stockbrokers are essentially honest, they are in a peculiarly tempting situation. Stockbrokers make money from commissions for buying or selling stock on behalf of their clients. If they don't encourage their clients to keep busy buying stocks and, soon after, selling them, they may not do enough business. In fact many stock brokerage firms maintain systems whereby brokers are fired who don't meet the quotas.

This places customers in the position of being encouraged to trade in the stock market on a short-term basis. Short-term trading has been statistically proven to increase investment risk and reduce investment returns. Investment returns are reduced, if for no other reason, because frequent trades erode investment principal by paying out a lot of brokerage commissions.

Discretionary accounts permit a stockbroker to buy and sell stocks at their discretion, without requiring approval from the customer for any particular transaction. The potential for abuse under this arrangement is large because it can often lead to the "churning" of accounts. Churning refers to the practice of stockbrokers buying and selling stocks for the sole purpose of generating commissions. This practice is illegal but hard to detect, if the stockbroker is careful not to overdo it.

A stockbroker may set up many discretionary accounts, and when things slow down among his active customers, execute a few trades among his discretionary accounts, just to pump up his commission income and meet quotas.

A better approach to stock market investing is to use mutual funds, or invest through an adviser with an incentive arrangement. An incentive arrangement pays the registered investment adviser only a percentage of the total funds under management, on a periodic basis. Thus the more effectively the adviser invests the funds, the greater her fee, since any increase in the amount of funds under management automatically increases the fee paid.

Final Words of Advice

Building wealth through business ventures and investments can be a slow and painstaking process. It requires study, discipline and effort. Common-sense approaches to business and investment opportunities are usually simple and straightforward and will bypass any problems. Here is a final list of guidelines. If you will follow these, you will be invulnerable to all of the tricks, scams, hype, and cons you might run into:

- Do not listen to or participate in any business or investment offers received by telephone from unknown parties.
- Do not read or participate in any business or investment offers received through the mail.
- Do not allow any stranger to solicit you for any business or investment opportunity at your home.
- When you are interested in pursuing business or investment opportunities, seek them out on your own initiative. Deal with large firms with established reputations who have no complaints registered against them with the Better Business Bureau.
- Make sure you understand the proposition thoroughly and that only reasonable and realistic investment returns are offered.
- Refer to other chapters of this book for sound principles of business and investment that don't involve foolish get-rich-quick schemes.

CHAPTER TWELVE

Motivation and Success

The key to making money, becoming wealthy, and succeeding in life is to identify with the high level of potential that already exists inside each one of us. We are each a vessel of vast potential, made of the same muscle and bone, sinew and brain, as the geniuses who created all the treasures of human culture. Not everyone can achieve the brilliant leaps of intuition and insight of an Albert Einstein. But all of us can achieve much more than we think is possible. Like your parents and teachers, I urge you to "realize your potential." Not because you *should* be all you can be. But because you *can* draw on the potential within yourself to fulfill your dreams and achieve wealth—quality of life.

The principles of wealth-building which I have outlined in this book all depend on *you* for their success. Understanding the secret of making money and the wealth-building equation is not enough. Understanding the right approach to your career or business, or how to invest your wealth, is also not enough. You must take action. You must be motivated to succeed.

The main obstacle to direct action is despair of wealth. We fall into despair of wealth when our beliefs and emotions tell us that we are not capable of achieving our dreams.

Hopelessness and despair are not completely negative emotions. They help us bring an end to pointless effort. If you find yourself on a treadmill going nowhere, hopelessness and despair tell you to *get off!*

There is nothing wrong with feeling discouraged and deciding not to waste your time on fruitless activity. But if you give up on what you truly want out of life because you don't feel worthy of it, or you don't feel capable of achieving it, then you have given up something very precious. You may be giving up your heart's desire.

The decision to give up our dreams—accept our lot in life and bow to adversity—is the most profound decision we can ever make. It has the finality of the cell door slamming shut in a prison. It seals our fate. It is a decision that all of our past failures convince us to make, but it is an uninformed decision. The power of our own experience overwhelms belief in any reasoning to the contrary, and it draws a dark shade over our vision of reality and the future. We have to reinform our decision to fail. We must become properly informed about our true potential.

I always dreamed of living in a beautiful home in the country, where I could raise my kids in a wholesome setting, close to nature. Ten years ago I was living with my wife and baby in a cramped little apartment in a middle-class neighborhood of Los Angeles. I had a dream, but I saw no way of fulfilling it. If I had given up on that dream, I might still be living in a dumpy little apartment somewhere, wishing I had some money left over at the end of the month. Instead, I believed in the one thing I knew could make my dream a reality, my own potential for success. I knew that if I did not believe in myself and realize my full potential, I could never make that dream a reality.

You may feel that others are luckier than you, and blame your bad fortune for your failure to have all you desire. You may blame your own unworthiness, perhaps even hating yourself for who you are. Or you may blame the injustice of the world in which you live, feeling that others have conspired against you to thwart your needs and desires.

All of these attitudes revolve around who you think you are as a person. They are forms of negative self-imagery that sap your strength and lead to despair of wealth. Our level of self-confidence and our will to action are directly controlled by our self-image, how we see ourselves, who we think we are, how we feel about ourselves.

I grew up feeling like an outsider. My parents were raised in poverty and suffered from low self-esteem. They passed that same low self-esteem on to me. It was always difficult to view myself as worthy or worthwhile. There were many things I was unwilling to attempt in life because I felt like a failure. It seemed futile to ask for what I could never hope to have. I was shy and afraid to put myself forward in social situations because I "knew" nobody found me attractive, or was interested in me.

All of this discouragement about myself, who I was, and what I could get out of life was based on self-image. The message of low self-esteem, which arises from our subconscious and unconscious, is the message of failure. It says that we are unable to achieve our goals, that we lack the necessary qualities to be successful. And this message colors all of the difficult challenges we face in our lives. If you see yourself as a failure, you will fail. You will never try hard enough to succeed. Or you will avoid the spotlight so you are not noticed and can never be rejected for who you are.

Money, wealth, and success come from others. Unless you are a thief or a robber, you don't get money by taking it. You get it because someone wants to give it to you. That means you have to have something of value to exchange. That can really put your self-confidence and self-esteem on the line. You have to consider what you have to offer.

Many of us don't feel we have a whole lot to offer. This can be a vicious cycle that is carried on our whole lives. The less we feel we are, the less we are willing to become. Without valuing and accepting ourselves for who we are, we are discouraged from applying ourselves to become more and greater. To believe in what you are is also to believe in what you can become.

People who become great are not rejecting who they are in order to become someone better or greater. Great people believe in themselves and are excited about what they can accomplish with their lives. It's kind of a paradox. To *become* great, you have to believe that you *are* great. You have to love and accept yourself enough to give yourself everything you want and deserve.

The human potential movement and its motivational speakers and authors often focus on low self-esteem and the negative self-image many people suffer. The standard solution to these obstacles, which bar the path to success, is to attack the attitudes, "false beliefs," and misperceptions which contribute to negative self-imagery. Low self-esteem is portrayed as simply a false self-image to be replaced by a new and better self-image, which can be created by new beliefs.

Despite the popularity of this approach and its appeal of offering a quick cure for a lifetime of negative self-imagery, it suffers a fatal flaw. It fails to acknowledge our modern understanding of how the brain and mind actually work.

The brain does not need the conscious mind to "tell it" what is happening, it gathers facts on a much more basic level. You cannot simply tell yourself to be self-confident, to value yourself, to believe in yourself, in your dreams, and your future. Stewart Smalley, the "Recovery" addict on *Saturday Night Live,* is forever repeating affirmations to himself, "I'm good enough, I'm smart enough, and doggone it, people like me." There is something futile and pathetic about this shallow ritual.

The conscious mind participates in only a small fraction of the information processed by the brain. Modern psychology has repeatedly proven that the unconscious mind records reality as vivid snapshots of every moment. The conscious mind filters or processes that reality through the mechanism of repression, to make a more acceptable "reality."

The motivational speaker is basically telling you to reinforce the mechanism of repression, which is natural to us all, and replace negative perceptions with positive imagery—a brighter outlook.

This technique is doomed to failure because it pits the conscious mind against a lifetime of unconscious meaning and memories stored in the brain. This creates a kind of warfare between what the unconscious mind *knows* is true, as a result of the actual experiences that the brain has recorded from the senses, and what the conscious mind *says* is true, through the use of affirming, optimistic thoughts and images.

Low self-esteem is the product of our upbringing and education; it is the experience our brain has recorded with every failed effort of our life. Wherever we did not find the resources within ourselves or from the support and encouragement of others to overcome obstacles, our brains recorded that as a failure. A failure of ability. A failure of possibility. A fact of reality, and a limitation of our opportunities.

All of this experience of failure was not a measure of our aptitude or potential; it was a record of our personal experience, what happened to us, what was. Positive attitude and affirmations will never reprogram all the experiences of failure recorded in the unconscious.

You can drive yourself crazy if, every time you feel bad about yourself, you try to replace the bad feelings with some nicer idea of who you are or should be. Trying to take on some new bubbly upbeat kind of personality, as a replacement for whatever you are now, is a waste of time.

The secret to conquering low self-esteem requires the courage to face up to who you are. To hold yourself in high esteem, you have to believe in yourself. What you have to do is prove to yourself, one small step at a time, that you are becoming the kind of person that can accomplish the goals you have set for yourself.

A neurosurgeon does not walk into a brain surgery operation telling herself, "I know I can do this; I just know I can." She proves to herself through past experience that she can do it. She does not tell herself she can do it, she *knows* she can do it.

And you know you can drive a car, balance your checkbook, cook a nice meal, dress yourself in the morning, keep up a lively conversation, play music, paint a picture, help a friend. These may be challenges yet to be overcome for some people, but most people are reasonably capable of functioning in ways that seemed almost impossible to them as young children. And they acquired their abilities only one step at a time, piece by piece.

That is where self-confidence comes from, and that is how you raise self-esteem and build self-confidence. Break big tasks into little ones that you can succeed at, gradually overcoming greater and greater challenges until the big ones are not so big, and you can manage them.

Begin with simple achievements, something you could not quite bring yourself to do before, but that is not too hard. Clean up that closet that has been nagging at the back of your mind, wash your car, plant that flower bed, read a chapter of that book that has been gathering dust. Then brag about it to yourself, and give yourself a big pat on the back. See whether there is a small reward you feel in the sense of accomplishment, the way it lifts your self-esteem, the way you feel better about yourself.

Keep doing this until you get results. Do not give up when you fail. Just remember you are unlearning a program of failure and learning a new program of success. And the new program is to make that one fundamental and most profound choice: to believe in your dreams and to follow them. The new program is to push out the boundaries of your knowledge, abilities, and self-confidence, a little bit more each day.

Work at all the little challenges that you keep stumbling over, one at a time. And keep experimenting with them until you start to feel a little better about yourself. Low self-esteem is not just an idea; it is an emotion. And to change that feeling you have to recognize it, not cover it over. Be careful of the motivational speakers and success stories that hype you into a frenzy one day and lower you into a depression the next. You can mask your feeling of low self-esteem so that you do not recognize it, but it will still be there in your subconscious, programming your actions for failure. You are better off if you can recognize that feeling. Become more familiar with it and how it controls you.

Then begin to chip away at it a little at a time, with small successes, little achievements that dispel the message of failure. Experiment with success and find out what helps to motivate you toward it. When do you feel good about yourself? What gives you the courage and the inspiration to go on and meet new challenges? Become resourceful and use whatever tools you can find to help you. Sometimes a friend can give you the sympathy and encouragement you need to go on. Sometimes just doing something nice for yourself as a reward can encourage you to take the next step. But you have to constantly expand the boundaries of your achievements. Once you overcome one challenge, up the ante and move on to the next. Continue to test yourself and your abilities to discover a new level of self-confidence, self-esteem, new ability, new knowledge. This is how you gradually transform yourself into the kind of person who can achieve his or her dreams.

Don't try to take on too much all at once. If you dream of becoming a movie star, and then try calling the studio president and ask for an audition, you are setting yourself up for failure and rejection. If your dream of becoming a movie star is the mountain peak, realize you cannot bound to the top in one giant leap. Instead look for the bottom of the mountain. Use the top to show you in which direction to head, but start out by heading for the bottom. Where does the climb begin? The journey of a thousand miles starts with one step, says the book of ancient Chinese wisdom, the Tao Te Ching.

I once heard an interview with Madonna in which she was asked what she thought was the secret of her success. Her response was, "Believe in your dreams." Whatever you may think of Madonna as a personality, she *is* successful. Not just a little bit successful. She is fantastically successful. She has done outlandish things in her career and produced a lot of negative publicity. But she continues to believe in herself and what she is doing, and to succeed at it.

If you follow your dreams they may not come true. But if you don't follow your dreams they will certainly not come true.

It is difficult to get access to the intimate lives of those whose stories would prove that success is possible for anyone, regardless of the adversities of their lives. You can read inspiring stories in books and magazines, and see successful people on television. But the details and the reality are never communicated as directly as our own every day, moment-to-moment experience.

The way to reinform your experience, your own vivid daily reality, is not to gaze in the distance at the faraway lives of others who may have succeeded. The way to reinform your own experience is to succeed one day at a time, one step at a time, until it becomes a rock-solid foundation for your own success.

The excitement of the human potential movement is that there is no limit to what one person can accomplish. This has been proven again and again by people who have confronted and surmounted the most difficult challenges imaginable.

Helen Keller was deaf, dumb, and blind. She lived like an animal until a brave woman took her in hand and taught her to communicate. Eventually, Keller wrote her autobiography and became internationally famous as a symbol for human potential and the challenges the human spirit can overcome. Our individual potential is unknown to each of us, a mystery blocked by the negative messages of failure and uncertainty we carry around in our subconscious.

I am an information systems consultant and I am fascinated by studies of how the brain works. What excites me the most as a computer professional is that I own the most powerful computer ever built—my own brain! You may take your brain for granted, since you have had one all your life. It may not seem like such an amazing device when you forget someone's name or phone number, or you can't find your car keys. But your brain has the same power to think, imagine, and create as Einstein, Michaelangelo, Madame Curie, Confucious, Mozart, or other brilliant men and women of history.

The key to appreciating the power of your own brain is putting it to use. It does not matter how powerful a computer is, if you don't tell it what to do and push the **GO** button, not much happens. The more you exercise your brain for every type of activity—thinking, imagining, doing—the more it will accomplish for you.

The brain thrives on accomplishment. It is an ultra-powered, 24-hour, one-million-achievements-per-second success machine. The brain is a super robot slave to thousands of goals it must accomplish every few seconds. To do this the brain starts with a goal. It controls a set of actions which can achieve that goal. And it continually measures its success by matching the outcome of its activities against the goal to be achieved. It uses your bodily senses, memories of past successes and failures, and its built-in programming to tell it how close it has come to achieving its goals. The brain contains an automatic feedback system for achieving success.

When your mind sets a goal for itself, and your self-esteem says, "No, forget that one, I have already failed at that," the system for achieving the goal has been short-circuited.

Now here is where positive thinking and positive action really work. If you set a goal for yourself, and you frequently reaffirm that goal in your mind, then the subconscious and the unconscious will keep adding it back to your agenda.

The point that all of the positive thinkers and motivational speakers miss is that the mind votes on the agenda at hand. If one goal conflicts with other goals that have a higher priority, then the first goal is always relegated to the back burner, put on hold. Your dreams, your self-esteem, and your habits convene a meeting, and your dreams get voted down.

Your habits are the path of least resistance, all the ways you have already succeeded, and all the ways you already know to enjoy your life. There is nothing wrong with habits; you just need to continually create new and better habits which will vote with your dreams, instead of with your low self-esteem. By raising your self-esteem, you encourage it to vote with your dreams as well.

Continually reaffirm your dreams and goals and take positive steps toward achieving them. Every time you do this, you are making a statement to your subconscious and unconscious mind that you are serious about success. The subconscious and unconscious are where the unlimited potential and genius of every individual are locked away, waiting to be unleashed.

We are all geniuses—every one of us. We all arrive with pretty much the standard options. Some may have a few frills thrown in with the package but that does not matter much, overall. The main difference between us is not genetic, it is not what we are born with; it is software, the programming. We are programmed by our experience to fail. Our self-image, or self-esteem, is programmed from the earliest age with proscribed limits, limits to our knowledge, our abilities, our possibilities, our potential achievements.

It is not as simple as "You are what you believe. Just affirm what you want and it will happen. Just say yes." We are all programmed in infinite ways to be who we are now and where we are now. You cannot reprogram all of that by thinking, "Now I am a terrific person, and I will say and do whatever I want, because I believe in myself."

Instead, you have to set a new agenda and reprogram yourself to accomplish it one step at a time, one day at a time. Sit down and evaluate what you want from your life, what you enjoy, what you desire, what you want to escape, where you want to go, who you want to be. Then look for the foot of the mountain. Where is the first foothold? Where do I take the first step? Build your self-esteem gradually by taking on small challenges and overcoming them one at a time. Do not try to convince yourself that in six months you are going to become a movie star or a millionaire, and then when six months rolls around, downgrade your self-esteem by adding another failure to the list. Start with small accomplishments and gradually build your self-esteem to the point where you know you can make your dreams a reality.

No brain surgeon ever said, "This is it. Today's the big day. I've thought about it long enough. I'm just going to go in there and operate." That would be a disaster. What the surgeon did was start out in high school emphasizing science in his coursework. In college he took premed and learned to cut up frogs. In medical school, he cut on cadavers and watched operations. As an intern, he helped with operations and began to do simple procedures. Gradually, he proved to himself what he was capable of, building his self-confidence and self-esteem, until one day he just knew he was ready. And eventually, the day-to-day brain operation was not even a challenge anymore. It was just a job, just a matter of course.

That is how it is for anyone, no matter how successful she or he has become. She or he slowly programmed themselves to fulfill a potential that was always there.

We all have habitual ways of behaving, patterns to our lives that repeat themselves, over and over. Habits are formed through repetition. An action is performed over and over until we don't even have to think about it. It is just automatic.

When we need to change our habits, the way to do it is by replacing old habits with new ones. This means consciously acting in a new way despite old habits. The easiest way to do this is to perform the new habit over and over again, until it begins to happen automatically, and the old habit just falls away.

Some old habits are very difficult to break because they involve addictions or pleasures which we don't really want to give up. Smoking is a good example of that kind of habit. Because it is a drug addiction, smoking requires more than just new habits. Ultimately what it takes to quit smoking is tremendous willpower and the conviction that it is a habit too dangerous to continue. A lot of bad habits are like smoking. They have to be seen for the self-destructive effects they have on our lives before they can be tackled and broken.

It is not a good idea to try and clean up your life all at once. A list of New Year's resolutions is almost guaranteed to fail in the first week. It is much more effective to take on your bad habits one at a time and replace them with better habits.

If you are in the habit of dropping in for a drink with the gang every Friday night after work, do not decide to stop by saying, "I will not go for a drink on Fridays anymore" and just go home to mope. Think of something new and better to do with your time on Friday afternoons. Find a friend who likes to work out, and start going to the gym every Friday afternoon. Or find a friend who likes to go to the movies, and make every Friday night movie night. Create a new habit to replace the old one. In no time at all, people will stop asking you out for drinks. They will remember that you have a new routine. And you will not even think of heading for the bar, because you will have become so used to heading for the gym or the theater.

If you want your habits to vote for success when your mind convenes a meeting, establish habits for success. If you are in the habit of reading at bedtime, read for education, not just romance novels and science fiction. Read books on topics that will further your goals and enhance your knowledge of yourself and the world you want to live in. If you like to watch TV, check out some educational videotapes from the library or watch educational television programs. Do something that will enhance your perspective on things that interest you, things that are relevant to your success. If you like to take long drives, or you have to commute to work, and you are in the habit of flipping on the radio or playing some music, keep some instructional tapes in the car and listen to them part of the time.

To establish new habits, we sometimes have to change our environment. If you are trying to start a new business, do not work on it in the same room with a TV. Television is a time vampire. It will suck every bit of free time and creativity right out of you, if you let it. Instead, clear out a special corner in a bedroom or the garage where you can get organized, and set up a little space for your business where you keep all of your books and papers. Make it comfortable, with good lighting—a place to sit, think, and work, in peace and quiet.

There are many different ways to create a setting for new habits and success-oriented activities. If you live in a noisy home, get out and take a walk and think. Make a habit of it. Do it every day for fifteen minutes at the same time. Walk around the block and review your day. Daydream about what you want to accomplish in the future, and wait for new ideas and strategies for success to come. Whenever you feel frustrated or stuck, try changing the scenery. Never just stay in one spot and beat your head against the wall.

Creating new habits can be difficult and frustrating. It requires effort to break out of old patterns and replace them with new and better ones. It will not work to just want to change; you have to put it into action. The most common cause of failure in life is the refusal to take action. You must learn to convert your *desire* to change into concrete *action* for success. It requires effort to take those first few steps to change. Habituate yourself to success, to a new way of being. And every challenge you overcome, every bit of progress you make, should be celebrated and used to raise your self-esteem, as a vote of confidence in favor of your dreams. Fortunately your success does not depend on just effort and hard work. It also depends on powerful forces in your unconscious.

The unconscious mind is where the brain does most of its work. It is like the research department of a corporation. Nobody else in the company really knows what goes on there, but every now and then it tosses out a great new idea. The principle of goal setting, and steering your way to the goal, relies on the automatic problem-solving skills of the unconscious mind. But the unconscious needs plenty of raw materials to work with. Just like a research department—which needs money, talent, laboratory equipment, and a mission—the unconscious mind needs you to set goals for it and feed it information.

The unconscious mind is an information-processing, skill-building genius. It can learn how to speak without any formal training. All it needs are the raw materials of a lot of conversation and it will gradually catch on and pick it up. The same thing is true for learning success. If the unconscious mind is given a mission for success, if it is told what your goal is, what your dreams are, what you seriously intend to achieve, it will guide you there. If it is fed the raw materials for creating your success, and the knowledge and experience necessary to solve the success problem, then it is surefire. Your unconscious will manufacture success. It will guarantee it.

All great thinkers can tell stories of where their greatest ideas came from, sometimes appearing in dreams or flashes of inspiration. They understand the power of their own minds, and of their unconscious, to solve problems. They learned to trust these tools and to rely upon them for their most important work.

One of the amazing things about the brain and unconscious is their ability to do some of their best work when you are relaxing and not concentrating. There is a rhythm to personal growth and achievement that sometimes requires great concentration and activity, but at other times needs relaxation and repose—time for the unconscious to work without demands from the conscious mind. That is why we sleep at night, and why it is so important to relax at times during the day and just let your conscious mind drift.

In order to use the power of the unconscious to its fullest, you must know who you are and what you want out of life. You must come to grips with how you feel about yourself and how this affects you subconsciously and unconsciously. Low self-esteem and shame are the most destructive feelings we have, and these are the greatest emotional obstacles to personal success. The most disturbing psychological condition that accompanies low-self esteem and shame is disintegration of personal identity.

The more things we dislike about ourselves, and the more things we want to disassociate from about ourselves, the more our personal identity disintegrates. We become vulnerable to the thoughts and opinions of others because we don't trust ourselves. We seek out qualities outside ourselves, and try to identify with them, and to disassociate from our own qualities. In the worst case, we forget who we are, and become identified with what we are not, or sometimes with nothing at all.

If we don't like the way we look, we listen when someone says, "You really shouldn't wear your hair like that; it doesn't become you." Suddenly we are in a quandary about how to wear our hair, and it gets worse when we ask for suggestions and everyone has a different opinion. We end up wanting to please everyone else, because we cannot please ourselves.

If we don't trust our ideas, we are afraid to have any ideas. We are afraid to share our ideas, and if anyone questions them, we collapse in self-doubt.

If we don't trust our behavior, we feel guilty when our actions are challenged or criticized, and perhaps we begin to analyze all of our behavior, constantly trying to improve it to please others. We no longer have just one person to please, ourselves; we have a whole group of people to please. And they all have different ideas of what is acceptable.

By rejecting our own qualities, and fishing around for new qualities that would satisfy the inconsistent opinions of others, our identity—who we are—fragments and disintegrates.

Personal identity is what makes us whole and gives us purpose. Personal identity is a singularity of thought, action, and purpose that is integrated and consistent with who we are and what we want. Personal identity is everything that makes us "us." Personal identity is the bedrock of life. It is the core from which all of our beliefs, attitudes, choices and actions emanate. If we are weak in our personal identity, then all of our goals and actions will be weak. To be successful, you must integrate who you are with what you do and whom you intend to become. A strong personal identity, a clear sense of purpose and personhood, and a deep sense of meaning and selfhood are essential to success in life.

Whether you like it or not you have to accept yourself. Nobody really has a choice in the matter, because, as the old saying goes, "In the end, you are all you have got."

If you are not sure of yourself, if your looks are not quite good enough, if you don't think you are so smart, if your speech and movements are not graceful, if you feel like a twit instead of a wit, then remember, the person you need to love you the most is you. No one is better equipped to do it than you. No one knows you better than yourself. No one knows what you need more than you do. And if you cannot love yourself, why the hell should anyone else?

Integrate yourself by accepting yourself for who you are and where you are. You don't have to like it, but you do have to love it. Give love to yourself, to nurture yourself. This is not "selfish." This is your most important job in life—looking out for number one. Lucky children have good parents and friends who love them and who look after them. But as we grow up we gradually take responsibility for our own lives. If our primary care giver, us, is not doing the job, who is going to?

The secret to accepting yourself for who you are is in discovering that people like you more when you are yourself. Nobody likes a phony. Nobody trusts a phony. We have a kind of sixth sense that we develop for recognizing sincerity or authenticity, and we get very nervous when it registers falsehood.

To be yourself, to maintain personal identity, you must know yourself.

When you have thoughts, ask yourself, "Are these my thoughts, is this what I truly believe?" And see how it feels. Does it feel "right"? Is that "you"? Is that what feels right for you? When you act, consider whether you are acting for yourself, or in the interests of others. If you are acting for others, that is OK, as long as you know that is what you are doing and want to do it. But if you are doing it just to please others, in order to gain acceptance, then you are giving up on yourself and your personal identity.

Establish a boundary or perimeter in your mind around who you are and what you stand for. You are not going to offer any more excuses for who you are or what you do. You are who you are and that is it!

Stand up for your right to mediocrity, your right to laziness and sloth, your right to be a slob. Or stand up for meticulous cleanliness, if that is your thing. Do your own thing! Be who you are and be proud of it.

A strong personal identity makes it possible to empathize with others and develop rapport. If you feel confident about who you are and where you are headed, you don't feel threatened by the attitudes and problems of others. You are able to distinguish your selfhood as separate from theirs and are not threatened by them.

Through rapport you find common ground and communicate on the same wavelength with others. Through empathy you find ways to appreciate the attitudes, opinions and actions of others—to understand them.

Establishing rapport and empathizing with others are skills that can be learned which will give you powerful tools for success. Whenever you need the consent or help of others in completing your goals, you will be able to use these tools to understand others and how to motivate them to help you.

Two of the most common areas of discussion in motivational seminars are "goals," and "desire" or motivation. Without clear-cut goals, you have nowhere to go, no end in view, nothing to give direction to your subconscious success mechanism. But the problem with talking about goals and desire is that many people don't know where to get them if they don't have them. Lack of motivation, desire, and goals is the product of despair of wealth. If you have a bad case of apathy toward your life then you are going to have to look for inspiration anywhere you can find it. Educate yourself on the opportunities life offers. Read inspiring books that show you what can be accomplished. Get out and meet people who are inspiring and who will sprinkle some of their pixie dust on you. Don't hang around with deadbeats who are going nowhere with their lives. Meet people who are excited by life and interested in their future—people who are doing great things.

Our minds and brains are powerful tools with vast potential for achieving wealth. To believe that, all you have to do is contemplate the history of human accomplishment. Consider the space program, the products of technology and invention, the great works of art, and the great ideas contained in world literature and philosophy. Once you accept humankind's unlimited potential, the challenge becomes identifying with that potential in yourself. **You are that.**

Your self-image, goals, and attitudes program you for success or failure. To make use of the vast potential designed into your humanity, you must unleash it from within. The greatest obstacles to personal growth and accomplishment are negative self-images and self-destructive behavior. To overcome these obstacles, you must explore who you are and what you want. Through recognizing your potential and taking action to move through your negative attitudes and self-limiting assumptions, you can fulfill your potential and achieve all the wealth you deserve.

CHAPTER THIRTEEN

When Dreams Come True

When I announced to my friends that I was going to write a book about making money, I encountered varying reactions. Some of my friends started making jokes about how much money I could make selling a book about making money. The implication was that since I couldn't have anything new or useful to tell people about making money, I must be doing it just for the money. When we attempt to strike out beyond our previous accomplishments and self-imposed limitations, there will always be people who feel threatened by our efforts to become more. They may feel they are being left behind.

Other friends were very encouraging and supportive. Some were obviously impressed and in awe of such a venture. They were anxious to receive autographed copies of the book, seeing that my status was now rising to that of an "expert" or "author."

When you set about doing something out of the ordinary, there is always some risk associated with it. You must live with the uncertainty of what might result from aiming beyond the known quantities of your life. People may begin to see and treat you differently. You may achieve a new level of respect among your peers, or you may discover ill will which you never expected.

This is my first book, so there were many challenges to be faced. I did not know if I had the knowledge, writing ability, self-confidence, or persistence to complete such a project. I encountered many crises of self-doubt and frustration. I wanted to share something very important with others. I wanted others like myself, who had never been given the knowledge and tools to become wealthy, to have them. But to accomplish my goal I had to believe in myself, despite the ridicule of others, my inexperience as a writer, the uncertain prospects of success, and the possibility of failure and humiliation.

This experience is typical of wealthy and successful individuals. Many people, no matter how successful, can never shake the feeling of being an impostor about to be exposed. They continually repeat or increase their successes, in the hopes of proving to themselves and others, once and for all, that they are worthy and deserving.

Ultimately, we all have to give up seeking the approval of others and turn to ourselves for validation. That is what this book is about—taking responsibility for your own successes and failures, knowing yourself, believing in yourself, and trusting yourself to get what you want out of life.

My goal has been to give you the knowledge and tools necessary to succeed in managing your own life enterprise, without unnecessary dependence on people and forces outside your control. If you wait for a spouse, parent, teacher, employer, or the government to improve your opportunities for wealth and quality of life, you deny yourself the power to control your own destiny and fulfill your dreams.

The wealth-building equation, the secret of making money, and all the other knowledge and tools in this book will empower you to become wealthy. The only thing that might separate what I have accomplished from what you can accomplish is that I have applied the knowledge and principles contained in this book to my life and have reaped the rewards.

Religion, philosophy, and psychology often downplay the importance of material well-being. We hear a lot about the immorality of greed that predominated during the 1980s. And that the solutions to our problems depend on improving our values and embracing spirituality. We are told that the superficiality of consumerism and shallow-minded popular culture is destructive to the moral fiber of our nation.

I don't entirely disagree with these assumptions. Certainly the most important thing in my life is the love of my family and friends. But there is also another part of my life that I never appreciated until I could try it on for size—the material part.

I have found that money and material comforts provide a deep sense of security, well-being, and freedom. It is a spiritual sensation, but I don't think there is anything spiritual about it. The primordial needs of all animals and people are physical safety and earthly sustenance. Food, shelter, warmth, companionship, and exciting diversions are basic to life. And with enough money, you can guarantee an almost perpetual supply of the basics of life. They are just the basics; I admit that. But without the basics, it is difficult to thrive on morality and spirituality.

This is common sense to most of us, but we experience mental conflict about it anyway. We wonder how much we deserve from life, and whether we will be judged selfish and greedy if we ask for too much.

Many people today explain that "consumption" and "greed" are immoral, because of the terrible damage that has been done to our environment in the name of "progress" and "prosperity," that is, money. The admonition against money and greed is not a new concept of sin. Long before humankind recognized the destruction of the environment that results from irresponsible industry and consumption, avarice was considered a serious sin. It has even been proclaimed that "love of money is the root of all evil." I think there is truth to this. I would say love of money and power is the root of most evil. There is a side to human nature which seeks to dominate and manipulate others, and to acquire and hoard as much wealth as possible. In order to do so, unscrupulous individuals will deceive and exploit others, to achieve their own selfish ends.

But the solution to evil in the world and to our environmental problems is not to extol the virtues of poverty and human misery, preaching against human "selfishness" and "greed," as so many environmentalists and social moralists do. The solution is to understand what people are seeking from money and wealth.

Wealth is everything of value to humans. A healthy environment represents a form of wealth, a better quality of life. Living in harmony with others, not exploiting and abusing them, is also quality of life. When you recognize that the true meaning of wealth is quality of life, and that money is just a tool for storing and exchanging wealth, then you can have all the money you want, without exploiting others or abusing the environment. You can enjoy money, material well-being, spiritual well-being, and inner harmony, without conflict.

Dreams come true when our hopes are fulfilled and we find happiness. I knew before I ever made a lot of money that money is only a symbol for happiness, and that materialism is not a solution to spiritual poverty. Few people who suddenly come into a lot of cash find lasting happiness. I was always suspicious of my longing for money, and wary of relying on it to provide happiness or fulfillment. But I must confess, when I finally paid off my debts, accumulated money, bought my dream house, and created the circumstances in my life I had always fantasized about, it was fantastic!

And it still is.

My goal throughout this book has been to impress upon you the importance of understanding that wealth is quality of life. My purpose has also been to demonstrate in countless ways that despair of wealth is despair of life. Any "average" healthy person can overcome this despair, once he or she discovers the endless possibilities that life offers. The knowledge in this book can expand the range of your possibilities in life, and offers the tools to make your possibilities a reality.

I continue to discover attitudes in myself that limit my thinking and discourage my efforts. I am amazed at how changing my attitudes increases my wealth-building power and my effectiveness. I am now excited and optimistic about my life, because there is so much more to come. I can't wait to see how it turns out.

New knowledge comes to me every day. I am having so much fun discovering new ideas and thinking of new ways to accomplish my goals.

I used to see the world as shrouded in mystery, full of secrets. I was seeking answers that would never come, while despairing of opportunities. Now I see the world as a library of knowledge, full of information that will help me learn and be more.

Skills continue to fascinate me. I see more and more potential in myself as I improve my skills. I have cleared the roadblock of low self-esteem and now enjoy the challenge of building new skills and putting them to work. I trust my skills and know that as long as I continue to practice and apply myself, I will accumulate more skills—more wealth-building competence.

I am still challenged by effort. I like to be lazy. It takes a lot of willpower to rev up my engines and get cranking. But once I am warmed up, I get excited, because I see so much getting accomplished. The need for effort no longer overwhelms me because I am so confident of what I will achieve, and the rewards which come from effort. Effort is the magic potion, the secret ingredient of my success. Without effort I would never have persisted beyond my gloom and despair of wealth, to achieve wealth and happiness.

I now have all the resources I need to stay wealthy and become wealthier. I have knowledge, self-confidence, optimism, the truth about wealth, skill, willpower, and self-esteem. Nobody can take these essential resources away from me.

Finding or creating value, and earning a good return on my time, effort, and money year after year is a simple but penetrating formula for financial success.

I encourage you to make use of the information in this book to create your own wealth-building program. Use the world's most fabulous computer, your own brain, to jump-start your program for success. Then you will not need to read how others reached their dreams, because you'll be living the reality of your own dreams.

RESOURCES

Suggested Reading

Allen, Robert G. *Nothing Down for the '90s: How to Buy Real Estate with Little or No Money Down,* rev. ed. New York: Simon and Schuster, 1984.

Baumback, Clifford M. *How to Organize and Operate a Small Business.* 8th ed. Englewood Cliffs, NJ: Prentice Hall, 1988.

Bolles, Richard Nelson. *What Color Is Your Parachute? A Practical Manual for Job-Hunters and Career Changers.* Berkeley, Ca: Ten Speed Press, 1988.

Drucker, Peter. *Innovation and Entrepreneurship: Practice and Principles.* New York: Harper and Row, 1985.

Engel, Louis, and Brendan Boyd. *How to Buy Stocks,* 7th ed. Boston: Little, Brown and Co., 1982.

Clason, George S. *The Richest Man in Babylon.* Reprint. Toronto: Bantam Books, 1976.

Graham, Benjamin. *The Intelligent Investor: A Book of Practical Counsel.* 4th ed. New York: Harper and Row, 1973.

Gunderson, Gerald. *The Wealth Creators: An Entrepreneurial History of the United States.* Reprint. New York: Plume, 1990.

Lynch, Peter. *One Up on Wall Street: How to Use What You Already Know to Make Money in the Market.* New York: Simon and Schuster, 1989.

Quinn, Jane Bryant. *Making the Most of Your Money: Smart Ways to Create Wealth and Plan Your Finances in the '90s.* New York: Simon and Schuster, 1991.

Ringer, Robert J. *Million Dollar Habits.* New York: Fawcett Crest, 1990.

Debt Counseling

If you have a serious problem with debt and are looking for advice or counseling, the National Foundation for Consumer Credit, Inc., can provide a referral to an office near you. It offers free or low-cost counseling for people who cannot get control of their personal debts.

The National Foundation for Consumer Credit, Inc.
8611 2nd Avenue, Suite 100
Silver Spring, MD 20910
(800) 388-2227

Family Service America can supply referrals to a variety of local nonprofit organizations that provide family counseling services, including credit counseling.

Family Service America
11700 West Lake Park Drive
Park Place
Milwaukee, WI 53224
(414) 359-1040

Business Investments

To find a business broker contact:

Institute of Certified Business Counselors
Eugene, OR 97401
(503) 345-8064; fax (503) 726-2402

To locate your nearest Better Business Bureau office contact:

Council of Better Business Bureaus, Inc.
4200 Wilson Boulevard
Arlington, VA 22203
(703) 276-0100

Investment Fraud

For consumer information about investment fraud contact:

North American Securities Administrators Association, Inc.
1 Massachusetts Avenue, Suite 310
Washington, D.C. 20001
(202) 737-0900

Write or call the National Futures Association to request the free pamphlets "Investment Swindles: How They Work and How to Avoid Them," "Swindlers Are Calling," and "Buying Options on Futures Contracts: A Guide to Their Uses and Risks":

National Futures Association
200 West Madison Street, Suite 1600
Chicago, IL 60606-3447
(800) 621-3570 or (312) 781-1410.

To obtain a list of coin dealers authorized by the Professional Coin Grading Service contact:

Professional Coin Grading Service
P.O. Box 9458
Newport Beach, CA 92658
(714) 833-0600

To obtain a membership list of gem dealers and for guidelines for buying gems and jewelry contact:

American Gem Society
5901 West 3rd Street
Los Angeles, CA 90036-2898
(213) 936-4367

To obtain information pertaining to fraud or misrepresentation in gem dealings, and to get their consumer information packet:

American Gemological Laboratories
Gemline Recovery Service
580 Fifth Avenue
New York, NY 10036
(212) 704-0727

The International Foundation for Art Research is a nonprofit organization dedicated to preventing the circulation of stolen or forged works of art. It provides aid in the authentication of art and recovery of stolen art.

International Foundation for Art Research
46 East 70th Street
New York, NY 10021
(212) 879-1780

Financial Planning

Write or call the Institute of Certified Financial Planners for their pamphlet "Selecting a Qualified Financial Planning Professional: Twelve Questions to Consider." It can recommend a list of financial planners in your area.

Institute of Certified Financial Planners
Two Denver Highlands
Denver, CO 80231
(800) 282-7526 or (303) 751-7600

Call or write the International Association for Financial Planning for its pamphlet "Consumer Guide to Comprehensive Financial Planning." It can also recommend a list of financial planners in your area.

International Association for Financial Planning
Two Concourse Parkway, Suite 800
Atlanta, GA 30328
(800) 945-4237 or (404) 395-1605

Call or write to receive the pamphlets "Financial Planner Interview: How to Choose a Financial Planner" and "Directory of Fee-Only Financial Advisors."

National Association of Personal Financial Advisors
1130 Lake Cook Road, Suite 105
Buffalo Grove, IL 60089
(800) 366-2732 or (708) 537-7722

To get information about federal student financial aid programs, contact the Federal Student Financial Aid Program. It will answer questions on student eligibility, help in completing financial aid applications, and help with student loan problems.

Federal Student Financial Aid Program
Department of Education
P.O. Box 84
Washington, DC 20044
(800) 433-3243

Securities Investments

To obtain consumer information on buying securities, verifying membership of securities dealers, and for help with complaints:

National Association of Securities Dealers
1735 K Street NW
Washington, DC 20006
(800) 289-9999 or (202) 728-8000

For information on public companies, stocks, bonds, and other securities; securities fraud; and to verify registration of securities brokers and investment advisors contact:

Securities and Exchange Commission (SEC)
450 Fifth Street NW
Washington, DC 20549
(202) 272-7440

To get information on buying savings bonds contact:

United States Savings Bonds Division
Office of Public Affairs
Department of the Treasury
1111 20th Street NW, Room 302
Washington, DC 20226
(800) US-BONDS

Small Business Owners

The Small Business Administration provides numerous publications and services to help small businesses. Call your local SBA office or the national 800 number listed here.

United States Small Business Administration
Office of Consumer Affairs
1441 L Street NW
Washington, DC 20416
(800) 827-5722

Mortgage Rate Comparisons

Here are some services that publish mortgage rate comparisons:

HSH Associates
1200 Rte. 23
Butler, NJ 07405
(800) 873-2837 or (201) 838-3330

Gary S. Myers & Associates
308 W. Erie St., Suite 300
Chicago, IL 60610
(312) 642-9000

Miscellaneous Free Information

Handbook
Consumer Information Center
Pueblo, CO 81009

This book is FREE and is a gold mine of useful addresses and phone numbers.

DEBT RESTRUCTURING PLAN

The following exercise will set you up to negotiate with your creditors and get them to leave you alone. You may find this complicated, confusing, tedious, or scary, but you must stick to your guns and follow it through. This plan works.

Make a list of all your creditors—credit cards, student loans, doctor bills, family, friends, etc.—and how much you owe them. Do not include your house payment or your car payment. Let's say you owe $1,000 divided among three creditors. Your list might look like this:

Creditor A	$ 360.59
Creditor B	467.89
Creditor C	171.52
Total debt	$ 1,000.00

Now figure out what percentage of the total you owe each creditor.

- Take the amount you owe creditor A and enter it to a calculator.
- Press the division button [÷].
- Next enter 1000 and press equals [=].
- Now multiply by 100 to get the percentage.

36.059% of the total debt is to creditor A. Round off to the nearest 1% and write down the percentage next to the name of the creditor. The list now looks like this:

Creditor A	$ 360.59	36%
Creditor B	467.89	
Creditor C	171.52	
Total debt	$ 1,000.00	

Continue with each creditor, dividing the amount you owe by the total and multiplying by 100 to get the percentage of the total you owe for that creditor. The list ends up like this:

Creditor A	$ 360.59	36%
Creditor B	467.89	47
Creditor C	171.52	17
Total debt	$ 1,000.00	100%

Now decide how much money you can pay your creditors every month. Do *not* pick too large an amount. That is a major mistake. Choose an amount you *know* you can come up with every month without fail!

Let's say you feel confident that you can pay $50 a month in total to your creditors. Divide up the pie so that each of your creditors gets its fair share.

- You owe Creditor A 36% of the total of your debts. So you enter .36 in your calculator.
- Then press the multiplication key [×].
- Next enter the total of what you can afford to pay: 50.
- Then press the equals key [=].
- The answer you get is 18. So you will pay $18 to Creditor A every month without fail.
- Do the same for Creditor B and Creditor C, adding the payments on to the list as follows:

	Debt		**Payment**
Creditor A	$ 360.59	36%	$ 18.00
Creditor B	467.89	46	23.00
Creditor C	171.52	17	8.50
Totals	$ 1,000.00		$ 49.50

Now make up a budget that uses up all of your monthly income except $50. For example, your take-home pay after taxes is $1,770.83 a month. So you list your expenses like this:

Rent (or mortgage)	$ 750	
Food	300	
Utilities	130	
Doctors	35	
Car payment	180	
Gas	70	
Clothing allowance	45	
Entertainment	10	(keep this low)
Car insurance	125	
Other insurance	75	
Total monthly expenses	$1,720	

In this example, your take-home pay is $1,770.83, and your monthly expenses are $1,720, leaving you with $50.83 to pay your debts. What you are trying to do is show your creditors that all you have is $50 a month left to pay your bills. Notice the $10 a month for entertainment. It is reasonable for your creditors to assume you are going to use a little money for entertainment. If you have to have $60 a month for entertainment, that is OK. Just fudge in the extra by adding five dollars here and there onto the other categories. Be sure to state your real car payment and rent, as these amounts can be easily verified by your creditors.

Type up this budget and make copies of it to send to your creditors. Include a cover letter that goes something like this:

> Dear Creditor:
>
> I regret that due to personal financial difficulties, I have fallen behind on my payments.
>
> I know this is a matter of concern to you, as it is for me.
>
> After reviewing my income and monthly expenses I find that I am unable to meet the schedule of payments under the terms of my agreement with you.
>
> As you can see from the attached budget, I have only $50 a month left over from my income after meeting other necessary expenses.
>
> Also note that my total debts add up to $1,000. Because I am anxious to honor my debts, I have worked out a plan of repayment. I am apportioning what little extra income I have to pay off my debts. I have divided my payments up to reflect the proportionate amount I owe each of my creditors.
>
> Henceforth, I will send you the following amount each month until my obligation to you is repaid: (Write here amount you will pay)
>
> Thank you for your patience in this matter.
>
> Sincerely,
>
> Jane or John Doe

Send this letter out to all of your creditors, then follow up with a phone call a week or so later. If you don't want to call them yourself, get a friend or family member to help you. You could start just sending the money, but it works a little better if you can give it the personal touch by calling.

Your goal is to get all of your creditors to agree to your payment plan and leave you alone. You do not want them calling you and making your life miserable.

If your creditors don't agree to your repayment plan, explain that you would be happy to exclude them from the plan and not send any payments, if they so desire. This is your leverage against your creditors—they want your money. Even if it is only a small amount, if you keep making payments as you promised, it shows your good faith and they can move on to the real deadbeats who don't pay them anything.

After sending your creditors regular payments for several months, you have even more leverage. If they continue to harass you, explain that if they keep bothering you, you will stop sending payments.

Do not hire a credit repair service to deal with your problems. That is a waste of your money, since they will charge you for the service. My plan works, and it is all that a credit repair service would do for you anyway. The only added advantage of a service is that they will negotiate with your creditors for you.

Don't let your creditors intimidate you, and don't try and threaten or insult them. Just stick to your terms. If they want to be included in your debt repayment plan, you have so much a month you will pay them, every month, without fail, until the debt is cleared up.

They will probably try to talk you into paying more. If you cannot cope with them yourself, as I said, get someone else to talk for you. But be simple and clear about what you are offering. Show your sincerity in dealing with the problem and leave it at that. If they refuse to listen to reason, stay calm and politely end the conversation: "I am sorry, we do not seem to be making progress here. I do not wish to receive any more phone calls from you. I am sending you a check today in the amount I have specified. I will continue making payments on the debt as long as you do not harass me. Thank you for your time. Good-bye."

If they call you back, hang up on them without a word. Call the Better Business Bureau and request the name of the agency in your state that has authority over creditors. Call these authorities and ask them what steps you can take to get troublesome creditors not to call you.

If your creditors send you mail, read it only if you need some information from it. If they are just threatening letters, don't throw them away. Set up a box to toss them into. You may want to have them later if you decide to take legal action.

The whole point is to stay cool and work the plan until all your creditors stop hassling you. I know from my experience as a bill collector that once you get things set up so that you are steadily paying off the debt—even with small payments—your creditors will back off and look for bigger fish to fry.

If you try to avoid your creditors, you just infuriate them more. I was working on commission as a bill collector. If people were running from me, there was something personally insulting about that. They were attacking my livelihood. But if they sent in $5 a month, it was better than nothing; it was almost a compliment. I know this sounds silly, but that is just how people are. I am sure you would rather not give that nasty bill collector the satisfaction of getting your money, and you hate sending off the check every month. But do yourself a favor; get this simple program going, and your debt problems are over.

BIBLIOGRAPHY

Ackerman, Martin S., and Diane L. Ackerman. *Money, Ego, Power: A Manual for Would-Be Wheeler-Dealers.* Playboy Press, 1976.

Allen, Robert G. *Nothing Down for the '90s: How to Buy Real Estate with Little or No Money Down.* Rev. ed. New York: Simon and Schuster, 1984.

Baida, Peter. *Poor Richard's Legacy: American Business Values from Benjamin Franklin to Donald Trump.* New York: William Morrow and Company, 1990.

Baumback, Clifford M. *How to Organize and Operate a Small Business.* 8th ed. Englewood Cliffs, NJ: Prentice Hall, 1988.

Beckley, Ed. *No Down Payment Formulas.* Reprint. Toronto: Bantam Books, 1987.

Bolles, Richard Nelson. *What Color Is Your Parachute? A Practical Manual for Job-Hunters and Career Changers.* Berkeley, Ca: Ten Speed Press, 1988.

Boorstin, Daniel J. *The Discoverers.* New York: Random House, 1983.

Burrough, Bryan, and John Helyar. *Barbarians at the Gate: The Fall of RJR Nabisco.* New York: Harper and Row, 1990.

Clason, George S. *The Richest Man in Babylon.* Reprint. Toronto: Bantam Books, 1976.

Cottle, Sidney, Roger R. Murray, and Frank E. Block. *Graham and Dodd's Security Analysis.* 5th ed. New York: McGraw-Hill Book Co., 1988.

Downes, John, and Jordan Elliot Goodman. *Barron's Finance and Investment Handbook.* 2d ed. Woodbury, New York: Barron's, 1987.

Dreman, David. *The New Contrarian Investment Strategy.* New York: Random House, 1982.

Drucker, Peter. *The New Realities.* New York: Harper and Row, 1989.

Drucker, Peter. *Innovation and Entrepreneurship: Practice and Principles.* New York: Harper and Row, 1985.

Drucker, Peter. *Managing for the Future: The 1990s and Beyond.* New York: Truman Talley Books, 1992.

Ducovny, Amram M. *The Billion $ Swindle: Frauds Against the Elderly.* New York: Fleet Press Corporation, 1969.

Ellis, Charles D., editor, with James R. Vertin. *Classics: An Investor's Anthology*. Homewood, Il: Dow Jones-Irwin, 1989.

Engel, Louis, and Brendan Boyd. *How to Buy Stocks*. 7th ed. Boston: Little, Brown and Co., 1982.

Finkler, Steven A. *The Complete Guide to Finance and Accounting for Nonfinancial Managers*. New York: Prentice Hall, 1983.

Fisher, Kenneth L. *Super Stocks*. Homewood, Il: Dow Jones-Irwin, 1984.

Frank, Al. *The Prudent Speculator: Al Frank on Investing*. Homewood, Il: Dow Jones-Irwin, 1990.

Gardner, Robert M. *The Dean Witter Guide to Personal Investing*. New York: New American Library, 1988.

Getty, J. Paul. *How to Be Rich*. Reprint. New York: Jove Books, 1983.

Gilder, George. *Wealth and Poverty*. Toronto: Bantam Books, 1982.

Givens, Charles J. *More Wealth Without Risk: How to Develop a Personal Fortune Without Going Out on a Limb*. New York: Simon and Schuster, 1991.

Graham, Benjamin. *The Intelligent Investor: A Book of Practical Counsel*. 4th ed. New York: Harper and Row, 1973.

Gunderson, Gerald. *The Wealth Creators: An Entrepreneurial History of the United States*. Reprint. New York: Plume, 1990.

Handy, Charles. *The Age of Unreason*. Boston: Harvard Business School Press, 1990.

Hawken, Paul. *Growing a Business*. New York, Simon and Schuster, 1987.

Hawken, Paul. *The Next Economy*. New York: Ballantine Books, 1983.

Hoffman, Mark S. *The World Almanac and Book of Facts, 1989*. New York: Pharos Books, 1988.

Hooper, Judith, and Dick Teresi. *The Three-Pound Universe*. New York: Dell Publishing Co., 1986.

Hyman, David N. *Economics*. 2d ed. Homewood, Il: Irwin, 1991.

Korda, Michael. *Success!* New York: Ballantine Books, 1977.

Lapham, Lewis H. *Money and Class in America: Notes and Observations on Our Civil Religion*. New York: Weidenfeld and Nicolson, 1988.

Lefèvre, Edwin. *Reminiscences of a Stock Operator*. Burlington, Vt: Books of Wall Street Edition, 1980.

Lowry, Albert J. *How You Can Become Financially Independent by Investing in Real Estate*. New York: Simon and Schuster, 1977.

Lynch, Peter. *One Up on Wall Street: How to Use What You Already Know to Make Money in the Market*. New York: Simon and Schuster, 1989.

Machiavelli, Niccolo. *The Prince*. Translated and edited by Thomas G. Bergin. Arlington Heights, Il: Harlan Davidson, 1947.

Mackay, Charles. *Extraordinary Popular Delusions and the Madness of Crowds*. Reprint. New York: Farrar, Straus, and Giroux, 1932.

Mandino, Og. *The Greatest Salesman in the World.* Reprint. Toronto: Bantam Books, 1974.

McCormick, Mark H. *What They Don't Teach You at Harvard Business School.* Toronto: Bantam Books, 1984.

Meigs, Walter B., Charles E. Johnson, and Robert F. Meigs. *Accounting, The Basis for Business Decisions*. New York: McGraw-Hill Book Co., 1977.

Naisbitt, John, and Patricia Aburdene. *Megatrends 2000: Ten New Directions for the 1990s.* New York: Avon Books, 1990.

Needleman, Jacob. *Money and the Meaning of Life.* New York: Doubleday Currency, 1991.

Nickerson, William. *How I Turned $1,000 into Three Million in Real Estate—in My Spare Time.* New York: Simon and Schuster, 1969.

Noonan, David. *Neuro-Life on the Frontline of Brain Surgery and Neurological Medicine.* New York: Simon and Schuster, 1989.

Peters, Thomas J., and Robert H. Waterman, Jr. *In Search of Excellence: Lessons from America's Best-Run Companies*. New York: Warner Books, 1982.

Peters, Tom. *Thriving on Chaos.* New York: Harper & Row, 1987.

Pilzer, Paul Zane. *Unlimited Wealth: The Theory and Practice of Economic Alchemy.* New York: Crown Publishers, 1990.

Plocek, Joseph E. *Economic Indicators: How America Reads Its Financial Health.* New York: New York Institute of Finance, 1991.

Quinn, Jane Bryant. *Making the Most of Your Money: Smart Ways to Create Wealth and Plan Your Finances in the '90s.* New York: Simon and Schuster, 1991.

Ringer, Robert J. *Million Dollar Habits.* New York: Fawcett Crest, 1990.

Roberts, Wess. *Leadership Secrets of Attila the Hun.* New York: Warner Books, 1985.

Schumacher, E. F. *Small Is Beautiful: Economics as if People Mattered.* Reprint. New York: Harper and Row, 1973.

Sloan, Alfred P. *My Years with General Motors.* Edited by John McDonald with Catherine Stevens. Reprint. New York: MacFadden-Bartell Corporation, 1965.

Smith, Adam. *The Money Game.* New York: Random House, 1968.

Spencer, Milton H. *Contemporary Economics.* New York: Worth Publishers, 1971.

Stein, Herbert, and Murray Foss. *An Illustrated Guide to the American Economy: A Hundred Key Issues.* Washington, DC: AEI Press, 1992.

Stevenson, Howard H., Michael J. Roberts, and H. Irving Grousbeck. *New Business Ventures and the Entrepreneur*. Homewood, Il: Irwin, 1985.

Terhorst, Paul. *Cashing In on the American Dream: How to Retire at 35.* Toronto: Bantam Books, 1988.

Tobias, Andrew. *The Only* Other *Investment Guide You'll Ever Need.* Toronto: Bantam Books, 1987.

Train, John. *The Midas Touch: The Strategies That Have Made Warren Buffet America's Pre-eminent Investor.* New York: Harper and Row, 1987.

Train, John. *The Money Masters.* New York: Harper and Row, 1980.

VanCaspel, Venita. *Money Dynamics for the 1990s.* New York: Simon and Schuster, 1988.

Watson, Thomas J., Jr., and Peter Petre. *Father, Son, and Co.: My Life at IBM and Beyond.* New York: Bantam, 1990.

Weiss, Geraldine, and Janet Lowe. *Dividends Don't Lie: Finding Value in Blue-Chip Stocks.* Longman Financial Services Publishing, 1988.

Young, Jeffrey S. *Steve Jobs: The Journey Is the Reward.* Glenview, Il: Scott, Foresman, and Co., 1988.

INDEX

To purchase additional copies of this book visit your local bookstore, or call Publishers Distribution Service
(800) 345-0096

To inquire about other publications by Shane Roberts, or his availability for speaking engagements, contact:

Shane Roberts
c/o McMahon Publishing
P.O. Box 96
Nevada City, CA 95959